DISCARD

# UNITY AND DEVELOPMENT IN PLATO'S METAPHYSICS

# UNITY AND DEVELOPMENT IN PLATO'S METAPHYSICS

## WILLIAM J. PRIOR

OPEN COURT PUBLISHING COMPANY
La Salle, Illinois

OPEN COURT and the above logo are registered in the US Patent and
Trademark Offices
OC845   10   9   8   7   6   5   4   3   2
Published by arrangement with Croom Helm Ltd, Beckenham, Kent

Library of Congress Cataloging in Publication Data

Prior, William J.
    Unity and development in Plato's metaphysics.
    Bibliography: p. 194.
    Includes index.
    1. Plato – Metaphysics.  2. Metaphysics – History.
I. Title.
B398.M4P74    1985    110'.92'4    85-5073

ISBN 0-8126-9000-1

Printed and bound in Great Britain

# CONTENTS

# Contents

This book is dedicated to my parents

# ACKNOWLEDGEMENTS

This book would never have appeared in print without the assistance and encouragement of several people and institutions, which I gratefully acknowledge here.

The Institute for Research in the Humanities at the University of Wisconsin in Madison awarded me a post-doctoral fellowship, during the tenure of which I was able to complete an initial draft of this work. The Institute provided not only financial support but an ideal environment in which to conduct research. Loretta Freiling of the Institute patiently, promptly and cheerfully turned my hand-written pages into typed copy.

The University of Colorado supplemented my income during my fellowship year; my own department gave me a reduced course load while I revised the first draft completely. Final revisions were completed while I enjoyed a sabbatical leave from the University.

Alex Mourelatos provided encouragement and helpful criticism at every stage of this project. More than anyone else, he gave me the confidence to see the book through to completion. Alex has served as my mentor for over a decade, and I could not have asked for a better one.

Several scholars have commented on various drafts of this book. I would mention in particular Charles Kahn and Kenneth Sayre, who gave me detailed comments on the penultimate draft, and saved me from many mistakes. My department chairman, Wes Morriston, prodded me to send the manuscript to Croom Helm Ltd; left to my own devices, I would probably have reworked it forever.

Several students, both graduate and undergraduate, both at Colorado and elsewhere, and several colleagues in other fields and other areas of philosophy have read the manuscript and bolstered my hope that it may be useful to more than professional Plato scholars.

A portion of Chapter 3, Section IV of this book originally appeared, in a somewhat different version, in Supplementary Volume IX (1983) of the *Canadian Journal of Philosophy*, in an article entitled, '*Timaeus* 48e–52d and the Third Man Argument'. A smaller portion of Chapter IV, Section II originally appeared in the *Southern Journal of Philosophy* 18 (1980), in an article entitled, 'Plato's Analysis of Being and Not-Being in the *Sophist*'. I thank the editors of both journals for their kind permission to reproduce this material.

My deepest thanks go, of course, to my wife, Peg, who happily undertook to move our family to Wisconsin for my fellowship year and who has given me constant support for the entire duration of this project (and indeed, well beyond).

Boulder, Colorado

In Plato's work there is both unity and development — unity, because he has a sharply defined manner of viewing things and securing an intellectual grasp of them, and this manner *is* the Platonic Idea or 'vision'; and development, because there is a change in the kind of objects on which his main interest rests at different times.

Julius Stenzel, Plato's Method of Dialectic, p. 23.

# INTRODUCTION: THE PROBLEM OF PLATO'S DEVELOPMENT

This book contains an account of the development of Plato's metaphysics. I focus on two metaphysical doctrines of central importance in Plato's thought: the Theory of Forms and the doctrine of Being and Becoming. I discuss Plato's epistemology, psychology, theology and other topics only when they are relevant to the metaphysical doctrines just mentioned. My approach is therefore selective. It is selective also in that I deal primarily with only six dialogues: the *Euthyphro, Phaedo, Republic, Parmenides* (part I), *Timaeus* and *Sophist*. I discuss other dialogues only when their contents illuminate or augment the metaphysics of these six.

This selectivity is not required by my topic, which certainly admits of more comprehensive treatment. It is well suited to my general thesis concerning Plato's development, however, which may be stated as follows. Plato develops in his early and middle dialogues a metaphysical view which has at its centre the Theory of Forms and the related doctrine of Being and Becoming. According to the Theory of Forms, there exist certain abstract objects of knowledge, called Forms. By virtue of a relation of participation which holds between these Forms and the phenomenal objects with which we are familiar, these phenomena acquire their names and characteristics. According to the doctrine of Being and Becoming, the Forms are eternal, intelligible and utterly insusceptible to change, whereas their phenomenal participants are generated and destroyed, sensible and in constant change. Plato not only makes this categorical distinction between Forms and phenomena, he portrays them as inhabiting separate worlds.

The Theory of Forms receives its first real treatment in the *Euthyphro*, an early dialogue. The theory is developed and the Being-Becoming distinction introduced in the *Phaedo* and *Republic*, dialogues of Plato's middle period. In the first part of the *Parmenides*, these doctrines are subjected to criticism. This criticism does not constitute a refutation of either doctrine, but it does raise serious questions about both, questions to which the middle dialogues do not contain definitive answers. In the post-*Parmenides* dialogues, and in particular, in the *Timaeus* and

*Sophist*, Plato does deal with the questions raised in the *Parmenides*. Without altering either the Theory of Forms or the doctrine of Being and Becoming in their essential natures, he augments and clarifies his metaphysics in such a way that the objections of the *Parmenides* are met. Thus, the dialogues I shall deal with exhibit a genuine development in Plato's metaphysics, a movement from an initial statement of his views through a critique of them to a refined final position.

This thesis is far from uncontroversial. It must be contrasted with two other views of Plato's thought which have been defended in the scholarly literature. I shall label the first of these views 'radical revisionism', both because it posits a change in Plato's position more radical than the one I propose and because the view itself constituted a radical departure from the orthodox conception of Plato's thought when it was first put forth. The second view is generally labelled 'unitarianism', because it emphasises the unity of Plato's thought throughout the dialogues. Whereas radical revisionism insists on a greater change in Plato's metaphysics than I allow, unitarianism insists on less. I shall discuss both views briefly below.

The question of Plato's development has concerned Plato scholars at least since the early nineteenth century. Any view that proposes some development or change in Plato's thought must deal with the question of the relative chronological order of the dialogues. Unless it can be determined which dialogues were written at what period in Plato's career, there is no objective basis for any claims about now his thought developed. Such a chronology of the dialogues was absent in the first two thirds of the nineteenth century, and the proliferation of rival hypotheses concerning Plato's thought demonstrated more clearly than could any abstract discussion of methodology the need for one.[1]

Such a chronology was provided as the result of numerous studies of Plato's style, undertaken in the later part of the nineteenth century and early in the twentieth by Campbell, Lutoslawski, von Arnim, Ritter and others.[2] These investigations, for which the term 'stylometry' was coined, showed that five dialogues — the *Timaeus, Critias, Sophist, Statesman*, and *Philebus* — were remarkably similar in style to the *Laws*, which was known to be one of Plato's latest works. These six dialogues constituted a 'late group'. Prior to them stood one or more 'middle' or 'Platonic' groups of dialogues, including at least the

*Phaedo, Symposium, Republic, Phaedrus, Theaetetus*, and *Parmenides*; and still earlier still was a group of 'early' or 'Socratic' dialogues, such as the *Apology, Crito, Euthyphro, Lysis, Laches, Charmides, Protagoras, Euthydemus*, and *Gorgias*.

The results of stylometry put an end for a time to wild speculation about Plato's development. They greatly reduced the number of accounts of Plato's thought that were historically possible; and, though rival accounts persisted, there was general agreement among scholars in the early part of this century that any development of Plato's metaphysics took the form of a gradual unfolding and refinement of that metaphysics.

This consensus was challenged in 1939 by one of the major exponents of radical revisionism, Gilbert Ryle.[3] Ryle argued that the critique of the *Parmenides* was fatal to any version of the Theory of Forms and that Plato in fact abandoned the theory following that critique. Ryle's argument succeeded in convincing many Plato scholars that the *Parmenides* presented a strong, perhaps unanswerable challenge to the Theory of Forms; but the later dialogues employed the theory so freely that it seemed impossible that Plato had abandoned it.

Ryle's account of Plato's development appeared historically impossible. There was more hope for a less extreme version of the radical thesis, which was propounded and defended by G. E. L. Owen in 1953.[4] Owen said that the *Parmenides* refuted not the Theory of Forms, but the interpretation of the Forms as *paradeigmata*, 'paradigms', and the doctrine of Being and Becoming. This version of the theory and the Being-Becoming dichotomy are propounded in the late dialogues chiefly by the *Timaeus*; thus, Owen sought to make his view plausible by proposing to remove the *Timaeus* from the late group and place it among the middle dialogues, after the *Republic* but before the *Parmenides*.

Owen lauched a many-pronged attack on the traditional late dating of the *Timaeus*. He said that the political philosophy of the dialogue differed from that of the *Statesman* and *Laws* but was the same as that of the *Republic*, and that its astronomy also differed from that of the *Laws* and resembled that of the *Republic*. He argued that both the view that the Forms are paradigms and the sharp dichotomy between Being and Becoming were abandoned in the later dialogues as the result of criticism in the *Cratylus, Theaetetus*, and *Parmenides*. He attempted to undermine the credibility of the stylometric evidence for the late date of the

*Timaeus*, and he attempted to refute a claim of Cornford's that a particular passage of the *Timaeus* presupposes the previous composition of the *Sophist*. The crux of Owen's argument, however, was the same as Ryle's: that Plato could not have continued to hold his middle period Theory of Forms after the *Parmenides*.

A response to Owen's radical proposal came in 1957 from the leading champion of the unitarian camp of Plato scholars, H. F. Cherniss.[5] Cherniss conceded many of the points Owen made in criticism of stylometry (not surprisingly, as unitarians from Shorey on had been themselves critical of stylometry on the grounds that it imports into Plato scholarship a concern for development, whereas in reality Plato's thought was fixed from the start of his career). He did argue, however, that there was sufficient sound evidence of this nature to show that the *Timaeus* is late, and he criticised Owen's evidence to the contrary. Cherniss also argued, as one would expect unitarians to do, that Plato's later metaphysics did not differ in any important way from the metaphysics of the early and middle dialogues. The arguments of the *Parmenides*, and in particular the Third Man Argument, which Owen had used to show the need for Plato to abandon paradeigmatism, were in Cherniss' view not serious objections to the Theory of Forms, but had already been refuted in the *Republic* and other middle dialogues.

The exchange between Cherniss and Owen initiated a debate which has continued to this day. Both positions have won some support, but neither has emerged victorious from the fray.[6] The work of Ryle and Owen has effectively destroyed the consensus of scholars on the development of Plato's metaphysics and the date of the *Timaeus*, but it has not produced a new consensus. Nor has Cherniss' contrary position won the support of a majority of scholars.

It is against the background of this dispute between two views which are polar opposites that I have developed the position I propound in this book. I am of course not alone in holding a moderate position between these two extremes. The majority of Plato scholars in this century have held some version of the view I put forth; my differences from them are largely matters of detail. None the less, it seemed important to me to propound and defend this alternative to radical revisionism on the one hand and unitarianism on the other, in part because the debate on Plato's development has been largely carried out, in recent years at least, by members of one camp or the other. Yet it seems clear to me that neither extreme view can succeed in presenting a historically accurate picture of Plato's philosophy; both the radical view, which shows Plato giving up metaphysics in his later years for a prototype of philosophical analysis, and the unitarian position, which finds the later Plato fully present in the early, are serious distortions of the facts.

I do not think it necessary to subject either of these extreme views to criticism.[7] The members of one camp have in general done a more than adequate job of showing up the weaknesses of the other. My book is therefore not a commentary on the dispute between the two camps, but an attempt to lay out a plausible alternative to either. The only satisfactory way of doing this seems to me to be to ground my interpretation in the Platonic text. Thus, I have undertaken an exposition of the metaphysical sections of the six dialogues I mentioned above, an exposition which I hope brings out the essential nature of Plato's metaphysics.

I discuss these dialogues in what I take to be their actual chronological order. In Chapter 1 I deal with the central features of the Theory of Forms and the doctrine of Being and Becoming as they appear in the early *Euthyphro* and the middle period dialogues *Phaedo* and *Republic*. Throughout these dialogues Plato assumes that the Forms exist, and he assigns to them a causal role in the phenomenal world. He also treats them as paradigms, and at least suggests by his use of certain expressions that they are self-predicative (that they have the characteristics of which they are the Forms). In the middle dialogues he emphasises the role of the Forms as objects of knowledge, a role which requires their separation from the phenomenal world and which is the basis of the Being-Becoming distinction. The separate existence of the Forms appears to conflict with their function as causes in the phenomenal world; this in turn leads to some of the problems raised in the *Parmenides*. Plato uses two models for the relation of participation in these dialogues: the sharing model (which suits the conception of Forms as causes) and the resemblance model (which suits their role as objects of knowledge); his failure to decide on one model again leads to trouble in the *Parmenides*.

In Chapter 2 I consider the criticism of these metaphysical views presented in the *Parmenides*. I deal in succession with Socrates' statement of the Theory of Forms in that dialogue, the questions Parmenides raises about the extent of the world of the Forms, the arguments against the view that the Forms are immanent in things, the two versions of the Third Man Argument, and the final argument against the separate existence of the Forms. I argue that the objections Parmenides makes against the Theory of Forms can only be made valid if premises are assumed which differ subtly from those Plato actually accepted in the middle dialogues. Thus, they do not constitute a refutation of the Theory of Forms in those dialogues; but they do raise some serious questions about the correct interpretation of Plato's metaphysics. These questions lead directly to the later dialogues.

In Chapter 3 I deal with the response of the *Timaeus* to the critique of the *Parmenides*. Plato presents the Theory of Forms and the doctrine of Being and Becoming in much the same way here that he had done in the *Phaedo* and *Republic*; this shows that he has not abandoned these doctrines in the face of the criticism they have received. Rather, he adds some new doctrines which enable him to escape from the problems the *Parmenides* had presented. He introduces a new theory of causation, in which the causal function of the Forms is restricted and a new causal principle, Divine Reason in the person of the Demiurge, is introduced. The introduction of the Demiurge enables Plato to show what is wrong with the critique of the separation of the Forms in the *Parmenides*. Plato also introduces into his ontology a new entity, the Receptacle. With the aid of the Receptacle, he is able to exhibit more clearly than before the relation between Forms and phenomena, and this new statement of the Theory of Forms can be seen to be immune to the Third Man Argument in either version.

In the last chapter, I discuss the metaphysics of the *Sophist*. I argue that the *Sophist* does not, as some scholars think, give evidence of a change in Plato's mind concerning the viability of metaphysics in general or the Theory of Forms in particular. There are genuine advances in the *Sophist* from the metaphysics of the middle dialogues, and perhaps even from the position of the *Timaeus*; but these advances are made within the same basic metaphysical framework that characterised those dialogues. Plato argues for the inclusion of changing things in the realm of Being; but this modification of the Being-Becoming dichotomy is verbal rather than substantive. He still employs the pattern-copy relation to illuminate the nature of an image, though he does not apply this relation in discussing the Forms (a fact that is explained by the context in which Forms are discussed). He makes a real conceptual breakthough in his analysis of negation, but the breakthrough is made with a metaphysical apparatus of Forms which is little changed from the middle dialogues. He introduces a new relation among Forms but interprets it as the familiar relation of participation. I discuss the consequences of these changes for the Platonic metaphysics and conclude with a comparison of the *Timaeus* and *Sophist*.

The order of my discussion is based on the assumption that the *Timaeus* is one of Plato's latest dialogues; my aim is to show that the dialogue makes good sense when placed after the *Parmenides*. As the reader will already have noted, however, the controversy over Plato's development has produced controversy over the chronological position of the *Timaeus* among the dialogues. In the Appendix, therefore, I address the chronological issue, and give some of my reasons for believing that the traditional late date for this dialogue is correct.

The subject of this book, Plato's metaphysical development, has been of great interest to Plato scholars, particularly in recent years. Accordingly, I have at times found it necessary to discuss the secondary literature on the subject. I have done so sparingly, however. I have tried to avoid mentioning works which bear on the particular issues I discuss unless they have influenced my own view or they make a point which is indispensible to the advancement of the discussion. Whenever possible I have confined even these references to notes. I have followed this policy because I believe that, although Plato scholars may benefit from lengthy discussions of the scholarly literature, other readers generally find such displays of erudition distracting or (what is worse) intimidating. Though my theme is one that has preoccupied Plato scholars, I do not believe that it is of interest only to them; I have tried to write, therefore, for a wider audience. I hope, in fact, that anyone familiar with the dialogues I discuss and interested in the metaphysical themes contained therein may be able to read this book with understanding and with profit.

## Notes

The following notes contain only brief references, listing the author's last name and page number; when more than one article or book by a given author is cited in the notes, the year of publication is added to disambiguate the reference. A complete reference to each work cited is to be found in the Bibliography.

1. See Lutoslawski, pp. 35–63, for a discussion of these hypotheses.

2. For a summary of the results of these studies, see Ross, p. 2.

3. Ryle, pp. 97–147.

4. Owen (1953), pp. 313–38.

5. Cherniss (1957), pp. 339–78.

6. According to Skemp (1976), p. 53, 'the majority of British scholars take Owen's point of view at present, but American and continental scholars do not, for the most part, accept it.' Guthrie (1978), p. 243, states that Owen's article 'has aroused a great deal of comment, mostly but by no means entirely adverse'. The division among scholars is by no means wholly geographical; among the British scholars who reject Owen's view are Guthrie (1978, pp. 243, 266, n. 2, and 298. n. 1) and Skemp (1976, pp. 53–5; cf. 1967, pp. 124–7). Among the scholars in North America who accept Owen's view are Robinson (p. 59), Shiner, and White. For additional references, see Guthrie (1978), p. 243, n. 3.

7. I undertook a detailed critique of Owen's view in Prior (1975).

# 1 THE METAPHYSICS OF THE EARLY AND MIDDLE PLATONIC DIALOGUES

As I stated in the Introduction, it is my view that Plato's metaphysics developed from an initial statement of the Theory of Forms and the Being-Becoming distinction in the early and middle dialogues, through a critical examination of those doctrines in the first part of the *Parmenides*, to an ultimate reformulation and development of them, refined in light of that critique, in the *Timaeus* and *Sophist*. In this chapter I shall consider the initial stages of that development, as it is reflected in the text of three dialogues: the *Euthyphro*, *Phaedo*, and *Republic* (with occasional glances at other early and middle dialogues).

Virtually all scholars accept the relative chronological order which stylometric investigation established for these dialogues. This order places the *Euthyphro* among the early dialogues and the *Phaedo* and *Republic* among those of Plato's middle period, with the *Phaedo* preceding the *Republic* in date of composition. The *Euthyphro* contains the most extensive treatment of the Theory of Forms to be found in the early dialogues; it introduces aspects of the theory which are later expounded in greater detail in the middle dialogues. In many respects the Theory of Forms in the *Euthyphro* is identical to the Theory of Forms in the *Phaedo* and *Republic*. I have therefore chosen to deal with the metaphysical content of these three dialogues topically, rather than considering each dialogue in succession.

This topical treatment offers the advantages of clarity and conciseness, for all the passages bearing on a single issue can be discussed at once. It does, however, threaten to obscure a matter on which Plato's thought undergoes real development from the early to the middle dialogues. Although the Theory of Forms is as explicitly present in the *Euthyphro* as in the *Phaedo* and *Republic*, the earlier dialogue contains at most the implicit basis for the doctrine of Being and Becoming which is developed in the *Phaedo* and *Republic*. In this respect the middle dialogues show an advance over the *Euthyphro*, and indicate that Plato's thought, even at what I have described as the initial stage of his development, was not static.[1]

For this reason, though I shall deal with my subject topically in this chapter, I shall begin with the topics on which the early and middle dialogues present a more or less common viewpoint, and only when I have discussed these shall I go on to discuss the topics developed in the middle rather than the early dialogues. I shall look first at the question of the existence of the Forms; secondly, at their causal role; thirdly, at their status as paradigms; and fourthly, at the problem of self-predication. On all of these matters the early dialogues as well as the middle have something to contribute. I shall then examine the role of the Forms as objects of knowledge, which gives rise to the Being-Becoming distinction; the separation of the Forms from the phenomenal world; and the problem of participation. The last two topics lead directly to the critique of Plato's metaphysics in the first part of the *Parmenides*, but the fact is that all of the topics discussed in this chapter are relevant to that critique.[2]

## I. The Existence of the Forms

In the early and middle dialogues, Plato does not argue for the claim that the Forms exist. He rather assumes that they do and argues from this fact to other conclusions. There is no indication in these dialogues that he regards the existence of the Forms as problematic, as subject to serious philosophical disagreement.

In the early *Euthyphro*, Socrates asks Euthyphro, 'does not whatever is going to be unholy have a certain single Form with respect to Unholiness?' (5d3–5); and, a little later:

> Remember, then, that it was not this I asked of you, to teach me one or two of the many holy things, but that very Form by virtue of which all the holy things are holy; for you said that by one Form the unholy things are unholy and the holy things holy . . . (6d9–e1)

Although these questions are expressed in the language of the Theory of Forms (*idea* is used at 5d4 and 6d11, and *eidos* at 6d11) and, I think, carry the ontological implications that language has in the middle dialogues,[3] Euthyphro accepts the questions as unproblematic (although he may well not understand them as Socrates does) and does not object to the claims that there exist a Form of Holiness and a Form of Unholiness.

In the *Phaedo*, Socrates is speaking with two close associates, Simmias and Cebes; these two, unlike Euthyphro, are presumably aware of Socrates' metaphysical views. Their adherence to the existence of the Forms, though probably more informed than Euthyphro's, is at least as unequivocal. When Socrates asks: 'What, then, about things of this sort, Simmias: do we say there is something Just itself, or nothing?' (65d4–5), Simmias responds, 'We say so indeed, by Zeus!' (d6). A few pages later, Simmias responds affirmatively when Socrates says:

> We say, I suppose, that something is Equal — I do not mean a stick equal to a stick or a stone equal to a stone, or anything else of this sort, but another thing besides all these, the Equal itself; shall we say this is something, or nothing? (74a9–12)

From such exchanges we might conclude that for Greeks of Socrates' time the existence of Forms was not a strange metaphysical claim but a fact as unproblematic as the existence of tables and chairs. In *Republic* V, 476b–d, however, Plato shows that he is aware that most people do not accept the existence of Forms. It is significant, though, that even here he presents this fact as a matter of their failure to recognise what the philosopher sees clearly, not as philosophically based scepticism about certain theoretical entities. Diotima represents the failure of most people to apprehend the Form of Beauty in the same light (*Sym.* 209e–212a).

Yet Plato does also portray the claim that the Forces exist as a hypothesis and as part of a general theory. At *Phdo.* 92d6–7 Simmias, who has been asked to choose between the view that the soul is a harmony and the existence of the Forms, prefers the latter claim as 'a hypothesis worthy of acceptance'. Several pages later, when Socrates introduces his own account of generation and destruction in lieu of the physical theories of his predecessors and the *Nous* (Mind) of Anaxagoras, he presents the claim 'that there is something Beautiful itself in itself and Good and Large and all the rest' (100b5–7) as a hypothesis.

Although Simmias and Cebes express no doubts about the truth of this hypothesis, Simmias does raise a general sceptical question at the end of the final argument of the dialogue (107a–b). Socrates points out that the same doubt can be raised about the hypothesis that there are Forms, even if Simmias and Cebes did not raise it; but he holds out the hope that, when the hypothesis is itself examined (and presumably deduced from some higher hypothesis, as is recommended at 101d–e) and the argument is pursued to its furthest point, a satisfactory resolution of doubt will be found (107b).

Thus, although Plato shows in the *Phaedo* that he is aware that the existence of the Forms is hypothetical and in some sense subject to doubt, he does not present this doubt as a serious philosophical objection to the Theory of Forms. He clearly believes that any doubt about the existence of the Forms can be resolved in favour of the theory; and, for the most part, he treats the existence of the Forms as unproblematic and the failure of some people to acknowledge it as a sort of intellectual blindness.

## II. The Forms as Causes

In the early and middle dialogues the Forms function as the causes, in some sense,[4] of the characteristics of phenomena. In the *Euthyphro*, at 6d11–e1, Socrates says that it is 'by one Form' that unholy things are unholy and holy things holy. If we ask how it is that a Form can have such an effect on these things, the answer of the *Euthyphro* seems to be that it is by virtue of the Form's being 'in' the things affected by it (5d1–2), by virtue of its being a characteristic which the things 'have' (d3–5). This sort of explanation seems clear enough, however many problems may arise when we analyse it (cf. Aristotle, *Metaph.* A. 9, 991a14–19): Whiteness makes something white by being in the thing it characterises.

The fullest account of the causal role of the Forms in the middle dialogues is presented in the *Phaedo*. Though what he says here has been interpreted in different ways, I shall argue that the account is essentially the same as that given in the *Euthyphro*: Forms make things to have certain characteristics by being in them; by being, in the language of philosophers, *immanent* in things.

Plato's account of the Forms as causes is prompted by an objection of Cebes to the claim that the soul is immortal. It might be very long-lasting, Cebes urges, but not immortal; it might outlast several bodies, as a weaver outlasts several cloaks, and yet eventually perish (86e–88b). Socrates states that an answer to this objection requires a thorough examination of the cause of coming into being and destruction (95e). The Greek word *genesis*, here translated 'coming into being', can refer both to substantial change (e.g. birth) and change of attribute (e.g. the 'coming into being' of a red car from a white one by painting). Plato investigates both kinds of change in the following passage, but focuses primarily on the latter kind of *genesis*.

Socrates rejects two accounts of change before giving his own view. The first is the explanation of change through some sort of physical causation, an explanation of the sort that most of the pre-Socratic philosophers gave. Not only do explanations of this kind give rise to various puzzles (96e–97b), but they seem to be guilty of the same mistake Socrates later attributes to Anaxagoras (98c–99c): they confuse some material condition that it is necessary for a given event or state to occur with the true cause of that event or state (which turns out to be the attempt of Mind or Reason to achieve the best result possible).

The second account he rejects is that of Anaxagoras. Anaxagoras had claimed that Mind or Reason, *Nous*, was the cause of everything. Socrates was attracted to this explanation, because it seemed possible to show by means of it that everything was ordered for the best (97c–98b). He rejected it only when he found out to his disappointment that Anaxagoras had not put this excellent idea of his into practice but had fallen back on physical causes in his explanation of change. In fact, Socrates says that he would be happy to have such an explanation as Anaxagoras promised but did not deliver; however, he could neither produce one himself nor learn of one from someone else (99c). Thus, his rejection of Anaxagoras' answer is not like his rejection of the first explanation of change. That had seemed incoherent, confused; this one seems in fact to be the sort of explanation Socrates would prefer to have (he refers to his own explanation as 'second best' at 99c–d), but it appears to be unattainable. (The difference between the rejections is significant, for the sort of explanation Anaxagoras promised seems to be the very sort Plato attempts in the *Timaeus*.)

Socrates' own explanation is in terms of the Forms. As we have seen above (p. 11), he first hypothesises that the Forms exist. Next, he claims that, 'if anything else is beautiful except the Beautiful itself, it is not beautiful for any other reason than that it participates in that Beautiful; and I speak thus in all cases' (100c4–6). Participation in the Form of *F*, then, is the only cause of a given thing's being *F*, provided that thing is different from the Form of *F* itself.

Socrates accordingly rejects all other explanations of a thing's being $F$: it is not by colour or shape that something is made beautiful, but by Beauty; it is not 'by a head' that one person is taller than another or shorter, but by Tallness or Shortness; it is not by two that ten is greater than eight, but by Magnitude (Greatness); it is not by addition that one and one become two, but by Twoness. Other causes are too 'wise' for him; he clings instead simply and naïvely to his own view (100c–101d).

Socrates uses this hypothesis to explain both why things are $F$ and how they come to be $F$. The first examples he gives (100c–101b) are of something's being $F$; however, in the example of one and one making two, he switches to the language of becoming:

> in these cases you know of no other cause of its coming to be two than participation in Twoness, and anything that is going to be two must participate in this, and whatever is going to be one, in Oneness . . . (101c4–7)

By granting the Forms a role in the generation of things and their properties, Plato indicates that they are more than merely the *formal* causes of these things: they do more than give the criterion or standard for being $F$, or explain what it is to be $F$. Certainly the Forms, being incomposite and immaterial, do not function as the *material* causes of things: they are not the 'stuff' out of which things are made. It is unclear, however, whether Plato intends the Forms to function as what Aristotle would call *efficient* or moving causes of things, the agents that by their actions bring things about; as the *final* causes, the end states towards which things strive; or in both of these ways or neither. The description of the causal role of the Forms given in this passage fits rather well with the conception of the Forms as efficient causes, but some of the things Plato has said earlier in the dialogue (74d–75b; see below, sec. VII) about phenomena 'striving to be like' the Forms suggests that they are final causes.

Socrates goes on to consider a single example of the Forms as causes, an example that reveals much about the relation between Forms and phenomena. If Simmias is taller than Socrates but shorter than Phaedo, then both Tallness and Shortness must be in Simmias (102b4–6). It is not by virtue of being Simmias that he is taller than Socrates and shorter than Phaedo but by virtue of the Tallness and Shortness he happens to have. (In Aristotelian terms,

Tallness and Shortness are accidental properties of Simmias.)

Although Simmias can have both Tallness and Shortness at the same time (though in relation to different things), Tallness and Shortness are in different situation. Socrates remarks:

> It seems to me that not only will Tallness itself never be willing at the same time to be both tall and short, but also the Tallness in us will never receive the Short or be willing to be overtopped, but will do either of two things: flee and depart whenever the opposite, the Short, approaches it, or perish when it approaches. It will not be willing to be different from what it was, remaining and receiving Shortness. (102d6—e3)

Tallness, unlike Simmias, cannot receive Shortness; it excludes Shortness by its very nature. Shortness, likewise, excludes Tallness (102e—103a).

It is worth stressing, in part because it has been denied,[5] that Socrates throughout this passage explains facts such as Simmias' tallness by appeal to the presence of the Form in its instances (e.g. the presence of Tallness in Simmias). He appeals to the immanence of the Form several times. We have already seen that he explains the fact that Simmias is larger than Socrates but smaller than Phaedo by stating that 'both Tallness and Shortness are in Simmias' (102b5—6). In 102d—e (just quoted above), he speaks of 'the opposite, the Short' (i.e. Shortness) approaching Tallness in Simmias and causing it to depart or perish. Later, at 104b7—10, when modifying in an important way the theory of causation presented thus far, he puts his auxiliary claim thus: 'not only do those opposites not receive each other; but also whatever things, not being opposites to each other, always have opposites, are not likely to receive the Form (*idean*, b9) which is opposite to that which is in them.' At 104d he speaks of things which 'force whatever they occupy to have not only their own Form (*idean*, d2), but also that of some opposite always'. In the lines immediately following he cites the Form of Three (*hē tōn triōn idea*, d5—6) as an example of something that occupies an object and makes it not just three but also odd and in so doing excludes from it the opposite Form (*hē enantia idea*, d9). Not all the things that enter something bringing with them one opposite and excluding another are Forms; Socrates speaks of fire bringing heat to a body and fever bringing illness (105c). His account of causation thus covers things other than

Forms; but it should be clear from the passages cited above that Plato regards Forms as among the things which enter bodies and bring characteristics with them.

The passages quoted above indicate how Socrates expands his account of causation from its initial, 'safe and ignorant' form (as he refers to it at 105c), the account given at 100b−103a, to the 'more elegant' (*kompsoteran*, 105c2) version explained at 103c−105c. According to the first version, it is the presence of an opposite (usually but not always a Form) in a thing that gives that thing a certain characteristic: Beauty makes a thing beautiful, Tallness makes it tall. According to the refined version, it need not be the opposite itself which is referred to in the explanation; another entity may be cited as the cause of a thing's having a characteristic, so long as the thing mentioned always brings that opposite characteristic with it to whatever it occupies. Thus the presence in a thing of the Form of Three makes that thing odd as well as three, and the presence in something of fire makes that thing hot.

The point of Socrates' presentation of this causal theory is not to show how the Forms function in causal explanation; it is, rather, to establish the immortality of the soul (which is Socrates' aim throughout the dialogue). Accordingly, Socrates concludes by adapting his theory to the case of the soul. The soul, while not the opposite of death, brings that opposite, life, to whatever it occupies. Thus the soul itself will never admit death, and is therefore immortal and imperishable (105c−107a).

For our purposes, however, it is the role of the Forms in causation and not the immortality of the soul that is important. As we have seen, Plato presents a theory of causation in which the Forms play the role of 'sole cause' of the characteristics of phenomena. They are the causes both of a given thing's being $F$ and of its becoming $F$. The Form of $F$ makes something $F$ by being instantiated in that thing; the thing ceases to be $F$ when it ceases to instantiate the Form. Plato portrays the instantiation of a Form in something in terms of the Form's 'entrance' into or 'occupation' of that thing, an entrance and occupation which drive out the opposite Form. The language he uses is the language of immanence: the Form comes to be 'in' the thing it characterises. In the second stage of the argument, the theory of causation is expanded so that the being $F$ of a thing can be explained in terms of its instantiation of some form other than $F$-ness, but the language of immanence is retained throughout the passage.

This explanation of the role of the Forms in causation sheds some light on Plato's conception of the relations among Forms. As early as the *Euthyphro* Plato had portrayed the Forms as standing in relationship to one another. He described the Forms of Holiness and Unholiness as 'entirely opposite' to one another (*Euphr.* 5d3) and put forth the claim that Holiness is a part of Justice (12d2–3). These relations are reflected also in the theory of the *Phaedo* — according to which, as we have seen, some Forms exclude others whereas others 'bring with them' one of a pair of opposite Forms. The question of the relations between Forms is one that looms ever larger for Plato as his thought develops, but the recognition that the Forms are related to each other is certainly present in the early and middle dialogues.

## III. The Forms as Paradigms

In the early and middle dialogues, Plato not only treats the Forms as causes; he also describes them as *paradeigmata*, 'paradigms'. This description is closely connected with his interpretation of participation in terms of resemblance of a copy or image to an original (see below, Sec. VII). In fact, in the *Parmenides* he mentions both claims together:

> But, Parmenides, it seems most clear to me that it is like this: these Forms are set up in nature as paradigms, and the other things are like them and are images of these; and the participation the other things come to have in the Forms is nothing other than their resemblance to them. (132c12–d4)

Although Plato does not refer to the Forms as paradigms in the *Phaedo*, even in discussing the relation of resemblance between Forms and phenomena, he does so refer to them in the early *Euthyphro* and in the *Republic*. I shall shortly examine some of the passages where he does so.

First, however, we must ask what Plato means by the term, *paradeigma*. All Plato scholars would agree that the term means 'standard', and that by calling Forms *paradeigmata* he means to assert that Forms are standards in the sense that they are the sources of the criteria whereby we apply concepts to things. Forms tell us what it is to be $F$, or what $F$-ness is; in some sense of 'meaning', they explain the meaning of $F$, at least for those terms that designate Forms (see Sec. IV, below). Plato makes the same point in a different way when he says (at *Phdo.* 65d12–e1) that Forms are 'what each thing happens to be'.

There are, however, two sorts of standards. One sort is abstract, such as the current standard for the unit of length, one metre, 1,650,763.73 wave lengths of the red-orange line of krypton-86. Such a standard provides a rule for the application of the term 'one metre long', to anything, but it does so without relating the term to any particular object. The other sort of standard, however, ties a concept or term to a particular which exemplifies the concept. Such a standard was the previous standard for the unit of length, one metre, the metre-bar in Paris. I shall call the latter sort of paradigm or standard an *exemplar*, and the former sort a *pattern*.[6]

Most scholars who have written in the last three decades on the question of the paradigmatic function of Forms have assumed that Plato construed his Forms as the latter sort of standard, i.e. as exemplars.[7] According to this conception of the Forms, Forms are perfect instances or examples of the concepts they represent: the Form of Equality is an equal thing (or two equal things), the Form of Bed and a bed, and so on. It is easy to see how such a conception of Forms would lead to the problems of the *Parmenides*. For in order to be an exemplar of a property, the Form would have to have that property; and if the possession of a property by a phenomenal object is to be analysed in terms of that object's participation in a Form, it would seem that the possession of a property by a Form would have to be analysed in terms of that Form's participation in another Form, and so on.

There are reasons to think that Platonic Forms are standards of the former kind, patterns, rather than exemplars, however. We can see this best by examining two of the passages in which Plato describes the Forms as paradigms. The first is *Euthyphro* 6d–e, where the following exchange takes place:

> *Soc.* Remember, then, that it was not this I asked of you, to teach me one or two of the many holy things, but that very Form by virtue of which all the holy things are holy; for you said that by one Form the unholy things are unholy and the holy things holy — or do you not remember?
> *Euth.* I do.

> *Soc.* Then teach me what this Form itself is, in order that, looking at it and using it as a paradigm, I may say that whatever is such as the Form, of those things which you or anyone else may do, is holy, and that I may not say that whatever is not such is holy. (6d9–e6)

Socrates is chiding Euthyphro for having given an example of holiness, a particular kind of action that is holy, in response to Socrates' demand for a definition of the Form. Thus, he distinguishes the Form from examples of it ('one or two of the many holy things'), and implies that the Form is not itself an exemplar of holiness but the single common feature in virtue of which all exemplars of holiness are made holy. His insistence that the Form is not an example of holiness is tied in this passage to the claim that the Form is a 'one over many', an entity that retains its unity though exemplified or instantiated by many things. This also indicates that the Form is not itself an exemplar, but something exemplified, a general pattern.[8]

The second passage occurs in the *Republic*, at V, 472c. Socrates is attempting to deal with the objection to the political theory of the dialogue that the ideal state he has described could never be realised on earth. He points out that it is unnecessary to require that a just person conform exactly to the ideal of justice in order to be called 'just'; it is sufficient if he approximate closely to that ideal. In other words, 'It was for the sake of a paradigm, then, that we were seeking the nature of Justice itself' (472c4–5). It was not the purpose of the discussion to show that either an individual or a city-state precisely conforming to the Form could come to be. The perfectly just person and his polar opposite, the perfectly unjust person, were described as ideals with which we could compare ourselves in attempting to discern the relative portions of justice and injustice in our lives (472c–d). Just as a painter who had portrayed the ideally beautiful man could not be faulted on the grounds that his painting was not and could not be a portrait of any actually existing individual, the philosopher who describes in words the ideal of justice cannot be criticised if it turns out that this ideal is not completely realisable.

Plato seems here to be divorcing the idea of a paradigm of justice from any particular example or instantiation of it. The role of the Form as a standard or paradigm is that of an ideal to which examples approximate. Had he thought of Forms as themselves exemplars of the properties for which they are named, he could have said that on earth there might be no perfect instance of a Form, but as each Form is a perfect instance of itself we have a guarantee that such an instance exists. This is not his point, however; indeed, the passage trades on the contrast between a Form, which is an ideal standard or pattern, and any instance or exemplar of the Form.[9]

These passages show Plato thinking of the Forms as paradigms in contexts where it is extremely doubtful that he regards them as exemplars of themselves. We should be wary, then, of the interpretation of the Theory of Forms that makes each Form an exemplar of itself. Forms are paradigms in that they are standards, general patterns common to many things, and abstract ideals to which things approach; but not, it seems, in the sense that they are perfect instances or exemplars of the characteristics of which they are the Forms.

## IV. Self-Predication

We come now to the last of the four topics of this chapter on which the testimony of the early dialogues is as important as that of the middle period works. As I noted above (in Sec. III), problems arise for Plato's Theory of Forms if it turns out that the Forms in general have the properties of which they are the Forms. One of the reasons Plato scholars have thought Plato was committed to this view is that they have in general treated his claim that the Forms are paradigms as the claim that they are exemplars. I have already argued that this is not an accurate representation of Plato's view. The main reason scholars have assumed that Plato held this rather strange position, however, is that they have regarded certain statements in the dialogues of these periods as proof that Plato regarded the Forms in general as self-predicative.

There is some divergence in usage among scholars with respect to the term, 'self-predication'. As I shall use the term, two conditions must be met before it can be asserted that a given Form is self-predicative: (a) the term '$F$' must be applicable to the Form of $F$; and (b) the basis of the application of the term must be the possession by the Form of the property, relation, or kind named by the term.[10] Scholars have thought that Plato believed that his Forms were self-predicative because he often says things which satisfy condition (a). In the *Protagoras*, he asserts that Justice is just and Holiness holy (330c–d); in the *Phaedo* he indicates that the Form of Equality is equal (74c–d); in the *Symposium* he says that there is no respect in which Beauty does not appear beautiful, and indicates that it is far more beautiful than any of the things that participate in it (210e–212a; cf. *Phdo.* 100c); in *Republic* X, 597b he speaks of 'three beds', one of which is the Form; and there are other cases.[11]

It is clear, moreover, that Plato accepts my condition (a) as a general principle. For he holds that Forms and their participants are homonymous, that they have the same names and that phenomena derive their names from the names of the Forms in which they participate (*Phdo.* 102b, 103e).[12] What is not clear, what has in fact been the subject of a great deal of scholarly debate in the past thirty years, is whether my condition (b) is met.[13] This we must attempt to determine by examination of the relevant passages.

As I have stated at the start of this section, the early dialogues contain evidence on the question of self-predication that is as important as that in the middle dialogues. In fact, Gregory Vlastos has called *Protagoras* 330c–d 'the star instance of Self-Predication in Plato'.[14] Now Plato does have Socrates claim in this passage that Justice is just and Holiness is holy, and, though there is no explicit textual proof that he is speaking of Forms, this is a natural enough assumption. Thus, *Prot.* 330c–d satisfies my condition (a); but does it satisfy (b)? I shall argue that it does not. I hope to show that a hitherto overlooked clue in the context of the passage indicates that Plato understood these alleged cases of self-predication as identity statements rather than as predications.[15]

Let us place the claims that Justice is just and Holiness holy in the context of the dialogue. Socrates has been eliciting from Protagoras his views on the virtues. Protagoras has said that these include Justice, Temperance, Holiness, Wisdom and Courage, and that Virtue is a single whole made up of these as parts (329d–330a). He believes, however, in apparent disagreement with Socrates, that the parts of Virtue are dissimilar to each other. Socrates sets out to prove that they are either very similar or actually identical.

Protagoras assents when Socrates asks whether Justice is 'a certain thing' (*pragma ti*, 330c1), and also when Socrates says,

> What, then; if someone were to ask you and me, 'Protagoras and Socrates, tell me: this thing which you have just now named, Justice, is this itself[16] just or unjust?' I would answer on my

own behalf that it is just; how do you cast your vote? (330c2—6)

The same inquiry yields the same results concerning Holiness (330d—e).

Of course it is Protagoras' ready assent to these apparent self-predicational questions that has perplexed scholars. He balks only when Socrates switches the predicate terms, asking whether Justice is holy and Holiness just; but it is Socrates' own gloss on these new questions that shows, I believe, how the original questions are to be understood (and, incidentally, why they seem obviously true to Protagoras). Socrates, continuing the fiction that an anonymous 'someone' is interrogating both himself and Protagoras, says,

> What, then, Protagoras, shall we answer him, having agreed to these things, if he asks us in addition, 'Is not Holiness such as to be a just thing; or is Justice such as not to be holy, but such as to be not holy? And is Holiness such as not to be just . . . ?' What shall we answer him? I myself would say on my own behalf that Justice is holy and Holiness just; and on your behalf, if you let me, I would make the same answer, that Justice is either the same as Holiness or that it is most similar, and that most especially of all things is Justice such as Holiness and Holiness such as Justice. (331a6—b6)

When Socrates offers to make 'the same answer' on behalf of Protagoras as on his own behalf, he tells us that he regards the claim that Justice and Holiness are either identical or most similar as equivalent to the claims that Justice is holy and Holiness just. He interprets 'Justice is holy' not as an ordinary case of predication, but as a relational statement, 'Justice is either the same as Holiness or most similar to it'.[17] The apparent basis for the attribution of a general term, 'holy', to the Form of Justice is not the possession of a property by the Form, but its similarity to, or identity with, the Form of Holiness.

We shall see below that Plato develops in the middle dialogues an account of participation according to which the possession of a property by an object (and the corresponding application of a general term to that object) is explained in terms of the resemblance of that object to the appropriate Form. This account grounds properties in terms of relations to Forms, rather than basing the relation of an object to a Form on the possession by both of a property.[18] It is tempting to see Plato's treatment of 'Justice is holy' and 'Holiness is just' as instances of that general account. It is also tempting to take the fact that Plato mentions sameness and similarity together as evidence that he regards sameness or identity as, not a different relation from similarity, but the limiting case of it. If Plato indeed did look at the two relations this way, he would naturally regard the identity of a Form with itself as the best possible justification for the application of the appropriate general term to the Form.

Whatever may have been Plato's thoughts about the relation between identity and resemblance, his analysis of 'Justice is holy' enables us to understand 'Justice is just' as well. For he explained 'Justice is holy' as meaning 'Justice is either identical with or most similar to Holiness'. If we substitute 'just' for 'holy' in the statement to be analysed, we get the corresponding analysis for 'Justice is just': 'Justice is either identical with or most similar to Justice.' Since every Form is identical to itself, this statement would be recognised by Plato (and hence, presumably, by his Protagoras) as self-evidently true. This would explain why Protagoras readily accepts the statement in the dialogue.

We are apt to balk at the idea that 'Justice is just' can mean 'Justice is identical to Justice'. Were it not for the fact that Plato gives the analysis of 'Justice is holy' mentioned above, I would have found such an interpretation far-fetched. As it is, this passage of the *Protagoras* serves as a warning to the reader that not every application of a general term to an object in Plato is a case of what we would call predication.

The 'star instance' of self-predication in Plato has turned out on analysis to be a case of identity. Unfortunately, not every instance allows such treatment. Of the three passages we shall consider next, one (from the *Republic*) seems to preclude self-predication in general; another (from the *Symposium*) seems to treat one Form as straightforwardly self-predicational; and the third (from the *Phaedo*) seems to be in the crucial respects ambiguous. Let us look first at the *Republic* passage.

In the tenth book of the *Republic* (596a–598d) Plato distinguishes the Form of Bed from beds made by carpenters, on the one hand, and pictures of beds produced by painters. The three-fold distinction parallels the distinction among phenomenal images, phenomenal objects (including artefacts such as beds) and Forms made earlier in the Divided Line passage (see below, Sec. VII).

Forms are 'ones over many' (596a); the Form of Bed is 'what a bed is' and 'true being' (597a); and it is the product of God, if of anyone (597b). The carpenter uses the Form as a model when he makes the sort of bed on which we sleep (596b); this sort of bed is not, as is the Form, true being but something that resembles being and is rather obscure with respect to reality (597a). The painter uses the bed the carpenter makes as his model and represents only the appearance and not the reality of it (598a–b; cf. 596e); the painting produced is at the third remove from nature (i.e. the Form, which God is said to produce in nature; cf. 597c, e).

For our purposes, the most important distinction Plato makes between the Form of Bed and the bed made by the carpenter is this: the carpenter 'does not make the Form, which we say is what a bed is (*ho esti klinē*), but some particular bed (*klinēn tina*)' (597a1–2). By implication, the Form itself is *not* a particular bed; and this in turn shows that, although 'bed' is used as a name of the Form, it does not function as a predicate in the case of a Form. In order for 'bed' to function as a predicate term, it would have to classify the object it applies to as an instance of the artefact-type, bed. That is, we only use 'bed' as a genuine predicate when we say of something that it is *a* bed, or in Plato's terms, some particular bed. Since Plato states that the Form is one of three sorts of 'bed', but denies that the Form is a particular bed, we must infer that 'bed' is not predicated of the Form, even though it refers to it. Thus, though the use of 'bed' to apply to the Form of Bed meets condition (a), it does not meet condition (b), and therefore is not a case of self-predication.

In 597c–d Plato makes an argument for the essential uniqueness of the Form, and this argument also seems to rule out the possibility that the Form of Bed could be an instance of itself, i.e. self-predicative. There cannot be two Forms of Bed, he says. For suppose two to exist; they would in turn have to have a common Form, and it would be this, rather than they, which would really be the Form of Bed. The point of these brief and suggestive remarks I take to be this. Forms are essentially unique because of the kinds of things they are. Forms are 'what a thing is', the essences of things, rather than things which have essences. It is easy to conceive of a multiplicity of things having an essence or participating in a Form, but it is impossible to think of more than one essence for a given multiplicity. There can be two beds, but not two Forms of Bed, because it simply does not make sense to think of two essences having exactly the same definition and having the same set of participants but differing only in number. For one Form to be different from another the two would have to be different in definition, not merely in number; mere numerical difference is a possibility only for things that have Forms, not for Forms themselves. For this reason, even to attempt to conceive of two Forms of Bed is in fact to think, not of Forms, but of things having Forms; and thus to fail in the attempt. If this interpretation of the argument is correct, it is clear that it is wrong to think of the Forms in general as instances of themselves, as instantiations of their own essences.[19]

*Symposium* 210e−212a, however, suggests that the Form of Beauty, at least, is in fact a perfect instance of itself, a supremely beautiful thing. The explicit self-predicational language we found in the *Protagoras* is absent here: Plato does not say straight out that Beauty is beautiful. Rather, he begins by denying that it is beautiful in only some respect or relationship, in some part or at some time (211a). He goes on to say that it is not like gold or clothing or beautiful youths (211d). It seems reasonable to infer from these remarks that Beauty is absolutely (rather than relatively) beautiful, that its beauty is greater than that of other objects. As Vlastos has pointed out, for Beauty to be the ultimate object of desire, it must, on Plato's own account, be the most beautiful of things;[20] for this reason also we may assume that Beauty is beautiful. *Phdo.* 100c4−6 also implies that Beauty is beautiful when it states that 'if anything else is beautiful besides the Beautiful itself, it is so for no other reason than that it participates in that Beautiful'.

It would seem, then, that Plato, despite his prohibition on self-predication contained in *Republic* X, regarded at least one Form as an instance of itself. There is no particular harm in claiming that the Form of Beauty is beautiful, as there is in claiming that the Form of Largeness is large (which sets off the Third Man regress in the *Parmenides*): Beauty is a property something may have without thereby needing to be a physical object. Self-predication may be in cases like this, as Vlastos has urged, 'mandatory and innocent'.[21] None the less, if even one Platonic Form is self-predicational, and if the self-predication assumption is crucial in generating the regress of the Third Man Argument (see Ch. II, Sec. IV), Plato will need some way of stopping the regress for this case.

In the *Phaedo* Socrates distinguishes the Form of Equality from equal sticks and stones in the following way:

> Consider it this way: do not equal stones and sticks sometimes,
> though they remain the same, seem equal to one person and
> unequal to another?
> Certainly.
> Well, then; is there ever a time when the Equals themselves
> appeared unequal to you, or Equality Inequality?
> Never, Socrates.
> These equal things and the Equal itself are not the same, then.
> It does not at all seem so to me, Socrates. (74b7–c6)

This passage has been much discussed by Plato scholars in the past
thirty years, and the discussion of it has made several points clear.

First, the argument attempts to show that the Form of Equality is
different from equal sticks, stones, etc., by showing that the latter
have a property the former lacks. That property is appearing to be
unequal in some situations. Equal sticks and stones may occasionally appear to be unequal, but the Form never does; thus, the two
are not identical.[22]

Plato does not hold, as some scholars[23] have alleged, that the
sticks and stones in question aren't really equal; he says that they
*are* equal, but appear unequal. He does not defend or maintain, but
in fact denies, the view that no two phenomenal objects are ever the
same length, width, height, or weight. The appearance of
inequality does not reflect a difference in the objects, but (we may
assume) the fallibility of our sensory apparatus, which makes it
liable to deceptive or erroneous experiences. (We shall see below, in
Sec. VI, that Plato regards the senses as deceptive.)

Plato refers to the Form of Equality by three different names:
'the Equals themselves' (*auta ta isa*, 74c1), 'Equality' (*hē isotēs*,
ibid.), and 'the Equal itself' (*auto to ison*, 74c4–5). His use of the
plural in *auta ta isa* has been the subject of much controversy.
Some scholars[24] have assumed that this expression refers not to the
Form but to a class of perfect instances of the Form. There is no
reason to think that Plato would here introduce by the briefest of
allusions an entirely new class of entities, which some have
associated with the class of 'mathematicals' Aristotle attributes to
Plato in the *Metaphysics* (A. 6, 987b14–18). Moreover, reference
to such a class would be irrelevant to the argument, the cogency of
which requires that *auta ta isa* refer to the Form.[25]

It has also been alleged that the use of the plural shows that Plato
conceived the Form as a set of two equal things, but this does not

seem to be the case, either. The simplest explanation of the plural is a purely grammatical one: Plato has just referred to equal sticks and stones in the plural, so his use of a plural expression to designate the Form is a natural shift which has no metaphysical significance.[26]

Even when these points have been established, however, the sense of the passage remains unclear, and in a most crucial respect. Plato says that the Form of Equality never appears to be unequal. This presumably implies that the Form is equal, and Plato states as much at 74d5−6, when he asks, 'Does it seem to us, then, that these things [i.e. the equal sticks and stones] are equal in just the same way the Equal itself is?' But what does it mean to say the Form of Equality is equal?

There seem to be two possible interpretations, neither of which can be ruled out on the basis of the text. The first is the self-predicative interpretation. According to this view, the Form of Equality is equal in that it possesses the (relational) property of being equal. There are numerous difficulties with this view, not the least of which is that it subjects the Form of Equality to the criticisms of the *Parmenides*. It is also difficult to tell what the Form of Equality could be equal to, unless the Form were, after all, a pair of equal objects. These difficulties do not, however, rule out the possibility that the self-predicational interpretation is correct; indeed, this interpretation could be put forward by those who wish to show that the Theory of Forms *is* subject to the Third Man regress.

The second interpretation is that, when Plato says that the Form of Equal is equal, this only means that Equality is Equality. 'Equal', according to this view, functions as a name of the Form and not as a predicate term. This interpretation does not commit Plato to the doctrine of self-predication.

There are several points in favour of this interpretation, beyond the obvious one that it frees the Theory of Forms from the criticisms of the *Parmenides*. The first is that, although Plato admits at 74d that both the Form and the equal sticks and stones are equal, he also says that they are not equal in the same way. On this interpretation, the difference is easily explained: the Form is 'equal' in the sense that it is Equality, whereas the sticks and stones are equal in the sense that they participate in Equality.[27] This difference between a referential or identifying use of 'equal' and a predicative use fits well with the distinction Plato makes in *Rep.* X between 'what a bed is' and 'some particular bed', and with the interpretation of 'Justice is just' in the *Protagoras* as an identity statement.

The second point is that this interpretation enables us to explain a remark which would otherwise be irrelevant to the argument. We recall that Plato asks, 'is there ever a time when the Equals themselves appeared unequal to you, or Equality Inequality?' (74c1–2). We have seen that 'the Equals themselves' and 'Equality' are both names of the Form of Equal, and that the point of the argument is to distinguish the Form from its participants by showing that the latter have, as the former does not, the property of sometimes appearing unequal. The first part of the question, and Simmias' immediate negative reply, suffice to establish that Equality never appears to be unequal; what, then, is the last part of the question doing in the argument? What does the fact that Equality never appears to be Inequality have to do with the fact that Equality never appears to be unequal? On the self-predicative interpretation, the latter part of the question is simply irrelevant; but on the interpretation we are now considering, it makes perfect sense. For if Plato is using 'equal' as the name of Equality, and not as a predicate term, he should likewise be using 'unequal' as the name of Inequality. Thus, when he asks, 'Is Equality capable of appearing unequal?' he means, 'Is Equality capable of appearing to be Inequality?' Thus, the last part of the question would not be irrelevant but would be a restatement of the original question, specifying the sense in which one might ask of the Form whether it might appear unequal.

This brings up another advantage of the interpretation we are now concerned with. It is hard to see why, on the self-predicative interpretation, the Form of Equality should never be thought of as unequal. If it possesses the property of being equal, and if we can make mistakes in judging whether phenomenal objects possess this property, why could we not make mistakes in making the same sort of judgement about the Form? On the other interpretation, however, the mistake ruled out is not a judgement that a Form has a given property, but a judgement that one opposite Form is its own opposite. There is a great difference between confusing the concept of Equality with that of Inequality and failing to apply those concepts correctly in a given situation; the latter sort of mistake is common enough, while the former might well be thought impossible, at least for anyone who knew what the words 'equal' and 'unequal' meant.

Admittedly, the second interpretation of the claim that Equality is equal is not as natural to us as the first, self-predicative one. This is because we recognise, at least intuitively, a difference between general terms, such as 'equal', and abstract singular terms, such as 'equality', and think that the former can only be used as predicates, while the latter can only be used as subject terms. This distinction was apparently not one Plato recognised himself, however; for he commonly uses general terms and singular terms indiscriminately as names of Forms. At *Phdo.* 65d4–13, for instance, in the space of ten lines he uses the general terms 'Just', 'Beautiful', and 'Good', and the singular terms 'Largeness', 'Health', and 'Strength' as referring expressions for Forms; and the general terms are not accompanied by the definite article which we would require to make them into proper referring expressions. Thus it seems that it was entirely possible for Plato to assert that 'The Equal is equal' and mean by that 'Equality is Equality'.

In spite of the points in favour of the second interpretation, however, there seems to be nothing in the text of this passage that absolutely disqualifies the self-predicative interpretation from consideration. Thus, whereas the passage of the *Republic* we examined seems incompatible with the claim that the Forms are self-predicative, this passage is not. The self-predicative interpretation of this particular passage is not the likeliest one, but it is not impossible. It would seem from all of this that Plato does not accept self-predication as a general principle, but that he does accept the fact that some Forms (such as Beauty in the *Symposium*) are self-predicative. If this is so, the criticisms of the *Parmenides* will bear on some Platonic Forms, but not on all. How this affects their validity we have yet to determine.

## V. The Forms as Objects of Knowledge; the Being-Becoming Distinction

Plato in the middle dialogues distinguishes between the mental states of *epistēmē* and *doxa* or, as translators of Plato would have it, knowledge and belief or opinion.[28] Phenomena are the objects of *doxa*, whereas Forms are the objects of *epistēmē*. Phenomena are disqualified as objects of knowledge because they lack certain characteristics which Forms possess. Thus, the fact that Forms are the objects of knowledge *par excellence* for Plato is closely related to their nature.

Plato portrays the Forms as objects of knowledge in their first appearance in the *Phaedo*, at 65d–e. In the preceding passage (63e–65d), Socrates has been arguing that the philosopher desires death. Death is the separation of the soul from the body; the philosopher desires this separation because he disdains all the pleasures of the body and because the body hinders him in his quest for wisdom. Once the state of wisdom has been discussed, Socrates turns to the Forms as the objects of wisdom. As we have seen above, he first gets the assent of Simmias to the existence of 'something Just itself' (65d4–5); to this he adds in the next lines (d7–13) the Forms of Beauty, Goodness, Largeness, Health, Strength, and 'all such things' (d12). He points out that none of these things is perceptible to vision or to any of the other senses; they are not apprehended by means of the body, but rather 'whoever of us has prepared himself to think most fully and accurately about each thing itself which he considers will come closest to the knowledge of each thing' (65e2–4). The contrast between what is recognised by sense and what is recognised by thought is fundamental to the distinction between *epistēmē* and *doxa* and the related distinction between Forms and phenomena.

In *Republic* V, 475e–480a, Plato elaborates on the distinction between *epistēmē* (here also referred to by *gnōsis* and *gnomē*) and *doxa* and their respective objects. Knowledge and opinion are different mental faculties (*dunameis*, 'powers', 477d–e), and therefore have different objects (478a–b). The object of knowledge, which is infallible (477e), is being (478b), what is 'completely' (*pantelōs*, 477a3) and 'purely' (*eilikrinōs*, a7). The object of opinion, which is between knowledge and ignorance (477d), is what lies between complete being and absolute non-being, what 'is so as to be and not to be' (477a6). It turns out that the Forms, which only the phiiosopher recognises, are the objects of knowledge (479e); the many phenomena that participate in these Forms and the many conventions about beauty and other things are the objects of opinion (479a–d). These participants in the Forms are between being and non-being in the sense that, for any term '*F*' that can be predicated of them, there is some respect in which they can also be called 'not-*F*' (479a–c).

Thus there are two classes of objects: those which are 'completely' and which are the objects of knowledge, and those which are and are not, and which are the objects of opinion. In *Phdo.* 78b–80b, Plato lists the characteristics of these two classes. We should note at the outset that when Plato says that things in the second class 'are and are not', he does not mean that they only partially exist (whatever that might mean), but, as the passage from the *Republic* just discussed indicates, that they are both *F* and not-*F*.[29] Plato recognises a distinction between the temporally unlimited existence of the Forms and the temporally limited existence of phenomena, but he does not mean to deny that the objects of opinion and sensation are actual. In fact, although he usually reserves the term 'being' for the Forms, he explicitly states at 79a6–7 that there are two sorts of beings, the visible and the invisible.[30]

Invisible being, which Plato identifies with the Forms (78d) is 'uniform' (*monoeidē*, 78d5, 80b2); visible being, on the other hand, is 'multiform' (80b4). It is not clear what this means; literally, it would seem to mean that each Form is simple, that it has only one Form (presumably the Form which it is), whereas phenomena each have a number of Forms or attributes. Socrates espouses such a view in the *Parmenides* (128e–130a; esp. 129b–c, d–e), where it is shown to be incoherent. Yet this assertion of simplicity is at odds not only with the *Parmenides* and the *Sophist*, but with the *Euthyphro*, the *Republic* (cf. esp. V, 476a6–7, where it is said that the Forms 'commune with one another') and the *Phaedo* itself (esp. 103e–105b), where Forms are shown to be complex at least to the extent that they enter into relations with each other. Perhaps all Plato means here is that the Form is one, whereas its instances are many — a contrast that is basic to the Theory of Forms and is often made (cf. e.g. *Rep.* V, 476a–c).

Forms are also constant and invariant, never changing in any respect (78d), whereas phenomena are 'entirely opposite to those and so to speak never in the same state either relative to themselves or to one another' (78e2–4). Again, it is not clear precisely what is meant here. The constancy of the Forms is clear enough, but when Plato asserts that phenomena are never in the same state, does he mean that *every* property of every phenomenal object is in change at each moment, or merely that *some* property of every object can be found which is changing at a given moment? The former view we may call 'radical Heracliteanism'; it is the position Plato attributes to Heraclitus in the *Theaetetus* and which he shows here to be incoherent (182a–183c). Some scholars have attributed this view to Plato himself, at least in the middle dialogues; but, in so far as Plato believes in some similarity between phenomena and the

Forms, it would perhaps be unwise to saddle him with a view of phenomena which makes any similarity impossible, given that a less extreme interpretation of his claim in this passage is possible. If Plato is only claiming that phenomena are always changing in some respect, there is room for considerable stability in their nature and considerable similarity between them and Forms, and there is no need to see the critique of the *Theaetetus* as directed against a view Plato once held himself.

The absolute unchangeableness of the Forms is proof that they are incomposite and thus not subject to destruction (78b–c); the inconsistency of phenomena, in contrast, attests to their composite nature and liability to dissolution. By saying that Forms are incomposite, I take it that Plato means that they are not composed of *physical* parts. He need not be taken to deny here what he affirms in the *Euthyphro*, for instance, that Piety is a 'part' of Justice (12d2–3) in the sense that the Form of Justice includes in its extension the extension of the Form of Piety.

As Forms are impervious to any sort of change and not liable to destruction, their existence is not temporally limited,[31] as is that of phenomena, which are subject not only to qualitative change but to generation and destruction. Although Plato refers to the class of generable and destructible things as 'beings' at 79a6–7, as we have seen, he normally restricts the term 'being' to things that exist forever and uses 'becoming' (*genesis* and related terms, such as *to gignomenon*) for things whose existence is temporally limited. The contrast is drawn precisely in these terms at *Tim.* 27d–28a; and, thus, the contrast between the two orders of entities has come to be known as the 'Being-Becoming' distinction. Since '*genesis*' and its relatives can be used in Greek to denote both a change in property and substantial coming-to-be, the label of the distinction is appropriate in that it brings out two of the basic differences between Forms and phenomena in Plato's ontology: Forms are indestructible and unchanging, whereas phenomena become both in that they change their properties and in that they come into existence and pass out of it.

Plato does not explicitly state that imperviousness to change is a necessary condition for being an object of knowledge, though he links the two traits at *Phdo.* 79a. Aristotle, though, attributed to the Platonists the view that phenomena were unsuited to be objects of knowledge because they were constantly changing and 'there is no knowledge of things in flux' (*Metaph.* M. 4, 1078b16–17).

Though disagreeing with the Platonists about the existence of Forms, Aristotle himself denies that there is *epistēmē* of objects of perception: cf. *An. Post.* I, ch. 31). If this is an accurate representation of Plato's thinking, we can say that it is because the Forms are changeless that they are objects of knowledge.[32]

Whatever may be the truth of the matter, it is clear from the passages discussed above that Plato distinguished Forms from phenomena on several grounds. The Forms are the only genuine objects of knowledge, they have absolute being, they are uniform, invisible, incomposite, unchanging, and they are temporally unlimited in their existence. Phenomena, in contrast, are the objects of opinion, are between being and non-being, are sensible, multiform, composite, in constant change and exist only for a limited time. I shall in the following include all of these distinctions under the heading of the 'Being-Becoming' distinction.

## VI. The Separation of Forms and Phenomena

The distinction between Being and Becoming is a distinction between two sorts of entity, two orders of being. As so far discussed, it implies no physical or spatial separation[33] between the two orders; for all Plato has stated, the Forms might coexist with or even be elements in the composition of phenomena. Yet is is clear from the *Phaedo* and elsewhere that Plato does intend the Forms to be not merely ontologically distinct but actually removed from the phenomenal world.

Plato insists on the separation of Forms and phenomena in the first passage of the *Phaedo* in which he introduces the Forms. After pointing out that Forms are not apprehended by sense but by intellect (65d−e), he asserts that they can only be recognised by one who separates his intellect from his body:

> Then would he do this most purely who as far as possible approached each thing with the intellect itself, neither employing any vision in the thought process, nor dragging along any other sense with his reason; but using pure reason, itself in itself, would he try to hunt down each of the things that are, pure and itself in itself, getting rid of his eyes and ears and, so to speak, all of his body, in so far as it is possible, on the grounds that it causes confusion and does not allow the soul to possess truth and intelligence when it accompanies her? (65e6−66a6)

It may seem that the talk of separating the soul from the body in order to see the Forms is metaphor; the context, however, suggests otherwise. This passage occurs in the context of an argument that the philosopher should desire death (see above, p. 30). The separation of the soul from the body in death is the separation he is here concerned with, and he explicitly makes the claim that:

> either the possession of knowledge is nowhere possible, or it is so when we are dead. For then the soul, itself in itself, will exist apart from the body, but not before. (66e6–67a2)

The natural explanation of this claim is that the Forms do not exist in the phenomenal world, but elsewhere: in that 'other world' to which the soul journeys after death (cf. 61e, 63b–64a). There would thus be, not simply two orders of beings, or categories of entity, but two distinct worlds, separated from each other in such a way that the soul of a living person inhabits only one and the soul of a person who has died inhabits only the other.

This picture is confirmed by the first two arguments Plato presents in favour of the immortality of the soul. The argument from opposites (70c–72e) portrays two worlds between which souls travel in the course of birth and death (70c, 71e–72a). The argument from recollection (72e–77a) argues for the existence of our souls in another world before our birth. As this argument is based on an explanation of how we come to know the Forms in our lifetime and thus links the Theory of Forms explicitly to the doctrine of two worlds, we shall examine it in some detail.

According to the argument, learning or coming to know something is actually recollection (72e). Recollection occurs when the perception of one thing puts one in mind of another thing which one has previously known (73c–d). One may be reminded of something by virtue of seeing something similar or something dissimilar; in the case of recollection from similars, the similarity may be either perfect or imperfect (74a). We recollect the Forms (Plato uses the example of Equality) on the basis of sensory experience of phenomena that resemble them imperfectly (74a–e; for more detailed discussions of this passage, see Secs. IV above and VII below). Our recollection of the Form on the basis of our experience of things that resemble it shows that we knew the Form before we saw the resembling objects and recognised their relation to the Form (74e–75a). Since we have been using our senses from the time of birth, it must have been before we were born that we acquired knowledge of the Forms (75b–d). At birth we forget this knowledge, which we later recollect on the basis of experience (75d–76d). Since our souls did not acquire the knowledge of the Forms at any time after our birth, 'then our souls existed, Simmias, even earlier, before they were in human form, apart from (*chōris*, 76c12) our bodies, and they had wisdom' (76c11–13).

This rather elaborate theory of recollection softens somewhat the harsh critique of sensory experience given earlier, at 65a–66e, and evades the conclusion that knowledge of the Forms is possible only after death. Plato had previously condemned the senses utterly, stating that they were a hindrance to the acquisition of knowledge and that the philosopher was better off without them; but here he gives them the role of catalysts for recollection and states that our knowledge of the Forms is derived from nothing else but the senses (75a). It now appears that, although the senses are not adequate for knowledge, they are necessary for it, at least while the soul is embodied. Plato had also stated before that knowledge was possible only after death, although he had allowed that one might come close to knowledge in life by purifying the soul from the corrupting influence of the body (66e–67a). Now, since the claims that the soul exists before birth and knows the Forms in that time have been established to Plato's satisfaction, he can allow the possibility of knowledge for the embodied soul on the basis of recollection.

The theory of recollection does nothing, however, to lessen the separation of the Forms from phenomena. In fact, the argument for the pre-existence of the soul depends precisely on the view that the Forms are not directly available to the embodied soul. Recollection is required only if the Forms are not immanent in the phenomenal world and thus available to the experience of living humans, but separate from that world. Thus, the theory of recollection itself attests to the separation of Forms and phenomena.

Other passages of the middle dialogues also support the claim of separation. Throughout the famous analogies of sun, line and cave in the *Republic* (507a–521b; see esp. 508b–c, 509d, 517a–c) the intelligible order is portrayed as a world or region separate from the sensible world; and in the *Phaedrus* this world is located 'above the heavens' (247c; see 247b–248c), outside of the phenomenal realm. These passages, especially the *Phaedrus* one, are doubtless not to be taken literally; but it is clear from them and from other remarks in the dialogues (e.g. *Rep.* IX, 592b, where Socrates refers to the Form of the just city as 'a pattern set up in heaven') that Plato intends us to understand that the Forms are not immanent in the phenomenal world but separate from that world and transcendent.

The separation of the Forms is closely related to their role as objects of knowledge. If we were correct in assuming that knowledge for Plato required permanence, we may conjecture further that Plato removed the Forms from the phenomenal world in order to free them from any suspicion or taint of change. Yet if this purification of the Forms is required for them to fulfil their function as objects of knowledge, it seems that the separation of the Forms is incompatible with their role as causes of the characteristics of phenomena, a role which, as I have described it in Section II above, requires that the Forms be immanent in phenomena.

This raises the question (which seems to me to be of central importance for the Theory of Forms in the middle dialogues), how can the Forms be both separate or transcendent (as they must be to be objects of knowledge) and immanent (as they must be to be causes)? Plato exploits both the causal and epistemological roles of the Forms throughout the middle dialogues, without seeming to be aware of the conflict.[34] It is only in the *Parmenides* that the tension comes to light.

It would seem that the Theory of Forms is overloaded with tasks; Plato demands that it perform too many functions, some of which are incompatible with each other.[35] If that is the case, one way to resolve the difficulty would be to asign one of the tasks to another agent; and this is in fact what I think Plato does in the late dialogues, where the Demiurge takes over the causal role assigned to the Forms in the *Phaedo*. There is, however, the material for another resolution of the conflict in the distinction (discussed above, Sec. II) between the Forms 'in themselves' and the Forms 'in us'. By distinguishing two modes of existence for the Forms, Plato might have resolved the conflict between their transcendence and immanence, stating that 'in themselves' the Forms are separate and pure, while 'in us' they are immanent causes. (Aquinas uses a similar distinction between form in itself and as instantiated to show how form can be particular in one situation but not in another in his *De Ente et Essentia*.)

Plato does not, however, exploit the opportunity his own distinction gives him. It is tempting to speculate that he did not see this as a way out of the problem because he conceived the distinction between Forms and phenomena in terms of the spatial distinction between two worlds, described above. He would naturally have connected the idea of a 'mode of existence' with a location in one of the two worlds and might well have found the view that an object might have locations in both worlds absurd.

## VII. The Problem of Participation

We have seen already that Plato thinks of the Forms as not only distinct from phenomena but as existing separately from them, and that he also thinks of the Forms as causally related to phenomena, by virtue of being somehow 'in' them. For the former conception of the Forms, it is unimportant and in fact unnecessary to specify *any* relation that holds between Forms and phenomena; for the latter conception, it is vital that Forms and phenomena be related in some way.

Plato does hold that Forms and phenomena are related to each other, and he names this relation 'participation' (*methexis*). In explaining the causal role of the Forms, we saw that Plato had stated that participation in the Form of Beauty was the sole reason why anything other than the Form was beautiful; all other cases were handled analogously (100c). As to the nature of this all-important relation, however, Plato is strangely uninformative:

> nothing else makes it beautiful than either the presence of that Beautiful itself, or communion, or whatever is the manner whereby it attaches itself;[36] for I make no confident affirmation on this as yet, but only that it is by the Beautiful that all the beautiful things are beautiful. (100d4–8)

In the absence of a clear statement from Plato as to the nature of participation (and the other middle dialogues are as unhelpful in this matter as is the *Phaedo*), we must look for circumstantial evidence as to the nature of the relation.

It turns out that Plato exploits two different metaphors for participation, corresponding to the two different conceptions of the Forms which have already been delineated. We have seen that, when Plato speaks of the Forms as causes, he treats them as immanent in things. It is therefore not surprising that in this context he thinks of participation in terms of 'sharing' and 'communion'. This account of participation is close to the literal meaning of *metechēin*, 'to have a share in'. *Metalambanein*, another verb Plato uses in the sense of 'to participate in', also means literally 'to have a share in'. These two verbs have the welcome feature of fitting nicely with the concept of the Forms as immanent in things, since they suggest, in their literal sense, that the Forms are somehow 'parcelled out' or 'distributed' among the many phenomena that participate in them. This aspect of the metaphor of sharing turns out also to be a weakness, however, for it suggests that the Forms are divided up into spatially separate portions. This suggestion is exploited in the critique of the Theory of Forms in the *Parmenides*.

The notion of the Forms as divided is not implicit in the other terms Plato uses as substitutes for 'participation'. Two of these, which he uses in the passage quoted above (p. 37) are *parousia*, 'presence', and *koinōnia*, 'communion'. Although Plato stresses that he will not affirm which of the two is the proper substitute for or analysis of 'participation', it is significant that both terms he uses here, as well as the verb *prosgenomenē*, 'attaches itself', suggest that the Form is where its participants are. This is what we should expect, given that the context of the passage is the treatment of the causal role of the Forms, in which, as we have seen, Plato repeatedly insists on their immanence in things. Both 'presence' and 'communion' seem to hold out the hope that the Form could be immanent in things without being divided into portions: in both locutions, it is the Form and not some piece of it that is said to be related to the phenomenon characterised by it.

The other metaphor for participation that Plato uses is that of resemblance or imaging. As we find him speaking of sharing and communion in contexts where the Forms are treated as causes and as immanent, we find the language of resemblance in contexts where the Forms are treated as transcendent. One such context is *Phdo*. 74a–75b, where the Form of Equality is discussed in connection with the argument from recollection (see above, Sec. VI). The reader will recall that the purpose of this argument is to prove the ante-natal existence of the soul and that Plato relies on a conception of Forms as separate from the phenomenal world to accomplish this purpose.

Phenomenal equals, such as sticks and stones, put one in mind of Equality itself, which is different from them. The basis of the act of recollection is a defective resemblance that holds between the

Form and its phenomenal participants. Socrates and Simmias agree that phenomena 'are deficient . . . in that respect whereby they are such as the Equal' (74d6–7); and in the following lines the same theme is stressed with many variations. Phenomena wish to be like the Forms, but fall short and are unable to be like them and are inferior (74d–e); they resemble Forms, but defectively (74e); they strive to be like the Forms, but are deficient (75a, b); they are eager to be like the Forms, but are inferior to them (75b). Plato uses some of these statements to describe in particular the relation between Equality and equal things but it is clear from 75c–d that the argument applies to all other Forms as well. Not all of the statements are equivalent; Socrates seems to ignore the difference between trying and failing to resemble something and succeeding imperfectly. Still, they suffice to establish the point that phenomena imperfectly resemble Forms.

Plato does not in this passage specifically offer the relation of resemblance as equivalent to the relation of participation, or use resemblance to explain what participation is.[37] He does explain participation in terms of resemblance in the *Parmenides*, however, where the account seems to give rise to an infinite regress. Nor does he explain what he means by saying that Forms and phenomena resemble each other. A reader of Plato in English translation would be apt to interpret the claim that two objects resemble each other as the claim that they have at least one property in common. On this interpretation it is easy to see how the problems of the *Parmenides* arise. Clearly, the respect in which phenomenal equals resemble the Form of Equality is the relation of equality itself. If resemblance means sharing a property, then presumably both the phenomenal equals and the Form would have the property of being equal. But if having the property of being equal requires an explanation in the case of phenomenal equals, why should it not require an explanation in the case of the Form? And if the explanation in the first case requires the postulation of a Form of Equality, why should it not also in the second?

I shall discuss these questions in more detail in the next chapter. For the present, however, I should note that it is unlikely that resemblance, as Plato understands the term, can be analysed in terms of having a property in common. There are at least two reasons for thinking this; the first comes from the *Phaedo* itself. For in the lines quoted above (74d6–7), Socrates says that phenomenal equals 'are deficient . . . *in that respect* whereby they are such as the Equal'. In other words, it is not in their general ontological status or some other way that phenomenal equals are defective in relation to the Form of Equality; rather, the equality which the phenomenal equals possess itself defectively resembles the Form of Equality. It would seem from this that defective resemblance, at least, is not for Plato a relation that holds between two objects that have a property in common but a relation that can hold between a phenomenal property and a Form. A resemblance relation that takes a property, rather than an object that has properties, as one of its *relata* is already somewhat removed from our ordinary concept of resemblance.[38]

The second reason is hinted at in the *Phaedo* but is more fully developed elsewhere. We have already seen that Forms and phenomena are of different ontological orders or categories, and we might well expect the resemblance between such entities to be somewhat less straightforward than the resemblance between entities within a single order. Two red pieces of paper might well resemble each other by having the same colour, red; but if one were to claim (as Plato does in the case of Equality) that both had the same colour in virtue of resembling a single Form, Redness, could we infer from this that the Form itself was red; that, though an intelligible object, it had colour, a sensible property?

Plato rarely simply asserts that phenomena resemble Forms. Ordinarily, in spelling out the relation that holds between the two orders, he indicates that phenomena are images or copies of Forms. The relation of original to image brings out, as the relation of resemblance does not, the difference between the two orders of being and the inferiority of the phenomenal order to the intelligible. It also raises the question whether a relation of resemblance between the orders can be explained in terms of simple community of property.

Plato hints at the difference between the orders in the discussion of resemblance in the *Phaedo* by pointing out that the resemblance is defective: phenomena 'strive to be like' the Forms and succeed only imperfectly at best. This relation of defective resemblance is not, like the ordinary notion of resemblance, a reciprocal one. Normally, if A resembles B, B also resembles A; in the case of the relation between the Forms and phenomena, however, it makes sense to say that the phenomena 'strive to be like' the Forms, but not that the Forms 'strive to be like' phenomena.

The concept of phenomena as images of Forms is elaborated not in the *Phaedo* but in the *Republic*; specifically, in the second of the three famous analogies Plato uses to explain the nature of the Good, the Divided Line (VI, 509d—511e). Socrates has just distinguished the visible from the intelligible realms, much as we have discussed previously (Secs. V and VI above). Now he represents the two worlds in terms of a line divided into two unequal segments, the larger of the two representing the intelligible order (which is correspondingly greater in certainty than the visible order). Each segment is then divided again in the same proportion, producing a total of four segments (509d). The smaller of the two segments of the portion representing the visible world contain images (*eikones*):

> I call images first shadows, then appearances in the water, and on whatever things are made dense, smooth, and bright, and everything of that sort, if you understand.
> But I do understand.
> In the other segment, then, posit those things to which these are similar, the animals around us and the class of plant life and the entire class of artefacts. (509e1—510a6)

The things we ordinarily call images, shadows and reflections, are for Plato also images of phenomenal objects, such as animals, plants and artefacts. In distinguishing these two classes, Plato simply follows our common-sense conception of the world.

When we reach the intelligible world, however, we find that the originals in the sensible world are in turn images of the Forms:

> In one segment of it the soul is compelled to use as images those things which were previously imitated, and to search from hypotheses, not journeying to the beginning but to the end; in the other segment, the soul goes from hypotheses to an unhypothetical beginning, and without the images used in the other case, dealing methodically with the Forms in themselves. (510b4—9)

As Socrates explains, when one does geometry one uses diagrams and other visual aids but treats them as images of the intelligible object or Form they represent (e.g. the Square itself) rather than as independent objects (510c—511a). The Form of the Square is the original of which phenomenal squares are images. Distinct from this class of Forms is the highest class, which includes the Good, which is to be investigated without the aid of sensible images, in the abstract.

It is not clear why Plato subdivides the intelligible portion of the Line into two classes of Forms, or precisely how the two classes differ. It may be that the nature of the highest class of Forms is so abstract that Plato thinks that they cannot have, in any meaningful sense, sensible images, that their relation to the phenomena that participate in them is not the relation of original to image, but some other relation. Plato does not use the relation of original and image to explain how these two classes of Forms are related, as he did to explain how the two classes of phenomena were related; we may therefore assume that he does not think that the lower Forms are images of the higher.

It is clear, however, that Plato thinks that at least some Forms are related to phenomena as originals to images; in the same relation, that is, that binds phenomena and what we would ordinarily call images. The analogy of the Divided Line, in fact, is a good example of a fairly typical Platonic procedure in metaphysics, the adaptation of a familiar concept to an unfamiliar use by the extension of the concept from its ordinary setting to the setting of Platonic metaphysics. The restriction of the analogy of originals and images to the relation between one class of Forms and their phenomenal participants is a tantalising suggestion that Plato realised the limitations of applicability of the analogy.

For a certain class of Forms, at least, including the mathematical ones discussed in the Divided Line and in the argument from recollection in the *Phaedo*, Plato deems the analogy of original to image appropriate. If we ask ourselves whether the relation between a human being and his mirror image or the relation between a square and the concept of squareness can be analysed successfully in terms of the properties shared by both original and image, the answer seems to be that it cannot. This casts further doubt on the analysis of Plato's concept of resemblance in terms of sharing of properties and suggests that Plato's notion of resemblance is different from that one.

Plato himself discusses this very point in the *Cratylus*,[39] where he reaches the conclusion that, in cases of defective resemblance (the kind that holds between original and image), at least certain properties must *not* be shared by both objects. In this passage (432b–d), Socrates contrasts the image produced of Cratylus by a painter, who imitates his colour and shape, with the object that would be produced if some god recreated all the internal organs of Cratylus, his bodily softness and warmth, and his motion, soul and intelligence (432b–c). This latter product would not be an image of Cratylus at all but another Cratylus (432c). This shows that images are by no means perfect replicas of their originals, and Socrates concludes by asking Cratylus, 'do you not see how much images fall short of having the same [properties] as the things of which they are images?' (432d2–3).

This passage gives us no way of telling *which* properties of an object cannot be possessed by its image, but it is surely significant that in the example given the pictorial image of Cratylus lacks all the properties that are essential to Cratylus' being what he is essentially, namely a human being. What makes a picture of Cratylus an image of Cratylus is not simply the similarity in colour and shape between Cratylus and his picture but the fact that the picture somehow succeeds in representing a particular human being. Yet, though the picture is *of* a human being and may be said to resemble the individual of whom it is a picture, the picture does not share with its original the relevant properties that make the original a human. The picture is not a human being, despite the fact that we speak of 'the man in the picture'.

It would seem, given Plato's comments about defective resemblance and imaging in the *Cratylus*, *Republic* and *Phaedo*, then, that he does not understand resemblance solely or even primarily in terms of sharing a property. It is not clear, apart from the information we can get from his examples, what he does mean by the claim that phenomena are images of Forms, or by the claim that phenomena resemble Forms defectively. Plato does not offer an analysis of resemblance, just as he offers no analysis of participation. Apparently he regards the concept of resemblance as he uses it as sufficiently intuitive not to require an analysis; at least, he does invoke the concept of resemblance implicitly in the *Phaedo* and explicitly in the *Parmenides*, as an explication or interpretation of the more obscure or technical concept of participation.

Plato's use of two conflicting interpretations of participation, the resemblance model and the sharing or communion model, without any recognition that the interpretations are at odds with one another, is a problem with the Theory of Forms that closely parallels the problem of his attribution to the Forms of both a transcendent and an immanent mode of existing. Like the latter problem, the former comes to light in the *Parmenides*, where Plato is at pains not only to show that the interpretations of participation are different from each other but that specific problems apply to each interpretation.

To sum up the findings of this chapter: first, Plato assumes in the early and middle dialogues we have examined that the Forms exist. He recognises that the existence of the Forms is a hypothesis but he presents no arguments in its favour. He does not appear to regard the existence of Forms as philosophically problematic. Secondly, he treats the Forms as the immanent causes of the characteristics of phenomena. Forms are among the causes described in the *Phaedo* but their precise causal role is unclear. Thirdly, Plato regards his Forms as paradigms but seems to mean by this not that they are *exemplars* of themselves but rather that they are patterns shared in some way by things that exemplify them. Fourthly, Plato uses statements of the form, '*F*-ness is *F*' in connection with the Forms but this does not in itself prove that he accepts the doctrine of self-predication. To prove that one would need to show that '*F*' functions in the case of a Form as a genuine predicate, that it names a property the Form itself possesses. 'Beautiful' seems to function this way in the case of Beauty, but we found other alleged cases of self-predication to be doubtful.

Fifthly, Plato regards the Forms as the only genuine objects of knowledge and, as such, invisible, temporally unlimited in their existence and impervious to any sort of change. Phenomena, in contrast, he regards as objects of opinion, sensible, temporally limited in their existence and in constant flux. This distinction between Forms and phenomena is the Being-Becoming distinction. Sixthly, Plato treats the difference between Being and Becoming not merely as a conceptual or categorial distinction but as a distinction between entities in two 'worlds'. Despite the fact that he regards the Forms as immanent causes, he also treats them as transcendent or separate from the phenomenal world. This conflict between Plato's two conceptions of the Forms is paralleled by a conflict between two conceptions of participation. According to the sharing model, the Form or some portion of it is in the thing that participates in it; according to the resemblance model, the participant resembles the Form. Neither 'sharing' nor 'resemblance' is clearly explained in these dialogues.

All in all, these findings suggest that in his early and middle dialogues Plato was working with a set of intuitions about Forms and phenomena that he had not fully developed, and that he was unaware of certain tensions between different aspects of the Theory of Forms that appear to be implicit in his thought. It would be impossible to prove that this was the case, since it is also conceivable that Plato had a fully developed metaphysics which he had decided to display only in bits and pieces in his writings. If it is true, however, that the metaphysics of the early and middle dialogues is more a set of intuitions than a complete theory, this would hardly be surprising. For Plato in these dialogues focuses not on the Theory of Forms itself but on the application of the theory to the resolution of certain philosophical problems. We might well expect that awareness of the problems implicit in the metaphysical views expressed in these dialogues would only come to one who turned his attention from the applications of the theory to the assumptions and claims of the theory itself. It is precisely this shift of attention that produces the dialogue *Parmenides*, which we must now examine.

## Notes

1. Allen describes the difference between the metaphysics of the *Euthyphro* and that of the middle dialogues as follows:

> The philosophy of the middle dialogues is a nest of coupled contrasts: Being and Becoming, Appearance and Reality, Permanence and Flux, Reason and Sense, Body and Soul, Flesh and Spirit. Those contrasts are rooted in an ontology of two Worlds, separated by a gulf of deficiency. The World of Knowledge, whose contents are the eternal Forms, stands to the World of Opinion, whose contents are sensible and changing, as the more real stands to the less real, as originals stand to shadows and reflections. The visible world is an image, unknowable in its deficiency, of an intelligible world apprehended by reason alone.
>
> This is 'separation', and it is possible to fix with some precision the kind of separation it is. It assumes both that sensible instances of Forms are deficient resemblances of Forms, and that they are less real than Forms. There is no trace of either of these claims in early dialogues such as the *Euthyphro*, nor of the characteristic doctrines of the middle dialogues with which these claims are implicated — Recollection, and the radical distinction between Knowledge and Opinion. (1971, pp. 332–3)

I agree with nearly all that Allen says here, and have quoted the passage at length because it provides a nice summary of the claims I shall draw out in Secs. V and VI of this chapter. On one small matter, however, I disagree with Allen. At *Euphr.* 6d–e Plato has Socrates put forward the claim that the Form of Holiness is a paradigm and the related claim that various acts are to be judged holy if they are 'such as' (*toiouton*, e5) the Form. It is true that the passage contains no suggestion that such actions resemble the Form only defectively; none the less, I think that this claim is the origin of the theory of defective resemblance and the two-worlds metaphysics of the middle dialogues.

2. What follows is no more than a summary of the metaphysics of the early and middle dialogues, according to my interpretation. The topics I choose to discuss are precisely those that are taken up in the *Parmenides*; I do not claim to cover every

aspect of the Theory of Forms in the dialogues of these periods. Nor do I claim to give a full and fair treatment to all views different from my own on the matters I do discuss. I am well aware that a much lengthier treatment of the issues I raise here is possible and that the discussion of the scholarly issues could be much more extensive. I cited in the Introduction my general reasons for not engaging more in scholarly debate; I will only add here that I was especially wary in this chapter of becoming bogged down in such debate and never being able to proceed to the later dialogues. The reader who is not familiar with the vast literature on these topics will doubtless not miss such a discussion; none the less, I wanted to warn that reader that there is much more to be said on the issues of this chapter than can be said here.

3. Vlastos objected to the claim that the Theory of Forms is present in the early dialogues, saying that 'I cannot consider the employment of certain linguistic expressions as *sufficient* evidence of the concurrent assertion of the metaphysical theory' (1954, p. 249, n. 9). It is true that Plato often uses the words *idea* and *eidos* in contexts where it is clear that the Theory of Forms is not being discussed. I think it is significant, however, that these terms occur in the *Euthyphro* in a context where Plato is attempting to establish a number of points about Holiness and Unholiness that I can only call metaphysical. Not only does he use these terms to refer to Holiness and Unholiness, he describes them as universals, causes and standards. Allen (1970, 1971) has defended at length the contention that the *Euthyphro* contains an early version of the Theory of Forms; though his claims have been somewhat controversial, I can only say that they seem in the main right to me.

4. The Greek word is *aitiai*. Vlastos discusses the pitfalls of translating this term as 'causes' (1969b, pp. 134–7). Certainly, when Plato describes the Forms as *aitiai*, he does not mean to restrict the sense of that term to the modern notion of an efficient cause; equally certainly, 'reasons' is often a more apt translation of *aitiai* than 'causes'. The translation 'causes' is, however, so widely used that it seems to me futile to change it; I have chosen to retain it, therefore, with this warning note to the reader that the Greek word is not equivalent in meaning to its English substitute.

5. E.g. by Hackforth, who states that, 'in the *Phaedo* itself, whatever be the case in other dialogues, the Forms are not themselves immanent' (1955, pp. 143–4). The basis of Hackforth's denial of the immanence of the Forms is the distinction Plato draws at 102c–e (part of which is quoted above) and again at 103b between the opposite itself and the opposite in us (specifically in 102c–e, between Tallness itself and Tallness in Simmias).

Plato's distinction has led interpreters to claim that this passage of the *Phaedo* contains a tripartite ontology: in addition to individuals — such as Simmias — and Forms — such as Tallness, there are entities of a third sort, which have been called immanent characters. (For treatments of this view, see Hackforth, 1955, pp. 143–57; Turnbull, pp. 131–40, and Vlastos, 1969b, pp. 139–42.) The rationale for this distinction is given by Turnbull: 'it is inconceivable for the Plato of the *Phaedo* to consider seriously the possibility of the perishing of a form' (p. 131); yet his argument requires that he take seriously the possibility that Tallness in Simmias perish at the onset of its opposite. Thus the immanent character, Tallness in Simmias, cannot be identical to the Form.

There is no doubt that Plato does distinguish Tallness itself from Tallness in Simmias and little doubt that he does so for the reason Turnbull cites. The important question seems to me, however, to be the ontological status of these so-called immanent characters. Turnbull asserts, correctly, that 'characters are dependent both on individuals and Forms' (p. 133); but he goes on to state that 'if individuals "participate" in forms at all, they do so only *via* having certain characters in them' (ibid.). This suggests (at least to me) that Turnbull regards the real source of Simmias' tallness as the presence in him of the immanent character, Tallness in Simmias; Simmias' participation in Tallness itself would be a fact somehow derivative from this. Such a view would make immanent characters in some sense independent of Forms and causally primary; I suspect that Hackforth is relying on some such view when he denies that the Form is immanent, while claiming that the character corresponding to the Form is.

This interpretation makes too much of the distinction between Form and immanent character. Plato has already made it clear that he accepts no other explanation of something's being $F$ than its participation in the Form of $F$ (cf. 100c–101c). He goes on, as I note below, to describe participation in terms of the immanence of the Form itself in the things that partake of it. Tallness in Simmias is the product of the participation of Simmias in the Form of Tallness; it is thus totally dependent on the existence of Simmias and the Form for its existence. In other words, the third entities in the tripartite ontology of the *Phaedo* are not causal agents, doing the work that otherwise would have to be done by the Forms; they are products of the causal activity of the Forms (cf. also Gallop, pp. 195–6, and O'Brien, pp. 200–8).

The distinction between individual, Form and immanent character is found again in the *Parmenides* (130b). In the *Timaeus* (51e–2c), Plato makes a similar distinction between the Receptacle, the Forms and Becoming (which seems to comprise all of the immanent characters of the Receptacle). I discuss this tripartite ontology of the *Timaeus* in detail in Ch. 3; I want only to note here a major difference between the position of the *Phaedo* and that of the *Timaeus*. In the *Phaedo* and the *Timaeus* alike the immanent characters are the product of the participation of things in Forms; but in the *Phaedo* this participation is the result of the Form's entrance into the thing, whereas in the *Timaeus* it is the result of the thing's imaging the Form. The Forms of the *Phaedo* are immanent in things (though we shall see that they are also transcendent); the Forms of the *Timaeus* are wholly transcendent.

6. I make this distinction at greater length and defend the view that Platonic Forms are not exemplars but patterns in Prior (1983).

7. Among these are Allen (1970), p. 154; Brownstein, pp. 49–61; Cross and Woozley, p. 181; Geach, pp. 267–70, 276; Owen (1953), pp. 318–22, esp. p. 320, n. 4; (1957), p. 310; and (1968a), pp. 116–18, 121, 123; Strang, pp. 187–92; Teloh, pp. 115–17; Vlastos (1954), pp. 244–51; and Weingartner, p. 146.

Strang makes a distinction between what he calls an A-*logos* (for 'analytical') and a P-*logos* (for 'paradigmatic') which corresponds closely to my distinction between the two sorts of standard; however, he regards only the standard that makes use of an exemplar as a paradigm (pp. 190–1) and thinks that Platonic Forms are standards of this sort (p. 196).

Allen's view that Forms are exemplars is inconsistent with his denial of self-predication (see his 1960, pp. 43–7); I suspect he means something different than I do by 'exemplar'.

8. Plato rejects definition by example consistently in the dialogues; cf. e.g. *Meno* 72b ff.

9. Other passages of the *Republic* in which Forms are called 'paradigms' are: VI, 500e; VII, 540a; and IX, 592b. In none of these passages is there conclusive evidence in favour of either the 'pattern' or the 'exemplar' translation.

10. This is the way Vlastos has interpreted the phrase, which he coined; cf. (1954), p. 236, and (1971b), p. 258, n. 97.

11. For a list see Wedberg, p. 41, n. 18.

12. Plato's doctrine of homonymy has been discussed by Allen (1960), pp. 45–7; and by Nehamas, p. 102. As both note, Plato does not have, at any rate before the *Sophist*, the concept of a predicate term as distinct from a referring expression.

13. Most of the scholars cited above (n. 7) accept the self-predicational analysis of statements of the Form, '$F$-ness is $F$'. For alternatives to this interpretation,

cf. Allen (1960), pp. 43–7; Cherniss (1957), pp. 369–74; Nehamas, pp. 93–103; and Vlastos (1971b), pp. 259–64.

14. Vlastos (1954), p. 249.

15. The view that all alleged cases of self-prediction in Plato are actually identity statements has been defended by Cherniss (1944, p. 293; 1957, pp. 369–74) and Allen (1960, pp. 43–7). I do not think that the Cherniss-Allen view is correct for all such cases; I do think, however, that it is the right interpretation of *Prot.* 330c–d's instances of the '*F*-ness is *F*' formula.

16. The fact that Socrates refers to 'Justice . . . itself' rather than Justice in relation to its instances argues against the view of Vlastos (1971b, pp. 252–9) that this is a case of 'Pauline' prediction.

17. Recall that the aim of Socrates' argument was to establish the identity or at least the close similarity of the Virtues. This reading of 'Justice is holy' has the merit of making the statement relevant to the aim of the argument.

18. I discuss the matter of grounding properties in relations to Forms in Prior (1979).

19. It is difficult to determine the intended scope of this argument. Plato seems to be drawing a distinction that would hold for all Forms, a distinction between what is *F* and what has *F* that would preclude the possibility that anything that is *F* could also have *F* as a character; cf. Cherniss (1957), p. 372. Yet this would be a mistake. As we shall see below, Plato apparently regards the Form of Beauty as self-predicative, and some Forms *must* be (Being must exist, Sameness must be the same as itself, Rest must be at rest). The argument of *Rep.* X may be used to block the Third Man regress in the case of some Forms but a different strategy seems called for in the case of those Forms which are or must be self-predicative.

20. Vlastos (1969b), pp. 262–3.

21. Ibid., p. 259.

22. For a discussion of the interpretive issues involved in this passage, cf. Gallop, pp. 121–5 and Mills (1957–8).

23. Gosling makes this point.

24. E.g. Ross, pp. 22–3, and Bluck, pp. 118–19.

25. Mills (1957–8), p. 40.

26. Owen (1968a), pp. 114–15.

27. As Cherniss puts it, 'The idea *is* that which its particular participants *have* as a character' (1957, p. 372); the italicised 'is' being the 'is' of identity. Cf. Allen (1960), pp. 45–7.

28. The distinction between *epistēmē* and *doxa* is explicitly drawn in the *Meno* (96d–end), a dialogue written at the end of Plato's early period; the association of the two mental states with different objects is, however, a feature introduced in the middle dialogues.

*Epistēmē* and *doxa* correspond only loosely with knowledge and belief or opinion. Plato's view in the middle dialogues is that phenomenal objects are objects of *doxa* but not *epistēmē*; yet it would be unwarranted to saddle him with the view that, although I might believe that I own a car, for instance, I could never know that I do. The distinction between *epistēmē* and *doxa* is closer to our distinction between *a priori* knowledge, on the one hand, and belief or knowledge about empirical matters, on the other. As this distinction is not easy to describe, and impossible to find a pair of English synonyms for, I follow the conventional translations. We must be wary, however, of reading the connotations of the English terms back into the Greek originals.

29. See Vlastos (1965), pp. 66–73, for a discussion of this point.

30. Owen (1953, p. 322) bases part of his case for dating the *Timaeus* among the middle dialogues on the claim that the *Timaeus* (presumably in common with those dialogues) treats *genesis* and *ousia* as incompatible. The late dialogues, he thinks,

abandon this view. As Vlastos (1954, pp. 247–8, n. 4) has pointed out, however, there are several passages in which Plato attributes being to things that become. One of these is the *Phaedo* passage just mentioned; another is *Tim.* 35a, where Plato speaks of 'the divisible being which comes to be in bodies'. These passages show that Plato does not treat being and becoming as incompatible, in either the middle dialogues or in the *Timaeus*; and this, as Vlastos notes, 'spoils one of the major arguments offered by Owen' (ibid., p. 247).

31. In the *Timaeus* Plato makes it clear that the Forms are not in time at all, but have an eternal existence. In the middle dialogues, however, I think it uncertain whether he regards the Forms as eternal or as having an existence which is everlasting in time. I have therefore used phrases such as 'temporally unlimited' to reflect this indefiniteness.

32. The rationale behind limiting knowledge to changeless objects is discussed by Hintikka.

33. Separation seems to mean different things to different people. According to Vlastos (1954, pp. 245–6), the claim that the Forms are separate is equivalent to the claim that they are 'real'; this claim he thinks equivalent to the claims that the Forms are intelligible, changeless, not qualified by contrary predicates and the perfect instances of the property or relation their names connote. Allen (1970, pp. 130–3), explaining Aristotle's use of the term in his treatment of the Theory of Forms, says that to be separate a Form must be numerically distinct from its participants, capable of existing independently of them, and ontologically prior to them (cf. Allen, 1983, pp. 100–1).

As I use the term, separation presupposes not only the numerical distinctness of the Form from its participants, its ontological independence and priority, but also the claim that the Form is not to be found in the phenomenal world. That Plato believes this about the Forms is attested by the passages discussed in this section. My warrant for using 'separation' to denote this claim lies in Parmenides' critique of the separation of Forms from the phenomenal world in *Parm.* 133a–134e (see below, Ch. 2, Sec. V). There Parmenides draws out, as a consequence of the separate existence of the Forms, 'that none of these objects exist among ourselves' (133c5). I think this is a consequence of the account of the Forms given in the passages discussed in this section, so I have followed Plato's own usage in calling it an account of the separation of the Forms from the phenomenal world. (I do not, incidentally, think that 'separation' carries the implications that Vlastos assigns to it above.)

34. Moline (pp. 119–20) distinguishes between what he calls the 'power/mixture' and the 'paradigm/copy' models of the relation between Forms and their participants. His distinctions parallel closely my distinctions between the Forms as immanent causes (and the related conception of participation as sharing; see below, Sec. VII) and the Forms as separate objects of knowledge (which is compatible with the view that the Forms are paradigms and that phenomena resemble them). Moline, however, denies that the two models are in conflict, in part because he regards the talk of separation as metaphor (cf. his pp. 95–105), of epistemological but not ontological significance. I do not see how Moline's interpretation can be made compatible with the passages I discuss in this section and in particular with the argument of *Phdo.* 65–67, which concludes with the claim that we can only know the Forms after death. Nor do I see how what Moline calls the 'power/mixture' model can be made compatible with the insistence of the *Timaeus* (51d–52c) that the Forms do not exist in space. I take the talk of separation to have more than metaphorical or merely epistemological significance; therefore, I regard the conflict between separation and immanence as real.

35. Cf. Cross and Woozley, pp. 194–5.

36. Reading '*prosgenomenē*' with the MSS. Cf. Gallop, n. 63, pp. 234–5.

37. In this respect the middle dialogues resemble the *Euthyphro* again. Plato invokes the notion of resemblance at *Euphr.* 6e to explain how he will use the Form of Holiness to judge the many acts which purport to be holy. Earlier, at 5d, he had claimed that the Form of Holiness was 'in' actions; thus, as I noted above (n. 1) the conflict between Plato's two concepts of Forms is already implicit in the *Euthyphro*. Unlike the middle dialogues, however, the *Euthyphro* does not raise the problem of participation in an explicit way; indeed, none of the words Plato uses to denote the relation of participation appear in these passages.

38. I have indicated above (Sec. IV, pp. 22–3) that Plato seems to ground the possession of a property by an object (e.g. the property of being beautiful) in the relation between that object and a Form (in this case the Form of Beauty), rather than grounding participation in the common possession of a property. In other words, common properties are for Plato derivative entities, not primary ones; the relation of participation (which he often describes in terms of resemblance, as I am arguing here) is basic. If this is so, any attempt to ground participation in the sharing of a property would inevitably distort Plato's own intentions, as well as producing a vicious circularity (first we explain common properties in terms of resemblance, then we explain resemblance in terms of common properties). As I noted above (n. 18), I discuss this matter in Prior (1979); cf. esp. Sec. III.

What all of this shows is that we should be wary of approaching Plato's ontology with what I have called our 'ordinary' concept of resemblance. This ordinary concept contains just the assumption Plato would reject: that resemblance is to be explained in terms of sharing a property. When we think of cases of resemblance, we are apt to think of two objects (twin brothers, perhaps, or a pair of golf balls) which have many features in common; and we are inclined to think that Plato must have had this paradigm in mind as well. I have already suggested that he did not: but I would like to point out also that this paradigm does not do justice to all the cases of resemblance we ourselves recognise. For we hold not only that relations of resemblance obtain between objects but also that they obtain between the characteristics of objects. We say things like the following: 'The colour of this chair resembles the colour of the curtains', when the two colours themselves are similar but not identical; or 'Jack is similar in build to Jim', when their bodily structures are alike but not exactly the same. I think it unlikely that this sort of resemblance can be analysed in terms of the sharing of properties by these objects (which in this case would themselves be properties), unless we give up our intuitive conception of what a property is. In any case, it seems to me that the latter cases of resemblance are close to what Plato has in mind than are the cases of resemblance between objects.

39. I am endebted to Richard Patterson for pointing out to me the importance of this passage.

# 2

# THE CHALLENGE OF THE *PARMENIDES*

In Chapter 1 I described in outline the metaphysics of the early and middle Platonic dialogues; in this chapter I shall attempt to show how the critique of the Theory of Forms in the *Parmenides* affects that metaphysics. The *Parmenides* is divided into two parts: the first contains the critique of the Theory of Forms and ends at 135c; the second is an examination of eight hypotheses about 'the One', which takes up the remainder of the dialogue. There is perhaps greater disagreement on the nature, purpose, and meaning of the second part of the dialogue than about any other comparable Platonic text.[1] As the relevance of this part of the dialogue to Plato's metaphysics is at best a matter of dispute, I shall confine the discussion of this chapter to the first part of the dialogue.

Stylometric evidence places the *Parmenides* among the last dialogues of Plato's middle period. It was composed well after the *Phaedo* and *Symposium*, but it may well have been written before the *Phraedrus* and at least the tenth Book of the *Republic*.[2] A reference in the *Theaetetus* to the conversation between Socrates and Parmenides reported in the *Parmenides* (*Tht.* 183e–184a) makes it probable that the *Parmenides* was written before the *Theaetetus*. It certainly predates the dialogues of the late group, including, if my thesis is correct, the *Timaeus*. I shall treat the dialogue as if it were written after all of the middle dialogues, in which the Theory of Forms play a major role, including the *Phaedrus* and *Republic* X; but the reader should regard this decision as heuristic in character rather than historically sound.

Scholars are divided on the question whether any meeting between Parmenides and Socrates could have taken place. The traditional dates assigned to Parmenides (540 BC–c470) would seem to rule out this possibility, but these are highly conjectural. It does seem certain that, even if Parmenides and Socrates did meet, the actual conversation reported between them is fictional. For Socrates presents the Theory of Forms not as it appears in the early *Euthyphro*, but as it is developed in the middle dialogues, and it strains credence past the breaking point to attribute that theory to a Socrates who is presented here as very young (127c). Nor is it likely that the criticism of the theory could have been the product of Parmenides' mind; indeed, the only plausible candidate for authorship of the criticism, as well as of the theory criticised, is Plato himself.[3]

It is significant that Plato portrays this dialogue as taking place between a Socrates who is quite young and inexperienced in philosophy and a Parmenides who is both much older and a past master of philosophical argument. The Socrates of the dialogue is in fact a callow youth; he takes good stands and makes good statements in defence of them but is unable to defend those stands and statements when Parmenides attacks them. In many cases, as we shall see, he fails to respond to Parmenides' criticism in a way that we might expect any competent defender of the middle period Theory of Forms to be aware of. It is to Socrates that the task of defending the Theory of Forms falls; and, given his inexperience and youth, we should not infer from the fact that he fails in its defence that Plato thought the theory indefensible.

Parmenides is treated with more respect in the Platonic dialogues than any other historical figure save Socrates himself. Socrates refers to him in the *Theaetetus* as 'venerable and wonderful' (183e), and in the *Sophist* he refers to the discussion of the *Parmenides* as 'entirely good' (217c). Plato undertakes the criticism of Parmenides only in the *Sophist*, after having refused to criticise him in the *Theaetetus*; and, although an escape from Eleatic principles about non-being is essential for his purposes in that dialogue and for the development of Greek metaphysics generally, he enters into the criticism with great reluctance.

None the less, the Parmenides of this dialogue has some undesirable features. He is rather smug and superior in his attitude toward Socrates, whom he admires (128a−b), but whom he constantly criticises in patronising tones for his youthful inexperience (130e, 133a−b, 135c−d). Parmenides' air of superiority seems at times to prevent him from taking some good suggestions of Socrates seriously, as we shall see below. He also does seem to be above some rather obvious chicanery at the expense of Socrates; at least we must so interpret his misrepresentation of some of Socrates' remarks, if we are to avoid attributing philosophical ineptitude to a character Plato means to portray as a great philosopher. The element of chicanery is present in the arguments against the Theory of Forms themselves, some of which are obviously invalid as they stand. So, as in the case of Socrates, we cannot draw any conclusions about the strength of these arguments from the fact that they come from the mouth of Parmenides.

Behind both characters stands Plato himself, and his views are only with caution to be identified with those of the Socrates or the Parmenides of his dialogue. It is possible, as Gregory Vlastos has urged, that Plato was as perplexed by the arguments Parmenides presents as is Socrates in the dialogue;[4] it is equally possible that he might be completely aware of the quality of the arguments he puts in Parmenides' mouth and of their relevance to the Theory of Forms. One scholar has likened him to a chess master rehearsing in a programmatic way strategies and counter-strategies, which are represented here by the arguments of the dialogue.[5] It is important for us to determine what Plato in fact thought of these objections to his theory; and, though we must rely on the text of the dialogues to do this, we must use the text critically, without assuming in particular that this section of the *Parmenides* wears its moral on its sleeve.

Assessing the quality of Parmenides' arguments agains the Theory of Forms requires the answering of several questions. First of all, we must determine whether the arguments are valid; and here the techniques of logical analysis have been of some value, although they have not in general fulfilled the large claims made for them. If a given argument is not valid as formulated, can it be made into a valid argument without undue violence to the text? If the arguments are, or can be made valid, do they rely on premises to which Plato was in fact committed — that is, do they actually attack the Theory of Forms as it is portrayed in the middle dialogues? Do the arguments, whether valid or not, raise issues that it is important for Plato to resolve if he is to maintain the Theory of Forms? (An argument may do this, even though it is invalid as stated and a serious misinterpretation of the views expressed in the middle dialogues; this in fact seems to be the case with the last argument, which Parmenides regards as the most serious objection to the theory.) Can these issues be resolved in favour of the Theory of Forms? Finally, does Plato ever attempt to so resolve them? Only when we have answered these questions can we hope to know or confidently guess how Plato regarded the objections to the theory raised in the dialogue.

The rest of the chapter will be devoted to the answering of these questions with respect to individual arguments of the first part of the *Parmenides*. I shall treat these arguments more or less in the

order in which they occur in the text. I begin with an analysis of the
passage (128e–130a) in which Socrates, in response to an argument
of Zeno, states the Theory of Forms; we shall determine the
relation between this statement of the theory and the theory as
described in Chapter 1. Then I shall discuss Parmenides' questions
about the population of the world of the Forms, his arguments
against the immanence of the Forms, the Third Man Argument and
his argument against the separation of the Forms. Finally, I shall
attempt to summarise the collective effect of these arguments on
the theory. One argument, against the view that the Forms might be
thoughts (132b–c), I shall not discuss at all, as it seems to me to
have no bearing on the Theory of Forms as Plato actually held it.

## I. Socrates' Statement of the Theory of Forms (128e–130a)

The philosophical part of the dialogue begins at the point where
Zeno, Parmenides' disciple, has just finished reading his treatise
against the existence of a plurality of things (127c–d). Socrates
associates Zeno's claim that there is no plurality with Parmenides'
claim that all is one, and Zeno agrees (128a–e). Zeno has argued
that a plurality is impossible, on the grounds that each of the many
must be both like and unlike; but Socrates objects that there is
nothing impossible in that. In the course of making this objection
he states the Theory of Forms:

> Do you not think that there is a certain Form of Similarity, itself
> in itself, and again another something opposite to this sort, what
> Dissimilar is; and that you and I and all the other things which
> we call 'many' partake of these two Beings; and that the things
> that partake of Similarity become similar in the respect in which
> and insofar as they partake of it; and dissimilar things [insofar as
> they partake], of Dissimilarity; and things that are both [insofar
> as they partake], of both? (128e6–129a6)

This formulation of the theory will be familiar to any reader of
the *Phaedo*. Socrates uses the word *eidos* at 129a1 to refer to the
Form of Similarity (cf. *Phdo.* 102b1). He calls the Forms 'Beings'
(*ontoin*, 129a2; cf. *Phdo.* 78d4) and notes that the Form of
Similarity exists 'itself in itself' (*auto kath' hauto*, 128e6; cf. *Phdo.*
66a2). Later, at 129d7–8, he links the claim that the Forms exist

'themselves in themselves' to the claim that they are 'separate' (*choris*, d7) from the things that partake of them. As in the *Phaedo* and elsewhere he uses both abstract singular terms (*homiotētos*, 129a1) and adjectival phrases (*ho estin anhomoion*, a2) to refer to Forms. His use of the plural in referring to 'the Similars themselves' (*auta ta homoia*, 129b1) and 'the Dissimilars' (*ta anhomoia*, b2) parallels his reference to the Form of Equality as 'the Equals themselves' at *Phdo.* 74c1. Most important for the remainder of this part of the dialogue, things are said to have characteristics for the same reason they were said to at *Phdo.* 100c: by virtue of participation (*metalambanein*, 129a3; *metechein*, a8) in the Form of that characteristic. They may partake of a Form in one respect but not in another: as Socrates notes in 129c–d, he participates in Plurality with respect to the many parts of his body and in Unity with respect to his being a single human being. Things may also partake of Forms to varying degrees (cf. *tosouton*, 129a5), which recalls the analysis of participation in terms of defective resemblance (cf. *Phdo.* 74d–75b).

Once Socrates has put forward the basic distinction between Forms and their participants, he dismisses the 'impossibility' of Zeno's conclusion:

> Even if all things partake of both opposites, and are by virtue of participation in both similar and dissimilar, themselves to themselves, what is surprising about that? If, however, someone shows the Similars themselves becoming dissimilar, or the Dissimilars similar, I think that would be a marvel. (129a6–b3)

The next page of text is an elaboration of this point. As with Similarity and Dissimilarity, so with Unity and Plurality: it is no marvel, but the simple truth, that Socrates is both one and many; what would be a source of wonder is a demonstration that Unity itself is many and Plurality itself one (129b–d). If one proves in the case of stones and sticks that they are both one and many, says Socrates, 'we shall say that he proves that the same thing is many and one, but not that the One is many or the Many one; nor is this to say anything wonderful, but just what we would all agree to' (129d4–6). If one first separates the Forms from their participants, however, Similarity and Dissimilarity, Plurality and Unity, Rest and Motion and all such things, and then shows that they 'can be mixed and divided among themselves' (129e2–3), then Socrates says that he would be amazed. He concludes with a challenge to Zeno:

> I believe that you have accomplished these things altogether manfully; however, as I say, I would marvel much more if someone were able to prove that this very difficulty is intertwined in all sorts of ways with the Forms themselves — with those things we grasp by reasoning, as you have shown it to be with visible things. (129e4–130a2)

In a nutshell, Socrates' strategy is to answer Zeno's argument by accepting its conclusion but denying that it is contradictory. He claims that a true contradiction would result only if the same problems arose for Forms that Zeno attributes to phenomena; and he denies that they do. To make this denial stick, he must be able to show that Forms are different in their behaviour from the things that partake of them. The relevant difference was spelled out at *Phdo.* 102b–103a, where Socrates says that Simmias can participate in both Tallness and Shortness in being taller than Socrates and shorter than Phaedo (see above, pp. 40–3). Neither Tallness itself nor that instantiation of Tallness in Simmias can become short, however; nor can Shortness become tall; what is possible for a thing having an opposite is not possible for the opposite Form itself (cf. *Phdo.* 103a–c). As the prohibition against opposite Forms intermingling echoes the *Phaedo*, so does the reference to 'stones and sticks' (cf. *Phdo.* 74a). As throughout the middle dialogues, Plato distinguishes Forms from the phenomenal participants on the grounds that Forms are understood by reason, whereas phenomena are perceived by the senses.

As the theory Socrates puts forth here is identical in several respects to the theory outlined in Chapter 1, we might expect that it has some of the same problems. One of these surfaces as soon as we ask why the Forms are precluded from mingling with their opposites. Is Similarity unable to become dissimilar because it has the property of which it is the Form but has it essentially rather than accidentally? If so, then the Forms must be self-predicative. Or when Socrates says that Similarity cannot be dissimilar, might he mean what I suggested he might mean in the *Phaedo* when he said that Equality could never be unequal — namely, that the Form could not be identical to its opposite (see above, pp. 27–9)? Perhaps his view is a combination of these two positions: he may think that the Form of Similarity, for instance, *has* the property of being similar because it *is* that property, and that it could not come to *have* the opposite property without *being* that property and ceasing to be itself. In this case, the contrast between Forms and their participants would not be a contrast between properties and things that have them but between things that have properties in very different ways. This possibility is suggested by *Phdo.* 102e−103a; but our present text gives no hint as to which of these alternatives, if any, is Plato's own view.

In most respects this statement of the Theory of Forms, then, reflects accurately the theory as presented in the middle dialogues. There are, however, some notable anticipations of later developments. Plato lists Rest and Motion among the Forms he mentions at 129d−e; these reappear as two of the five 'Greatest Kinds' in the *Sophist*. Similarity and Dissimilarity are at least akin to two more of the Greatest Kinds, Sameness and Difference. Here, as in the *Sophist*, Plato refers to the Forms both as 'Kinds' and as 'Forms' (*genē* and *eidē*, 129c2; cf. *Soph.* 254c2, d4). These parallels at least create the suspicion, if they do not prove, that Plato may have had in mind at the time of the *Parmenides* at least some of the ideas he developed later in the *Sophist*. It is one of the major advances of the *Sophist* that it provides a clear and explicit distinction between statements of predication and statements of identity,[6] which is just the distinction required for us to determine what Plato means when he rules out the possibility that one Form could become its opposite. The *Sophist* also shows that, although no Form could be identical to its opposite, some Forms do participate in their opposites (e.g. Sameness and Difference) and thus 'can be mixed and divided among themselves'. This is of course what Socrates had challenged Zeno to prove; and the prohibition of mixing among Forms in the *Parmenides*, especially in light of the verbal anticipations of the *Sophist*, could be interpreted as Plato's intentional emphasis of a point of the middle period's metaphysics that he knows needs revision.

In any event, the later dialogues do show that Forms can combine with and be divided from each other in ways that Socrates may well mean to preclude here. Indeed, the method of Collection and Division, in which Forms are arranged in hierarchies of genera and species, seems at times in the *Phaedrus*, *Sophist*, *Statesman* and *Philebus* to be almost identical in Plato's mind to philosophy itself. Whether this passage anticipates this development or not, it certainly raises a problem with the Theory of Forms that the method of Collection and Division resolves. It may also be that behind Plato's prohibition of mixture among Forms lies a belief in the absolute unity (in the sense of simplicity) of the Forms, which the middle dialogues contrast with the complexity of phenomena (see above, p. 31). This is a position that the middle dialogues, no less than the later ones, show to be false, however: Forms are related to each other in complex ways in the *Phaedo* and even as early as the *Euthyphro* Plato recognised part-whole relations among Forms.[7]

Throughout his statement of the Theory of Forms, Socrates is concerned primarily not with the relation between Forms and their phenomenal participants (the question of participation) but with relations among the Forms themselves. Although this question is a dominant one in the later dialogues, it is quietly shelved for the remainder of part I of the dialogue at the conclusion of this passage. When Parmenides criticises the Theory of Forms, it is on the problem of participation that he focuses; relations between Forms only surface again in the final argument, and then as a side-light. It remains a significant fact, however, that, as Socrates states the Theory of Forms in a way that accurately reflects the theory of the middle dialogues, he emphasises a difficulty with that version of the theory that is dealt with systematically only in the late dialogues. As in many other respects, this passage of the *Parmenides* is transitional, looking as it does both backward to a theory already developed in some respects and forward to revisions and refinements in it.

## II. The Population Problem (130b–e)

Parmenides' first response to the Theory of Forms as Socrates states it is not an objection but a series of questions about the extent of the world of Forms. Socrates agrees readily to the existence of Forms such as Similarity and Dissimilarity, Unity and Plurality, and in general all the things of which Zeno had dealt with in his treatise (130b). He also agrees to the existence of Forms of Justice, Beauty, Goodness and the like; but when Parmenides asks about 'a Form of Human Being, apart from us and all who are such as we are', or a separate Form of Fire and Water (130c1–2), Socrates voices some doubt. When Parmenides mentions Forms of

Hair, Mud and Dirt, Socrates says that, though he has wondered whether, if there are Forms of some things, there ought not to be Forms for all, he none the less thinks that it would be 'too absurd' to posit Forms of such things, on the grounds that they are 'just what we see' (130d3–4).

Parmenides attributes this uncertainty to Socrates' youth:

> It is because you are still young, Socrates, said Parmenides, and philosophy has not yet taken hold of you as in my opinion it will do in the future, when you will disdain none of these things; but now you still have regard for the opinions of people, because of your youth. (130e1–5)

Parmenides' diagnosis has no justification in Socrates remarks in the text, and it ignores the philosophical reason for Socrates' doubt about such Forms, which is expressed, albeit briefly, in his claim that things like hair, mud and dirt are 'just what we see'. Parmenides' comments are an indication of his patronising attitude toward Socrates, which I mentioned above (p. 52). Socrates' inexperience is shown by his failure to develop this remark into a full-fledged philosophical argument.

The significant difference between Forms such as Similarity and Goodness, on the one hand, and Fire and Mud, on the other, a difference to which Socrates' remark that the latter are 'just what we see' alludes, is that the former are Forms of what have been called 'incomplete' predicates. An incomplete predicate is one which, 'accordingly as we complete it in this way or that . . . will be true or false of the thing to which it is applied'.[8] 'One' is incomplete in that it is true of Socrates as a human being but false of him as desparate bodily parts; 'tall' is incomplete in that it is true of Simmias in relation to Socrates but false of him in relation to Phaedo. Things may be 'one' or 'tall' in one or other relation or respect: but 'fire' and 'mud' apply or fail to apply to things without such qualifications. Something either is fire or it is not; being fire 'in one respect but not another' is, one is inclined to say, senseless.

As Plato puts the point in *Republic* VII, 523a–525b, some studies draw the mind toward reality and some do not. The mind is drawn toward reality when the senses produce contrary judgements. This does not happen when, for instance, we judge that something is a finger. The senses are adequate for discerning whether or not something is a finger because a finger is the sort of thing which is 'just what we see'. Questions about whether something is large or small, light or heavy, soft or hard, however, do produce contrary judgements, and these lead in turn to reflection about the nature of the attributes involved. That is, such judgements lead inexorably, in Plato's view, to reflection about the Forms of Large and Small, the intelligible counterparts of the sensible large and small objects from which we started. It would seem, then, that in the case of such incomplete predicates as those mentioned, Forms are in Plato's view absolutely necessary, whereas in other cases they are not. If this is true, Soctrates' doubt about the existence of Forms of Fire and Mud is philosophically well-grounded and not based on concern for public approval.

Even so, Plato does accept in the middle dialogues Forms of predicates that are not, as all those he acknowledges here are, incomplete. He posits a Form of Shuttle in the *Cratylus* (389) and, as we have seen, a Form of Bed in *Republic* X.[9] Such Forms are unlike Man or Fire in that they are of artefacts, not of natural substances, but are like in being straightforward in their applicability to things. Plato even puts forward in *Rep.* X (596a) the claim that there is a Form for every multiplicity of things having a common name, which would commit him to the existence of all the Forms Parmenides mentions and many more. He apparently later came to reject this criterion, for he notes in the *Statesman* (262d) that, although the Greeks call all foreigners 'barbarians', this name does not pick out a Form. It seems certain, though, that whatever Plato's philosophical reservations were about Forms for any but incomplete predicates, he had resolved those doubts in favour of such Forms before he wrote the *Parmenides*. Socrates' misgivings are not, then, a fair reflection of Plato's attitude at the time.

It must be admitted, however, that the later dialogues are far more sanguine about such Forms as Human Being, Fire and Water than are the middle dialogues. Forms of Man and Ox are mentioned in the *Philebus* (15a), side by side with Beauty and Goodness; and Forms of Fire and Water are accepted in the *Timaeus* (an indication in itself, though certainly not a conclusive one, that the *Timaeus* is later than the *Parmenides*). The *Theaetetus* even offers a definition, if it does not explicitly posit a Form, of clay (147c), which is not far removed from mud and dirt. In the *Seventh Letter*, which is quite late, there is an extensive list of the kinds of things of which there are Forms (342d), which includes fire, water and all living beings; though it refers to all bodies, whether natural or manufactured, there is no specific mention of hair, mud or dirt. It may well be that Plato's later confidence in the existence of Forms of natural substances was the result of his resolution of the problems raised by this passage of the *Parmenides*, even if the passage does not convey accurately Plato's view at the time of the dialogue on the extent of the world of the Forms or do justice to the expressed philosophical doubts of the Socrates of the dialogue.

## III. The Arguments against Immanence (130e–131e)

Parmenides now turns to the question that will, in one way or another, dominate the rest of this part of the dialogue: the question of the nature of participation. He begins with a very literal interpretation of participation as sharing (see above, pp. 37–8), and asks whether each participant in a Form partakes of the whole Form or only of part of it. This question he immediately (131a8–9) restates as the question whether the Form as a unitary whole is *in* each thing. When Socrates says, 'why not?', Parmenides replies that if the Form were present as a whole in each of several separate things, then it would be separate from itself. If the entire Form of Unity, for instance, were present in Socrates, who is in Athens, and also in Callias, who is in Corinth, the entire Form would have to be in two places at once, which seems absurd.

To this objection Socrates replies that the Form may be like a single day, which exists simultaneously in many places and yet is not separated from itself (131b). Parmenides immediately substitutes for this analogy the analogy of a sail spread over many people. When Socrates says that 'perhaps' the sail analogy is a good one (131c1), Parmenides shows that, although the whole sail may be said to be over the people, only a part of it was over each person. He concludes:

Then the Forms themselves are divisible into parts, Socrates . . . and the participants in them would partake of a part, and no longer would the whole Form be in each one, but part of each Form [would be in each]. (131c5–7)

Socrates agrees that this 'appears' to be the case (c8) and concurs also when Parmenides says that when the Form is actually divided it can no longer be one.

The remaining possibility, that things may participate in Forms by having in them a part of the Form, also has its awkward consequences. For if Largeness is divided each of its parts will be small in relation to the Form; and how can something small make a thing large (cf. *Phdo.* 101a–b)? Likewise, a part of Equality will have to be unequal to the whole Form and the parts of Smallness will be small in comparison to the Form of Smallness, which will be large. This last conclusion is particularly embarrassing, for it is just the result that Socrates had challenged Zeno to show: that a Form could mix with its opposite. Moreover, Parmenides points out, the part of Smallness that is added to each thing has the paradoxical property of making the thing smaller and not larger as added parts usually do (131c–e). Parmenides concludes with a question to which Socrates has no answer: 'In what way, then . . . Socrates, will you have the other things partake of Forms, as they are able to partake of them either as parts nor as wholes?' (131e3–5).

These two arguments are effective only against a view that treats Forms as physical individuals, entities with spatial dimensions and unique spatial locations. Only if one assumes that a Form is a physical object that is 'in' the thing that partakes of it — in the way that flour is in a loaf of bread — can one draw the conclusion from the fact that there are, say, two loaves of bread that flour is in two different places. Only if one assumes that the Forms of Largeness, Equality and Smallness are physical objects with definite sizes can one compare them in size with the portions of them that are in various things. Most important, only if one assumes that Forms are physical *individuals*, things whose identity depends on their possession of a single spatial location at a given time, can one draw the conclusion that if the Form is divided it will no longer be one. Physical objects such as flour, water and sugar, for instance, retain their identity in spite of being scattered about the surface of the earth in various disparate loaves of bread, ponds and cups of coffee, among other things.[10] (Of course, if one thought of the Forms as these sorts of mass substances, the other conclusions of the argument *would* apply: things could partake of only a portion of them, not the whole; Smallness would be larger than its parts, and so forth.)

Socrates seems to realise, at least dimly, that it is Parmenides' treatment of Forms as physical objects that causes the problems raised by the argument, since he attempts to substitute for this concept the analogy of the Forms with a single day. In one respect at least, this analogy is a bad one: for a single day is an abstract object and thus immune to the problems of physical division on which the arguments depend, but it is also a particular, an instance of a general concept and not the general concept itself. A day is also divisible into various smaller units of time, and it would be possible to exploit this aspect of the analogy against Socrates by saying that, after all, the entire day is not present at different places at a given time but only a segment of it. That Parmenides does not take this tack is another indication that he is conceiving the problem of division solely in spatial terms and Forms as physical objects. The analogy of a single day is good in the most important respect, however; for the identity of a day does not depend at all on whether the day occurs in spatially distant locations, such as Athens and Corinth. As a day is an abstract division of time, divisions in space are irrelevant to its conditions of identity.[11] This fact serves to point out the obvious illegitimacy of Parmenides' substitution of the sail analogy for that of a day. Assuming that Parmenides understands what he is doing and what Socrates is trying to do in response, one can only describe this sleight-of-hand trick on Parmenides' part as sophistry. It is another measure of Socrates' inexperience that he does not object vigorously to the substitution.

The arguments Parmenides presents, then, are valid, but only if we assume that Forms are physical objects. There is ample reason to think that Plato did *not* so think of them in the early and middle dialogues. He clearly did not accept the idea that the identity of a Form depended on its having a unique physical location; from the early *Euthyphro* (5d) to the *Republic* (V, 476a) we find him maintaining that the Form is a single thing, although it is found in may different objects. In terms of the Being-Becoming distinction, we should expect that Plato would confine physical objects to the realm of Becoming; certainly all sensible objects are confined there, and there is considerable overlap between sensible objects and physical ones. If physical objects are confined to the realm of Becoming, then Forms, which inhabit the realm of Being, cannot be physical objects. Although Plato accepts the claim that Equality is equal (see above, pp. 25−9), we cannot infer from this that he thought that the Form had some definite physical size or shape. Indeed, Plato stresses that equal physical objects (sticks and stones) are not equal in the same way that the Form is.

It must be conceded, however, that although Plato says things about the Forms that seem to rule out the possibility that he thought that they were actually physical objects, he uses language that has its natural home in the description of physical objects to describe them. We might say that Forms are conceived by Plato on the model of physical objects. The term 'participation' itself, literally understood, virtually requires one to think of the Form as a physical whole that is divided up among many participants (see above, pp. 37–8). We have seen that he speaks of the Forms as 'in' things when describing their causal role (see above, pp. 15–17), which again suggests that the Forms are physically present in the world of Becoming. When Plato thinks of the Forms as transcendent rather than as immanent, he often places them in an 'intelligible space' ('*noētos topos*'; cf. *Rep.* VI, 508c1, 509d2; and VII, 517b5; see also Ch. I, Sec. VI, above).

What the arguments of this passage show is that such talk is metaphor, and cannot be understood literally. Even if we do not assume (as we should not) that Plato ever thought that these claims could be interpreted literally, the arguments of this passage, by showing the problems inherent in a literal interpretation, would force him to ask himself what sort of interpretation they could have. If 'participation' is not to be understood literally, how can it be understood? If the Forms do not have spatial location, what sort of existence do they have, and how can they be related to things which *are* spatial? These are questions that Plato specifically addresses in the *Timaeus*. If he does not completely resolve the question of participation, either there or elsewhere, he does come to a clear realisation of the fact that Forms are abstract objects, with no location in space or time, and yet related to things that have such location. His comparative clarity on these questions in the *Timaeus* may well be the result of his exposure in the *Parmenides* of the bankruptcy of the literal interpretation of 'participation'.

## IV. The Third Man Argument (132a–b; 132c–133a)

We come now to the objection to the Theory of Forms that has been most discussed by scholars in recent years and that is generally regarded as the most damaging of those brought up in this dialogue. The Third Man Argument, as it has been called since the time of Aristotle, occurs in two versions in the *Parmenides*. Here is the first:

I think that you believe each Form to be based on this sort of consideration: when you judge that many things are large, perhaps there seems to be one and the same Form over all as you look at them, whence you judge that the Large is one.

You speak truly, he said.

What, then, if likewise you look at both the Large itself and the other large things in your soul; will not a single large thing appear again, by which all of these appear large?

So it seems.

Then another Form of Largeness will appear, besides the Large itself which has come to be and the participants in it; and over all these again another, by which all these will be large; and no longer, in fact, will each of your Forms be one, but indefinite in number. (132a1–b2)

This formulation of the argument is not, like the other objections Parmenides states to the Theory of Forms, directed against some particular version of the theory, or to some particular conception of Forms. The argument purports to establish an infinite regress, and a vicious one at that. In order to know what 'large' means and how it applies to individual things, the Theory of Forms claims, we must first know what the Large itself, the Form of Largeness, is. The argument attempts to show that, if we require a Form to explain the largeness of individual large objects, we also require a Form to explain the largeness of the first Form, and so on.

The conclusion cf the argument, that there is an indefinite number of Forms in each case, contradicts a basic assumption of the middle period theory, namely that the Form of each general characteristic is unique. Parmenides makes this assumption explicit at the start of the argument. Given this assumption, an infinite number of Forms of a given concept would be an embarrassment to Plato even if the regress were not vicious.

Gregory Vlastos pointed out in 1954 that the argument requires two assumptions that are not explicitly stated. The first of these is the self-predication assumption; as Vlastos states it: 'Any Form can be predicated of itself. Largeness is itself large. *F*-ness is itself *F*.'[12] The second is the non-identity assumption; as Vlastos states it: 'If anything has a certain character, it cannot be identical with the Form in virtue of which we apprehend that character. If *x* is *F*, *x* cannot be identical with *F*-ness.'[13] Without the self-predication assumption, we could not compare the Large itself and the other large things with respect to largeness, for they would not all appear large. Without the non-identity assumption, we would not be justified in positing *another* Form of Largeness, besides the Large itself; it would be possible that, if the Large itself were large, it would be so in virtue of itself.

Even with these two assumptions added, the argument is valid only in a peculiar sense. As the premisses required to deduce the conclusion are logically inconsistent, contradictory, and from a contradiction anything follows, the conclusion follows from the premisses.[14] Other scholars have responded to Vlastos by providing alternative analyses of the argument which are valid without being inconsistent;[15] but Vlastos has argued that at least the best-known of these analyses cannot be derived from Plato's text.[16]

The dispute over the proper formulation of the argument, and its resultant consistency, is a case study in the value and limitations of the application of the techniques of logical analysis to the study of ancient philosophy. If we are unable to show unequivocally whether the Third Man Argument is consistent or inconsistent, the reader may well wonder, how can we expect Plato, to whom such methods were totally unavailable, to be able to reach a firm position on the merits of the argument? Fortunately, Plato's assessment of the argument, and ours as well, need not rest solely on the question of its internal consistency as formulated.

The situation seems to be this. Vlastos has a strong case when he argues that the argument as formulated in the text is inconsistent. His critics have a strong case in their argument that a version of the Third Man not much different from the one Parmenides states is both valid and consistent. Plato, lacking the logical tools required to distinguish between the different formulations of the argument, might not even have been alive to the differences between them, and might as easily have accepted the consistent formulation of the argument as Vlastos' inconsistent one. It behoves us, then, to give the argument the benefit of the doubt and not to attempt to make much mileage out of the inconsistency of one formulation of it.

We might reformulate the argument in this way:

(1) A given object, a, has the property of being $F$.

(2) If anything has the property of being $F$, there exists a Form of $F$-ness, in virtue of participation in which that thing has the property; and the Form is not identical to the thing that participates in it.

From (1) and (2) we can infer:

(3) There exists a Form of *F*-ness, in virtue of participation in which *a* has the property of being *F*; and the Form is not identical to *a*.

(4) *F*-ness has the property of being *F*.

Then, from (2) and (4), we can infer:

(5) There exists a Form of *F*-ness, in virtue of participation in which *F*-ness has the property of being *F*; and the Form is not identical to *F*-ness.

This is the conclusion that Parmenides attempts to establish; that there are two Forms of *F*-ness, not identical to each other. All objects other than the first Form might well derive their property of being *F* from the first Form; but this must in turn derive its property of being *F* from another Form of *F*-ness, and so on.

The reader will note that the argument as thus formulated contains the two suppressed premisses Vlastos distinguished: non-identity is incorporated in the last part of premiss (2), and self-predication is made explicit in (4). As the argument depends on these two assumptions we must, in order to determine its effect on the Theory of Forms in the middle dialogues, determine whether Plato was in fact committed to them.

We have already considered the question of self-predication (see Ch. 1, Sec. IV). It seems doubtful that Plato was committed to self-predication as a general principle (i.e. as applying to every Form), and there is at least one passage where he seems to deny self-predication explicitly. That passage is the one containing the argument for the uniqueness of the Form of Bed (*Rep.* X, 597c–d, discussed above, pp. 24–5). In that passage Plato denies that the Form of Bed is something that has the property of being a bed and asserts that it is that which is common to all beds. Scholars have differed as widely on the relevance of this argument (sometimes called the 'Third Bed Argument') to the Third Man. Some[17] have claimed that the argument is a refutation of the Third Man; others have argued that, if Plato intended it as such, it fails.[18] A more accurate estimate of the argument's relevance to the Third Man would appear to be the following. The argument does not refute the Third Man, for it does not show that the Third Man is fallacious. If we could assume, however, that the 'Third Bed Argument' accurately reflected Plato's thinking at the time he wrote *Rep.* X, the argument would show that Plato was aware of one of the two suppressed premisses needed for the Third Man and that he rejected that premiss. The Third Bed Argument is in some ways quite similar in structure to the Third Man; not only does it deny self-predication, but it also seems to accept a premiss that is similar to Vlastos' non-identity assumption. It concedes that if there were two putative Forms having a giving character, the Form in virtue of which they had that character would necessarily be different from either of them.[19] The resemblance of the two arguments, each using in different ways the same or similar premisses to reach contradictory conclusions (one concluding that the Form of each character is unique, the other that it is infinite in number), is so striking that it is hard to imagine that Plato failed to compare one with the other. Had he done so, he would in all likelihood have realised that the Forms can be proved unique if one denies self-predication but infinite in number only if one affirms it. Even if he did not realise that self-predication was required if the Third Man regress were to be generated, he would have had to have been impressed by the fact that he had constructed an argument for the uniqueness of the Forms that was as impressive as the Third Man itself. This fact alone would probably have prevented him from regarding the Third Man as a knock-down refutation of the Theory of Forms.

If, then, we could take the Third Bed Argument as a reflection of Plato's views at the time he wrote the tenth Book of the *Republic* and if we could assume that Plato intended the argument to apply not just to the Form of Bed but in general, we would be justified in assuming that Plato was aware of an escape from the Third Man at the time he constructed that argument. There is a problem, however, with assuming that Plato, when he wrote *Rep.* X, wished to deny self-predication entirely. The problem is that he seems to have regarded at least some Forms (e.g. the Form of Beauty; cf. *Symp.* 210e–211b, *Phdo.* 100c) as genuinely self-predicative. Although the Forms play in the middle dialogues the role played in other systems by properties or concepts (for which role self-predication is not merely unnecessary but embarrassing), they also play the roles of objects of knowledge and standards, for which the attribution of certain properties to the Forms is necessary. Not only must the Form of Beauty be Beautiful, but the Form of Unity must be one, the Form of Being must exist, and so on.[20] A total denial of self-predication would rule out this possibility, and the result Aristotle mentions in *Metaphysics* Z. 6 would follow: 'If the essence of good is not good, neither is the essence of reality real, nor that of unity one; but all the essences are alike real, or none is, so that, if the essence of reality is not real, neither are any of the others' (1031b8–10).

Both textual and philosophical reasons, then, lead one to assume that Plato accepted the self-predication of some Forms, if not all. For these Forms, which include the most important Forms Plato deals with in the dialogues, the Third Man poses a genuine problem, a problem which apparently can be dealt with only by the denial of the second suppressed premiss on which the argument relies, the non-identity assumption. We must therefore ask whether Plato ever accepted this assumption. The answer seems to be that he did not, but that he accepted principles that are confusingly close to it. We have already seen that something similar to the non-identity assumption is implicit in the Third Bed Argument. Plato also insists on the non-identity of Forms and their participants (cf. *Phdo.* 74a–75b, 102b; *Rep.* V, 475e–476d), an insistence apparently based on the idea that participation is always a relation that holds between two *different* entities and never between a thing and itself. What is necessary for the Third Man to get off the ground, however, is not the non-identity of Forms and things that participate in them but the non-identity between Forms and objects that have the characteristics of which the Forms are forms. For suppose the Form of Beauty has the property of being beautiful, but *not* only because it participates in itself. (We may leave unanswered the question how it could have the property without participating in itself; perhaps Plato thought that the relation between a Form and its cognate property was in such cases primitive, unanalysable.) Then from the fact that Forms are non-identical to their participants we could not infer that Beauty was non-identical to the thing in virtue of which it had the property of being beautiful.

Plato in fact enunciates a principle concerning the attribution of properties to things in the *Phaedo*, and it is instructive to compare what he says to what the Third Man requires that he should say. The principle is this: 'if anything else is beautiful except the Beautiful itself, it is not beautiful for any other reason than that it participates in the Beautiful; and I speak thus in all cases' (100c4–6). If we combine this principle with the principle of the non-identity of Form and participant, we get a claim something like the following:

(2a) If anything other than the Form of $F$ has the property of being $F$, there exists a Form of $F$-ness, in virtue of participation in which that thing has the property; and the Form is not identical to the thing that participates in it.

(2a) is identical to (2) in my formulation of the argument (see above, p. 66), except in the crucial respect that it is restricted to things *other than* the Form of $F$. It leaves open the possibility that a Form may have the property of which it is the Form (and in the case of Beauty, at least, the *Phaedo* implies that it does) but without participating in something different from itself, or indeed in anything at all![21]

If we could assume that Plato was fully aware of the implications of this restriction in the principle of prediction he puts forth in the *Phaedo*, we could say with confidence that he was aware at the time he wrote the *Parmenides* of still another escape from the Third Man regress, namely the restriction of the non-identity assumption to Forms and their participants and the positing of Forms only for multiplicities of $F$ things other than the Form of $F$ itself. It is tempting to assume that Plato was aware of this escape route and that when he constructed the Third Man Argument he was aware that his Parmenides was ignoring a restriction on non-identity which he had himself clearly made. There are two facts which undermine the plausibility of this assumption somewhat, though they certainly do not destroy it entirely. The first is that the principle Plato enunciates in the *Phaedo* is, after all, rather close to the one one which he relies in the *Parmenides*; and, if the young Socrates of the dialogue fails to detect the omission of the crucial restriction, it is possible that Plato himself failed to notice it. The second is that the non-identity assumption is not explicit in the argument and was in fact not explicitly noted until Vlastos called attention to it in 1954.[22] The ancient interpreters seem to be well enough aware of self-predication but only Aristotle, to my knowledge, tries to stop the regress from developing by insisting on the identity of the Forms of Goodness, Reality and Unity with their cognate properties (cf. *Meta*, Z.6; the identification is not all that clear and would have been easier for an Aristotelian — who thought of goodness, being and unity themselves as properties — to make than for a Platonist, who thought of such things as substances).

What the discussion of self-predication and non-identity should make clear is that, although Plato is not clearly committed to either of these premises as general principles in the middle dialogues, he does not seem able simply to reject them totally. He apparently accepts (and ought to accept) self-predication in some cases, and he accepts a non-identity principle similar to the one he needs. Even if Plato saw clearly enough into the hidden structure of the argument to recognise what its necessary assumptions were and saw clearly also that he was not committed to them as general rules, the very exhumation of these buried assumptions would have naturally led him to ask some questions of himself. 'If I do not accept self-predication for all Forms,' he might have asked, 'for which of them do I accept it? and why? What distinguishes the Forms that are self-predicative from those that are not? Further, if a given Form does have the property of which it is the Form, what prevents me from treating it as if it were a participant in something other than itself? That is the way I treat predication in every other case; what is it that makes the Form different from the things that partake of it? Granted, I can evade the Third Man by denying self-predication or restricting non-identity; but what is the *philosophical* basis for such a denial or restriction?'

Thus, the Third Man Argument raises some genuine philosophical problems for the Theory of Forms. It does so in spite of the fact that it is not clearly valid as formulated and that it contains hidden premises to which Plato was probably never committed. We can take the Third Man, in fact, as another case of Parmenides' deceptiveness; for only by interpreting the Theory of Forms in a most unfavourable way is Parmenides able to generate the regress. Behind the apparent sophistry of the argument as stated, however, lie important philosophical problems which it is unlikely that Plato — however far he may have carried the logical analysis of the argument itself — overlooked.[23]

The second version of the argument is, unlike the first, directed at a specific version of the Theory of Forms, namely the view that Forms are paradigms and their participants imitations of them. Vlastos has argued that it relies on the same two suppressed premises as the first version and that its logical structure is the same as that of the first.[24] No scholar of whom I know regards one version of the argument as valid and the other not; it seems safe, therefore, to regard the second version as in the respects that concern logic a special case of the first.[25] Thus, the reader may take it that all the comments I have made on the first version apply to this one also.

There are, however, some interesting features of this argument in its own right, which stem from the fact that it is a critique of one particular version of the Theory of Forms. Whatever plausibility the Third Man may have in general as a criticism of the theory, it has less plausibility as an objection to the paradigm version than to others, due to the concept of a paradigm itself.[26]

The argument occurs at 132c–133a. Socrates, who has failed in every attempt to explain coherently the nature of the Forms and the relation of participation, tries again:

> But Parmenides, it appears to me at least most likely to be like this: these Forms are set up in nature as paradigms, and the other things are like them and are images of them; and this participation of the other things in the Forms becomes nothing other than their being made like to them. (132c12–d4)

Parmenides asks whether, if something is like the Form, the Form must not also be like the thing; and Socrates agrees (132d). Parmenides then goes on to claim that the Form and its image, as similar things, must participate in the same Form (132d–e). He concludes:

> Then it is not possible for anything to be like the Form, nor for the Form to be like anything else; if this is not so, another Form will always appear besides the Form; and, if that one is like anything, still another, and there will never cease to be new Forms coming always to be, if the Form becomes like to that which participates in it.
>
> You speak most truly.
>
> Then not by likeness do the other things partake of Forms, but it is necessary to seek some other way by which they partake.
>
> That is likely. (132e6–133a7)

The argument purports to establish the conclusion that Forms are not related to their participants by the relation of resemblance; it does not purport to establish that Forms cannot be paradigms. It would establish the latter conclusion only if it could be proved that by 'paradigm' Plato meant 'exemplar', and I have argued above (Ch. 1, Sec. III) that he means rather 'pattern'. If Forms are patterns, in the image of which phenomena are made, it would not in general be the case that the Form and its image would share the property required to generate the regress. If we think in terms of ordinary examples of the pattern-image relationship, this should be obvious: the pattern of a house is not a house but a blueprint or plan for the house; the pattern of a dress is not a dress; and the pattern common to many floor tiles or sheets of wallpaper is not a floor tile or a sheet of wallpaper.

As the argument requires that the paradigm Forms of the middle dialogues be treated as exemplars, rather than as abstract patterns, it also requires that the resemblance relation posited between them be the ordinary one, which is analysable in terms of sharing a common property. We have already seen (Ch. 1, Sec. VI), however, that when Plato notes that phenomena resemble Forms he does not mean that they share a property, but rather that the phenomenon has a property of which the Form is the essence. Thus, both the notion of paradigm and the notion of resemblance that Plato actually held are insusceptible to the Third Man's regress.

Scholars have devoted a good deal of attention to the claim of Parmenides that, if the image resembles the Form, the Form must resemble the image. Some have claimed that, as the relation Plato posits between paradigm and image is not the reciprocal relation of resemblance but the non-reciprocal one of original to copy, the regress cannot arise.[27] Others have responded that the original-copy relation at least includes the reciprocal relation of resemblance and that this is all Parmenides needs to generate the regress.[28] It must be pointed out, however, that the resemblance relation that holds between Forms and phenomena is, as Plato describes it, itself a non-reciprocal relationship, containing as it does the element of defectiveness. Phenomena resemble Forms, but defectively; from this we cannot infer that Forms resemble phenomena, but defectively.

Thus, this version of the Third Man, like the first, requires that we interpret Plato's remarks in the least attractive light. Only if we take paradigm Forms to be instances of themselves, and resemblance to be the sharing of a property, can we get the necessary assumption of self-predication, without which the regress cannot arise. Even if we interpret Plato's remarks about paradeigmatism and resemblance in this unfavourable way, however, we still need the assumption of non-identity to generate the regress; and this assumption seems incompatible with the very idea of a paradigm.

Suppose that Plato's Forms are perfect exemplars of themselves; that, rather than being patterns, they were more like models or prototypes from which other things were copied. Their copies would, so far as the skill of the copyist permitted, resemble the original in the ordinary sense: the two would share a property. The model for a vase could well be an individual vase, the model of a temple another temple, and so on. It would be legitimate to ask of the copy whence it derived the properties that made it a copy of the original model, and the correct answer would be, 'from the original'. If the model were truly a standard and an original, however, the same question would not make sense if asked of it. True originals and standards are precisely those objects that do *not* derive their properties from something other than themselves; if they did so, they would not be originals. If we think about the Forms in general terms, the question that generates the Third Man may make sense: if we think it makes sense to refer the *F*-ness of the many *F* things to a Form not identical to them, we may well think that it makes sense similarly to refer the *F*-ness of the Form of *F* to another Form. If we think about the Forms as originals, standards or paradigmatic instances of themselves, however, the question is at once seen to be idle. Not only is there no reason to accept the non-identity assumption if the Forms are paradigms, there is every reason to reject it, not simply to evade the Third Man but because of the very sorts of things paradigms are.

Again we must return to the question whether Plato realised that this was the case. Without discussing in any detail matters that will be the focus of the next two chapters, let me state in outline what I take the response of the late dialogues to the problems raised by the Third Man to be. In the *Timaeus* Plato retains and exploits the paradigm-image conception of the Forms and their relation to phenomena, so it is not likely that he thought this version of the Theory of Forms refuted by the Third Man. He also makes it clear that, although Forms and phenomena share a name, they do not share a property; the Forms are not in general self-predicative. (This shows in turn that when Plato speaks of the Forms as paradigms he does not mean that they are exemplars of themselves.) Just as clearly as he rejects self-predication for most Forms in the *Timaeus*, however, he accepts it for some forms in the *Sophist*. He hints that, for these self-predicative Forms, he would reject non-identity; but nowhere in the late dialogues does he address the issue of the non-identity assumption directly and conclusively. It may be that, in retaining the conception of the Forms as paradigms he had a sufficient rejoinder to the non-identity assumption; or it may be that he had not articulated it clearly and was thus unaware of its centrality to the argument. In any event, he does not seem to have thought the Third Man in either version to be a refutation of the Theory of Forms, as he continued to hold the theory and the particular interpretation of it attacked in the second version of the argument. Neither version of the argument seems to be a fair objection to the Theory of Forms as Plato held it, let alone a refutation; yet, just as the first version pointed to some serious philosophical questions about self-predication and non-identity, the second version also would have raised questions about paradeigmatism and resemblance. These latter questions are addressed, and clearer answers than Plato had before provided are given, in the *Timaeus*.[29]

## V. The Two-Worlds Argument (133a–134e)

The second version of the Third Man Argument was directed against the view that the Forms are paradigms and participation imaging. This concept of the Forms and participation is especially appropriate if, as Socrates and Parmenides have often insisted (129d; 130b, c, d; 133a), the Forms are separate from their phenomenal participants. The paradigm-image relation, unlike the relation of sharing, suggests no spatial contiguity between Form and participant.

The final argument of this section of the dialogue, which has been called the 'Two-Worlds' Argument,[30] is specifically directed against this conception of the Forms as separate from phenomena, as transcendent entities. Parmenides begins the argument with the assertion that the Forms *are* separate: 'I think that you and anyone else who posits the existence of an essence of each thing "itself in itself" will agree that none of these objects exist among ourselves' (133c3–5). Socrates agrees that the immanence of the Forms is incompatible with their existence 'themselves in themselves', and Parmenides goes on to claim that:

These Forms are what they are in relation to each other, and have their being themselves in relation to themselves, but not in relation to their likeness among ourselves, or in whatever way one posits them, of which we are participants and after each of which we are named. These things among ourselves, on the other hand, being homonymous to those, exist for their part themselves in relation to themselves and not in relation to the Forms, and are called what they are called in relation to themselves and not in relation to those. (133c8−d5)

To explain this principle, Parmenides uses the example of master and slave. The Form of Master is what it is in relation to the Form of Slave, whereas human masters are what they are (i.e. masters) in relation to human slaves (133d−e).

In like fashion, the Form of Knowledge will be Knowledge of Truth itself (i.e. the Forms), whereas our knowledge will be knowledge of the things among us (134a−b). Since we do not possess the Forms and they are not in our world, and since knowing the Forms involves possessing the Form of Knowledge, it follows that we cannot know the Forms: 'Unknown to us, then, are what the Beautiful itself is and the Good and all those things which we suppose to be Forms themselves' (134b14−c2).

Next Parmenides goes on to bring out a consequence of separation 'even more terrible than this one' (134c4). The Form of Knowledge must be 'more precise by far' (c6−7) than the knowledge which we possess. The only being fit to partake of it would be a god; but a god related to the Form of Knowledge and to the other Forms, by the initial assumption of non-relatedness, would be entirely cut off from our world:

Therefore if this precise Mastership and this precise Knowledge are with the god, this Mastership of the gods would never be mastership of us, nor would their Knowledge ever know us; but just as we do not rule them by virtue of the rule which is among us or know anything of the divine by our knowledge, they by the same argument are not masters of us, nor do they, being gods, know human matters. (134d9−e6)

This argument has not been favourably regarded by recent interpreters, who assume that it is invalid as it stands and cannot be made valid.[31] There are differences among them, however, on the question why it is invalid, and corresponding disagreements as to how the argument should be formulated. The first two steps of the argument are clear enough: the Forms exist 'in themselves', and this mode of existence precludes their existence among us. The next step is capable of different analyses, however. Some scholars[32] have thought that, when Parmenides makes the point that Forms are related to other Forms and not to their phenomenal counterparts, he is denying that any Form can be related in any way to anything but another Form; others have held that the restriction is more limited. Perhaps only relational Forms are being discussed and perhaps Parmenides' point is merely that the proper correlate of such a Form is another Form, just as the proper correlate of a phenomenon is another phenomenon.[33]

There are difficulties with each interpretation. It is true that Parmenides uses only relational Forms, Master and Slave and Knowledge, as examples; but surely he wishes the conclusion, that Forms have their being in relation to themselves, to apply to all Forms and not just relational ones. Otherwise, the argument would be at most an objection to some Forms and not to all. It is also true that Parmenides' examples only establish the valid point that Forms are the proper correlates of Forms, and phenomena of phenomena; but this point does not justify the conclusion that Forms and phenomena are totally unrelated, that we cannot know the Forms or that the gods cannot know and govern us.[34]

If we assume that Parmenides is denying at the outset that there can be *any* relation between entities in the world of Being and entities in the world of Becoming, then we can develop a valid argument for Parmenides' conclusions. As Forms are entities in the world of Being and we are entities in the world of Becoming, and knowledge is a relation, the separation of the two worlds would preclude the relation of knowledge from obtaining between us and the Forms. In like manner, as the gods are entities in the world of Being and we are entities in the world of Becoming, the separation of the two worlds would preclude their standing to us in the relation of knowers or rulers. The problem with this interpretation of the argument is that, though it is valid, it rests on a premiss that Plato would have no reason for adopting: the total separation of the two worlds.

The alternatives seem then to be a valid argument with premisses Plato is not committed to or an invalid argument with premisses he would have no reason to reject. In this respect, however, the Two-Worlds Argument is in no different position from the other arguments in this section of the dialogue, including the Third Man; for they also obtain their validity at the expense of plausible premisses. It may be that Plato is aware of this problem and portrays Parmenides as illicitly substituting the stronger but implausible separation principle for the weaker but valid principle of correlation in order to point out once again the chicanery of the philosopher. If so, we may take it that the divergence among modern interpreters of the argument reflects a genuine ambiguity in the text itself, on which Plato has his Parmenides trade.

Leaving aside the question of the validity of the argument, we may note that several of the premisses would have seemed objectionable to a proponent of the Theory of Forms of the middle dialogues. He would accept the existence of the Forms in separation from phenomena (see Ch. 1, Sec. VI) but he would not agree that this separation precludes the immanence of Forms in things (see Ch. 1, Sec. II). He would accept the claim that the Forms are what they are in relation to themselves or each other but not the claim that the same applies to phenomena. For the core of Plato's theory of causality is the claim that phenomena are what they are in relation to Forms, by virtue of participation (see above, p. 13). The example Parmenides gives seems to show that a man is a master if he stands in the relation of mastery to another man who is his slave; but the causal theory of the *Phaedo* rejects all such explanations in favour of the explanation that a man is a master if he participates in the Form of Mastery. Thus, the Theory of Forms in the middle dialogues maintains the independence of Forms but the dependence of phenomena.

Nor would the proponent of the middle period Theory of Forms accept the claim that we could not know the Forms. As Cornford points out,[35] he would deny that we are completely confined to the world of Becoming: because the soul is immortal, it can view the separate Forms in its disembodied state and recollect them when again embodied (see Ch. 1, Sec. VI). He would object also to Parmenides' claim that the kind of knowledge we have is confined to things around us, on the grounds that this relation is not properly called knowledge at all, but belief or opinion, whereas genuine knowledge must be a relation between souls and Forms (see above, p. 30). Finally, although the gods do not play much of a role in Plato's middle dialogues, the metaphysician of the middle period would certainly object to the confinement of the gods to the world of Being; even the Socrates of this dialogue manages the response that 'the argument would be too strange if it were to deprive the god of knowledge' of phenomena (134e7–8).

It seems, then, that the middle period theorist would have no reason to accept the conclusion of the argument or many of its premisses. For once, moreover, Plato allows his characters to express their views about the cogency of the argument, and the view they express is that it is not conclusive. Parmenides states at the very outset of this argument:

> If someone should say that it is not proper to know things such as we say the Forms must be, one would not be able to prove to one who said this that he lied, unless the disputant happened to be of great experience and not without natural talent, and were willing to follow the demonstrator a great distance, labouring over a great many things; otherwise the one proving that the Forms could not be known would be unconvinced. (133b4–c1)

As we have already seen, the Socrates of the dialogue protests that at least the ultimate conclusion of the argument is 'too strange', and Parmenides does not dispute this claim.'

Parmenides' warning indicates two things. The first is that Plato must be aware that something is wrong with the argument. In the previous arguments we have seen that things are frequently amiss, but the characters of the dialogue display little overt awareness of that fact. This creates doubt about what Plato's own attitude might be. Here, however, in an argument with problems akin to those present in the other arguments, Plato has the proponent of the argument himself show that he recognises some error in the reasoning. As there are errors in abundance, it is implausible to presume that here Plato puts into the mouth of Parmenides a judgement he does not himself share.

The second point is that Plato does not think that the argument can be refuted merely by pointing out, as I have done, a fallacy in reasoning or a premiss which the proponent of the Theory of Forms would deny. To show that one who claims that the Forms cannot be known is wrong, a long and laborious proof is required. If this is the case, Plato must think that the argument is a more serious objection to the Theory of Forms than the analysis so far has indicated. This judgement is supported by another remark Parmenides makes at the outset of the argument. No sooner has the second version of the Third Man reached its conclusion than the following exchange takes place:

> 'Do you see now, Socrates,' he said, 'how great is the diffi-
> culty if someone separates as Forms being themselves in them-
> selves?'
>
> 'Most assuredly.'
>
> 'Know well, then,' he said, 'that so to speak you do not yet
> grasp how great is the difficulty of this, if you posit one Form as
> something always separate from each thing.'
>
> 'What do you mean?' he said.
>
> 'There are many other difficulties,' he said, 'but the greatest is
> this.' (133a8–b4)'

He goes on to state the argument we have been discussing.

The exchange between Parmenides and Socrates shows that, at
least in Parmenides' eyes and probably in Plato's too, this
argument is the most serious objection to the Theory of Forms. It is
clearly said to be more serious than any of the problems yet unmen-
tioned; and Parmenides' claim that Socrates — even after having
heard the Third Man — does not yet know how great the problems
with the Theory of Forms are, seems to show that he regards this
argument as more serious than those which have gone before. We
must try to determine why this is so.

First of all, this argument is the first place where Plato explicitly
recognises a conflict between the immanence and the transcendence
of the Forms which is implicit in the middle dialogues (see above,
p. 36). Once this conflict is recognised, it is no longer possible for
him to treat the Forms as both immanent and transcendent, as the
context requires, without an explanation of how this is possible. If
such an explanation is not forthcoming, a choice would seem to be
required between immanence and transcendence. To abandon
transcendence would be to inject the Forms into the world of
phenomenal change and to destroy their claims to be objects of
knowledge; to abandon immanence would be to abandon the
causal role played by the Forms in the theory of the *Phaedo* (see
Ch. 1, Sec. II). Neither alternative is desirable.

Even more important than this, however, is the fact that the total
divorce of the phenomenal world from the world of the Forms now
looms as a real possibility. The responses of the theorist of the
middle period dialogues to this argument are, at this stage of the
*Parmenides*, largely otiose. The doctrine of recollection and the

immortality of the soul both are established by reference to the Theory of Forms and specifically to the participation of phenomena in Forms. Without participation, phenomena could not be the spurs to recollection; without participation of individual souls in the Form of Immortality, the claim of the soul to be immortal could not be established. The dependence of phenomena on Forms is analysed in terms of participation also. Thus, every attempt to relate the Forms and phenomena depends at bottom on there being some relation of participation between the two, whether it be explained in terms of resemblance, sharing, or in some other way. Yet at this point in the dialogue no analysis of participation has been found and all the analyses put forward have apparently been refuted. It is thus hardly consoling to know that an answer to this argument can be found in the relation of participation and other doctrines that depend on it. It may be that there is no such thing as participation at all; and, if that is so, the complete separation of the two worlds will be no idle claim. Moreover, if the worlds are totally separate, the world of Being will be completely extraneous from the viewpoint of someone in the world of Becoming, in much the way that the noumenal world turns out to be extraneous in Kant's philosophy (at least, according to his critics). So this argument, despite its apparent invalidity and the implausibility of its premisses, is none the less a serious objection to the Theory of Forms. The earlier arguments raise the question of the nature of participation; this one raises the question of its very possibility. The two questions are in fact closely related, however; for to show that participation is possible it is sufficient to provide an analysis of the nature of participation that is coherent (i.e. one that is free from the defects that appear to plague the analyses offered so far).

Plato responds to the challenge of this argument directly in the *Timaeus*. In that dialogue he abandons the immanence of the Forms in favour of their transcendence and presents the concept of participation as resemblance in such a manner that it is clear that the Third Man is avoided. Most important, however, is the fact that he modifies the theory of causality to accommodate the fact that the Forms are not immanent in things and in so doing presents a cosmological system in which God does know the phenomenal world and we the world of the Forms. There may be doubt as to whether this system was Plato's last word in response to this argument; it does, however, succeed in meeting the major problems the argument raises, as I shall argue in the next chapter. Thus, the *Timaeus* confirms Parmenides' estimation of the argument: that it is serious and requires a long argument to refute (which argument the body of the *Timaeus* provides) but that it is not irrefutable.

## VI. Conclusion

Having examined these objections to the Theory of Forms individually, we must now look at them together, in order to determine what their cumulative effect on the Theory of Forms of the middle dialogues is. As is the case of the Two-Worlds Argument, Parmenides' remarks in the dialogue give us a clue to Plato's own attitude toward the arguments. When he has finished stating the final argument, he makes three claims. The first is that the difficulties so far raised and others in addition are necessarily involved with the Forms (135a). There appears to be something to these arguments: they create doubt about the existence and knowability of the Forms and it is very difficult to win over someone who is convinced by them. In other words, the arguments are not extraneous to the Theory of Forms but, rather, serious and damaging objections to it.[36]

Parmenides' next claim is expressed in the following remark:

It takes a very talented person to learn that there is a kind and essence of each thing, itself in itself, and an even more wonderfully capable person to discover and teach all these things adequately to another who has made the correct distinctions. (135a7–b2)

This statement tells us that, though it takes a person of intelligence to realise the fact, there are Forms such as Socrates has described, and they exist 'themselves in themselves' (i.e. separately from phenomena). The arguments he has presented do not in Parmenides' view refute the Theory of Forms; they merely make it hard to convince people of the truth, that separate Forms exist. Parmenides thus affirms here the two theses he has most forcefully attacked, the existence and separation of the Forms, and it is hard to avoid the conclusion that this affirmation, in the mouth of the critic of the Theory of Forms, represents Plato's own view that the arguments, though serious, are not fatal to the theory.

Parmenides goes on to give an argument for the existence of the Forms:

'On the other hand,' said Parmenides, 'if someone does not in fact admit that there are Forms of existent things, Socrates, having looked at all of these arguments and others like them, and does not distinguish a Form of each thing, he will have no place to direct his intellect, not allowing a Form of each real thing to be always the same, and thus he will destroy entirely the power of dialectic.' (135b5–c2)

Here the Forms appear as the indispensible objects of thought and dialectic; without them there could be no rational activity, perhaps (on one interpretation of *dialegesthai*, 135c2) no meaningful discourse. Having made the claim that the Forms after all do exist, Parmenides buttresses that claim with an argument (similar to one we shall find in the *Timaeus*) that they must exist. The opponent of the Forms turns out at last to be in worse shape than the proponent; the latter must deal with several serious objections to the theory, but the former must, it seems, presuppose the Theory of Forms if he is to reason at all.

I think we may take all of these claims to represent not just Parmenides' last word on the arguments but Plato's. The estimation given here of the force of the arguments corresponds closely to what I have claimed is their true value. They are not conclusive refutations of the Theory of Forms as it is presented in the middle dialogues, because in order to be made into valid arguments they must be interpreted as containing premisses to which Plato is certainly not committed. On the other hand, they are not merely idle objections, for the premisses on which they rely are sufficiently similar to premisses to which Plato is in fact committed to create uncertainty about the nature of Plato's metaphysics. Though misinterpretations of Plato's claims, these crucial premisses are not implausible readings of those claims. Though the middle dialogues contain clear indications of how Plato would avoid the arguments presented in the *Parmenides*, these indications are presented as asides and hints more often than not and require further development if they are to be incorporated in a consistent, systematic theory. Moreover, the arguments do reveal genuine tensions and uncertainties in the metaphysics of the middle dialogues (e.g. about the extent of the world of the Forms, the relation between the transcendence and immanence of the Forms and the nature of participation) that require resolution.

Thus, the arguments of the *Parmenides*, though they do not refute the Theory of Forms, do expose certain problems, ambiguities and weaknesses in it. In so doing, they present a programme of sorts for the development of that theory in the late dialogues. Plato must attempt to determine and state clearly his view on the combination and separation of the Forms, the population of the world of Forms, the nature of participation, the question of self-predication, the question of non-identity and the immanence and transcendence of the Forms. The late dialogues and in particular the *Timaeus*, I shall argue in the remainder of this book, do a remarkable job of addressing these issues and forging a coherent interpretation of the Theory of Forms and do so in such a way that Plato's position on the issues seems to be not piecemeal and *ad hoc* but reasoned and systematic. The solution to these problems Plato gives indeed builds on the theory of the middle dialogues, but it is to that theory as the mature oak is to the seedling; the later metaphysics of Plato develops from the earlier in an integral, natural way.

## Notes

1. Cf. Sayre, p. 37. For a survey of the various interpretations, see Runciman (1959), pp. 167–77.

2. The *Phaedrus*, as noted in the Appendix, has many late traits. Else has argued that parts of *Rep.* X are later than the rest of the dialogue and in fact belongs to Plato's late period. Sayre holds that second part of the *Parmenides*, at least, is quite late, later in fact than the *Timaeus*. As he groups the *Timaeus* with the *Theaetetus* and *Sophist* as 'intermediate' dialogues, written after Plato's middle period but before the *Philebus*, and as he links the *Philebus* and the second part of the *Parmenides* doctrinally, I presume he regards the second part of the *Parmenides* as later than the *Theaetetus* and *Sophist* as well. He argues (in his Appendix B) that this placement is consistent with the stylometric data, but it seems inconsistent with the apparent references to the *Parmenides* at *Tht.* 183e and *Soph.* 217c.

3. Cf. Allen (1983), pp. 65–6.

4. Vlastos (1954), pp. 254–5. On the question of the relation between the views of Plato and those of the characters of the dialogue, the cautionary remarks of Sayre (pp. 18–25) are especially salutary. If Sayre is right, we cannot infer from the fact that Socrates is baffled that Plato was likewise.

5. Lee (1973), p. 117, n. 1.

6. Most major interpretations of the *Sophist* concur in this: cf. e.g. Ackrill; Crombie, p. 499; Frede; and Owen (1971), p. 256.

7. I argue this point, which seems obvious from *Euphr.* 12d, in Prior (1980).

8. Owen (1957), p. 305.

9. Teloh (pp. 113–14) denies that Plato accepts Forms for such things as beds and shuttles until the time of the *Phaedrus* and *Parmenides*. He denies (p. 83) that the reference in the *Cratylus* is to a separate Form and rejects the testimony of *Rep.* X (p. 114) on the grounds that the passage 'is not a reliable source of information about the Forms'. I am unconvinced by Teloh's arguments for these claims, the latter of which seems quite overstated to me; however, there is room for doubt about the dates of the *Cratylus* and, as I noted above (n. 2), *Rep.* X. Perhaps neither were written before the *Parmenides*; but if either or both were, they seem to me (*pace* Teloh) to provide evidence for Forms of complete predicates in the middle dialogues.

10. For a discussion of objects of this kind and their names, cf. Quine, pp. 91–5. Allen (1983), pp. 124–7, also notes that the argument turns Forms into physical objects.

11. At least for the most part. There are problems about the date, in e.g. Tokyo and Honolulu, that relate to the international dateline; but these problems do not affect the main point. Allen (1983), pp. 116–17, interprets Socrates' analogy of the Forms to day and Parmenides' response differently. He thinks that Socrates must mean, not the abstract unit of time, as I have assumed, but the light of day, and finds Parmenides' substitution of the sail analogy to be the helpful response of a good teacher. Allen's interpretation is an alternative to my own which cannot be ruled out on the basis of the text but I do not see the necessity of adopting it for which he argues.

12. Vlastos (1954), p. 236.

13. Ibid., p. 237.

14. Ibid., pp. 239–40.

15. E.g. Sellars and Strang.

16. Vlastos (1969a).

17. E.g. Cherniss (1944), pp. 295–7, and (1957), pp. 371–2; cf. Vlastos (1954), p. 259, n. 1.

18. E.g. Ross, p. 87, and Strang, pp. 192–3. Teloh (p. 165) follows Ross.

19. Vlastos (1963), p. 263, claims that the Third Bed Argument relies on non-identity; but all the argument states is that a multiplicity of *F* Forms needs a Form of *F* which is not identical to any of them, not that a single *F* Form needs one.

20. Vlastos (1971b), p. 259; (1970), p. 306; (1969), p. 337.

21. My (2a) resembles what Vlastos (1954), pp. 238–9, called the 'weak' non-identity assumption. Vlastos, in presenting this weak version of the non-identity assumption, does not call attention to the parallel between it and *Phdo.* 100c.

22. As Vlastos (1954) himself notes, p. 237.

23. Allen (1983) and Sayre treat the arguments of the first part of the *Parmenides* in a fashion similar to mine. Both reject the view that the arguments are valid and insurmountable objections to the middle-period Theory of Forms and the view that they are simple sophisms. According to Allen, they are examples of 'aporetic inquiry', raising serious problems which Plato later tries to solve (pp. 92–100, 177–80). According to Sayre, they are rhetorically but not logically powerful and reveal Plato's dissatisfaction with certain aspects of the middle-period Theory of Forms without containing Plato's actual reasons for being dissatisfied (pp. 22–3). Allen and Sayre differ in that Sayre believes that Plato eventually gave up the attempt to repair the theory of the middle period, whereas Allen thinks the later dialogues (and in particular the *Timaeus*) contain a satisfactory response to the *aporiai* raised here. On this matter I side with Allen against Sayre.

24. Vlastos (1954), pp. 241–4.

25. Owen's view (cf. that of 1953, pp. 318–22) seems to be that the Third Man refutes the view that the Forms are paradigms but not the Theory of Forms as a whole. If what I have said is correct, he cannot consistently maintain this position.

26. For a detailed discussion of this point, cf. Prior (1979).

27. For references cf. Owen (1953), p. 319.

28. E.g. Ross, p. 89.

29. As noted above (n. 23), Allen also thinks the *Timaeus* contains Plato's response to these difficulties (see Allen (1983), pp. 167–8; 180).

30. By Passmore, p. 40.

31. Cf. Cornford (1939), pp. 98–9; Forrester; and Lewis, p. 117.

32. For references cf. Lewis, p. 125, n. 11.

33. Lewis, pp. 107–9; cf. Forrester, p. 236.

34. As both Lewis and Forrester note.

35. Cornford (1939), p. 99.

36. According to Bestor, pp. 39, 68–72, they are merely exercises for pupils in the Academy to cut their teeth on. Though I agree with much of his analysis of the arguments themselves, I cannot accept this as the correct verdict on arguments which have engaged the serious attention of philosophers down to the present day. I take the passage just discussed as evidence that Plato did not so regard them either.

# 3

# THE RESPONSE OF THE *TIMAEUS*

In Chapters 1 and 2 I have described the metaphysics of the early and middle Platonic dialogues and the critique of that metaphysics in the *Parmenides*. Now it is time to investigate Plato's response to that critique in the *Timaeus*. We shall see that in the *Timaeus* Plato maintains some of the metaphysical doctrines attacked in the *Parmenides*, most notably the distinction between Being and Becoming and the view that Forms are related to their phenomenal participants as patterns to copies. These doctrines are considerably clarified in light of the *Parmenides*, however, and are in addition augmented by new metaphysical principles which enable Plato to meet and defuse the objections to the Theory of Forms as stated in the middle dialogues. Such, at any rate, is what I shall attempt to show in detail in this chapter. I shall be concerned only with the metaphysical doctrines of the *Timaeus* and with the part of the dialogue (27d–52d) in which they occur. I shall focus in particular on two passages within that part: 27d–31b and 48e–52d. I shall discuss the rest of the dialogue only in so far as it relates to the metaphysical scheme outlined in the passages cited above.

The *Timaeus* does not present the reader with the interpretative problems of the *Parmenides*: it is not hard to determine which of the characters speaks for Plato. With the exception of Taylor,[1] most ancient and modern interpreters have agreed that the character Timaeus represents Plato's views on cosmology, just as Socrates in the middle dialogues speaks for Plato. Plato's Timaeus, in all probability a fictional character, is introduced as a man who has held the highest offices in his well-governed native state and who stands at the acme of philosophy (20a); a few pages later (27a) it is pointed out that his special interests are astronomy and natural science. This combination of political, scientific, and philosophical wisdom recalls the philosopher-king of the *Republic*, and there is no hint of irony in the accolades given Timaeus. It seems safe to assume, then, that Timaeus is Plato's spokesman.[2]

The *Timaeus* is the first part of a projected three-part sequel to a discourse of Socrates on the state, which the dialogue presents as having been completed the previous day (20b). This discourse is

summarised at 17c–19a, and it contains many of the politica
doctrines of the *Republic*.[3] The second dialogue in the sequel is the
incomplete *Critias*, the Atlantis story of which is summarised a
*Tim*. 21e–25d. As is the case with another projected trilogy, the
*Sophist*, *Statesman* and *Philosopher*, the last dialogue in the
sequence was not even started, for reasons that remain unclear.

The insertion of a discourse on cosmology into a series of
dialogues on political themes may strike us as strange, but it reflects
Plato's view that wisdom is a single whole, no part of which is
independent of any other. For this reason the philosopher-rulers of
the *Republic* were required to spend years in the study of
arithmetic, astronomy, geometry, and harmonics before engaging
in philosophical dialectic. As the philosopher must know everything, in so far as possible, if he is to govern wisely, Plato would
certainly not have found a treatise on physics irrelevant to his
education.

The discourse of Timaeus is to begin with the origin of the
universe and conclude with the nature of man (27a). In the course
of it we are presented the most highly detailed cosmological theory
still extant from the period before Aristotle. In its details it often
resembles the accounts of the Presocratics but it is by no means a
representation of their thought. As Plato was not a highly original
natural scientist, it is no surprise that he drew on the insights of
others in matters physical. These insights are incorporated into a
metaphysical system that is purely Platonic, however; and the
metaphysics of the dialogue affects the physics and cosmology at
every stage.

Timaeus treats the cosmos as the product of two forces, Reason
and Necessity (48a). Reason, in the person of the Demiurge, orders
the intrinsically chaotic phenomenal realm in light of the Forms,
which serve as principles of order. The ordering is not perfect,
because the chaos on which the Demiurge works is recalcitrant; but
the Demiurge does the best job possible with the material he is
given. Scholars generally agree about the scheme so far described,
but there is much disagreement concerning the details in terms of
which it is worked out. Some of these disagreements I shall discuss
briefly below. As previously, I shall attempt no general treatment
of the dialogue; nor shall I proceed through the dialogue line by
line. Rather, I shall deal successively with the Being-Becoming
distinction and the two-worlds doctrine, the Demiurge and the new
theory of causation, the nature of Forms as paradigms and

the Receptacle (in relation to the question of self-predication).

## I. Being and Becoming; the Two Worlds

Plato in the middle dialogues made a categorial distinction between two sorts of entities: those that 'are' and those that 'become' (see Ch. 1, Sec. V). In addition, he treated those two categories as separate worlds, neither of which is contained in the other (Ch. 1, Sec. VI). One of the primary reasons for the separation of the two categories was the role of the Forms, the only unquestionable members of the realm of Being, as objects of knowledge, a role which in Plato's eyes required imperviousness to change (p. 41). The separate existence of Forms seemed at odds with their existence in phenomena as causes, and it was attacked in the Two-Worlds Argument of the *Parmenides* (Ch. 2, Sec. V). Yet Aristotle claimed that Plato did not abandon the doctrine of separation even in his later years (*Metaph.* A. 6, 987a34–b1); and this judgement is supported by the *Timaeus*.

The categorial distinction is affirmed in Timaeus' first question:

> In my judgment, first of all these things must be distinguished: What is always real and has no becoming? And what is always becoming, but never real? The one is apprehended by intelligence with a rational account, is always in the same state; the other is opined by opinion with unreasoning sensation, comes into being and perishes, but never really is. (27d5–28a4).

Plato draws the distinction in virtually the same words he used in the middle dialogues. As before, he associates the Being-Becoming distinction with the distinction between knowledge and opinion.

A few lines later, Timaeus asks of the entire 'heaven or cosmos, or whatever it would prefer to be called' (28b1–3):

> whether it always was, having no beginning of generation, or whether it came to be, having begun from some starting point. It has come to be; for it is visible and tangible and has body, and all such things are sensible; and sensible things, apprehended by opinion by means of sensation, appeared to become and be generated. (28b6–c2)

Here for the first time Plato explicitly locates physical objects within the dichotomy; and, as I speculated above (p. 63) he confines them to the world of Becoming. This implies that Forms, as members of the realm of Being, are not physical objects and that it is therefore not proper to treat them as such. This makes idle the objections Parmenides raises to the immanence of the Forms (cf. Ch. 2, Sec. III).

Plato also reaffirms the epistemological distinction between knowledge and belief and uses that distinction to issue a disclaimer about his cosmology:

> This distribution must be made concerning the paradigm itself and concerning its image, that the accounts are similar to the things which they expound: the account of the stable and firm and apparent to reason will be stable and unchanging — insofar as it is possible for an account to be irrefutable and unmoving, this account should fall short of that in no respect — but an account of that which is made in the image of that thing, being like an image is analogous to those things: just as Being is to Becoming, so is Truth to Belief. (29b3–c3)

Some scholars have seen in this warning an excuse for regarding all or part of the cosmological theory as myth, poetry or metaphor. This is not justified. Timaeus is simply observing the epistemological corollary of the Being-Becoming distinction and telling us that his cosmology, being about matters of opinion rather than of rational knowledge, cannot be known for certain. *Epistēmē*, scientific knowledge, is for Plato *a priori* rather than empirical and requires proof of the sort found in geometry. Cosmology, concerned as it must be with the world of becoming, is empirical and lacks proofs of this sort; it therefore cannot be 'science' in Plato's sense of the word. This does not imply, however, that the account put forth in the dialogue is not scientific, as we would describe it. Nor does the fact that Plato describes the account as a *mythos* entitle us to regard it as a 'myth', if that term implies that a myth must be a fiction. The cosmology is a myth only in the sense that it is a story; *Tim*. 30b8 shows that Plato is not unwilling to use the word 'true' in connection with its contents.[4]

We have seen, then, that Plato in the *Timaeus* maintains the categorial distinction between Being and Becoming and the related epistemological distinction between knowledge and belief. He also continues to maintain the separation of the two orders. The best evidence of this comes in the Receptacle passage, where Plato summarises the three elements in his ontology:

> These things being so, we must agree that there exist:
>
> (1) the Form, which remains in the same state, ungenerated and imperishable, neither receiving into itself anything else from elsewhere, nor itself going anywhere into another, invisible and in general imperceptible to sense, that which it is the task of intelligence to examine;
>
> (2) that which has the same name [as the Form] and is like it, sensible, generated, always borne about, and coming to be in some place and perishing again back out of it, grasped by opinion with the aid of sensory experience;
>
> (3) the always-existent genus of space, not admitting destruction, furnishing a seat for all that has generation, but itself grasped without sense experience by a certain bastard reasoning, scarely an object of belief . . . (51e6–52b2)

This summary does not simply repeat the already familiar elements of the Being-Becoming distinction; it adds a new distinction. Phenomenal participants in Forms come to be in some place and perish out of that place. The Receptacle (space) provides the place wherein phenomena come to be and perish. Forms, in contrast, do not receive other things into themselves, as does the Receptacle; nor do they enter into another thing, as do their phenomenal participants. Phenomena exist in space and are dependent on space for their existence (52c); Forms do not exist in space, or anything else. As Timaeus puts it at 52c5–d1, 'in the case of the true reality . . . as long as something is one thing and another thing another, neither will ever come to be in the other . . .' Our belief that everything that exists must be in some place or other is the result of our dreamlike state and is untrue (52b–c; cf. *Rep.* V, 476c–d).

As phenomena exist in space and Forms do not, the separation of the two orders is maintained. The view presented here is not quite the same as that defended earlier, however. In the *Republic*, Plato had used the notion of intelligible space as the locale of the Forms (see above, p. 64), and he had treated their existence as if it were analogous to that of phenomena. This may well have been metaphor; but in the middle dialogues Plato made use of the metaphor, whereas here he explicitly rejects it. By insisting on the nonspatiality of the Forms, Plato clearly (more clearly than before) shows his awareness of their abstract nature. It is tempting to think that this increased awareness is at least in part the result of the critique of the *Parmenides*, and that Plato in this passage is recording his own awakening from the dreamlike state of the middle dialogues.

It appears, then, that Plato in the *Timaeus* actually widens the gap between Forms and phenomena. This is only partly true. He recognises more clearly than before the difference in mode of being between Forms and phenomena; but the earlier disparagement of the phenomenal world is largely absent from this dialogue. In the middle dialogues, Plato regarded the phenomenal world as unworthy of the philosopher's serious attention (cf. esp. *Phdo.* 65a–68b); now he treats it with considerable respect. The cosmos is now a suitable object for serious philosophical study (if still inferior to the Forms) and has acquired attributes at least similar to those of the Forms.

Many passages attest to Plato's new attitudes. The cosmos is the best of the things that have come to be (29a); it is a living creature with soul and reason (30b–c); it is complete, comprehensive, unified and free from illness and age (30c–33b); its existence is everlasting (38b–c). Throughout the dialogue, Plato uses mathematics to describe the structure of the phenomenal world (see esp. 31b–32c, 35b–36d, and 53c–57d); as mathematics is a paradigm of rational knowledge for Plato, these passages must be taken to mean that at least some aspects of the phenomenal world can be rationally understood.

As Plato's estimation of the value of the phenomenal world goes up in the *Timaeus*, so does his estimation of the value of sensory experience and in particular of vision, the instrument whereby the phenomenal world is apprehended. In the *Phaedo* Plato had deprecated all sensory experience, emphasising its illusory character (see esp. 65b). In the *Republic*, he had conceded that the 'artificer of the senses' had been extravagant in providing for vision (VI, 507c); but he also stated that experience of the visible heavens was simply irrelevant to the study of astronomy (VII, 529b–530b). Although Plato also admitted that the senses were necessary to spur the process of recollection or dialectic (*Phdo.* 72e–75e; *Rep.* VII, 523a–524d) and though he modelled the process of reasoning on the visual process (*Rep.* VI, 507a–509c), his realisation of the value of the senses has been at most grudging and limited.

In the *Timaeus*, however, he composes an encomium to sight:

> Sight, then, according to my account, has become the cause of
> the greatest benefit to us, since no one who had seen neither the
> stars nor the sun nor the heavens would ever have uttered the
> present discourse concerning the universe. But now the sight of
> day and night and months and the cycles of the years and
> equinoxes and solstices has devised number, and has given us the
> concept of time and the investigation of the nature of the
> universe, from which we have provided for ourselves the nature
> of philosophy, than which no greater good has come or ever will
> to the human race as a gift from the gods. (47a1–b2)

Now vision is given a role in scientific inquiry and is said to be the
ultimate cause of the existence of philosophy. As Plato regards
philosophy as 'the greatest benefit' to mankind, the estimation of
the value of vision that results is very high. He goes on to claim
(47b–c) that observation of the rational cycles of the cosmos can
lead us to stabilise the revolutions in our own souls and thus
become better persons. This gives vision moral and psychological
efficacy as well as cognitive. In all, the attitude Timaeus expresses
toward vision is a rather radical departure from the attitude
expressed by Socrates in the *Phaedo*.

In summary, Plato maintains both the categorial distinction
between Being and Becoming and the separation of the two worlds
in the *Timaeus*. He recognises that the Forms are abstract, non-
spatial entities and that phenomena are concrete, spatial ones. In
spite of his recognition of the difference between the two orders,
however, he now regards Becoming as an appropriate object of
philosophical investigation and the senses as valuable instruments
of thought.

Plato's recognition of the non-spatial existence of the Forms, as I
have noted, makes idle the arguments against the immanence of the
Forms raised in the *Parmenides*. It does so, however, by ruling out
the possibility that the Forms might be immanent in phenomena in
any literal sense. This raises two problems. If the Forms are not
immanent in things, how can they be causes? And if the Forms are
separate from the phenomenal world, how can the Two-Worlds
Argument (see Ch. 2, Sec. V) be answered? Both of these problems
are addressed, if not entirely resolved, by Plato's new theory of
causation.

## II. The Demiurge and the New Theory of Causation

In the *Phaedo*, Plato had offered the Theory of Forms as the sole explanation of how and why phenomena had their characteristics and he had adopted this theory in lieu of an explanation in terms of the benevolent purposes of *Nous*, Divine Reason (an explanation promised but not provided by Anaxagoras; see above, p. 13). In the *Timaeus*, he offers just the sort of explanation he had abandoned in the *Phaedo*. It is clear from his account of the theory itself that it is a new theory and not just a restatement of the theory of the *Phaedo*.

Immediately after the passage discussed above, in which Plato reaffirms the Being-Becoming distinction, Timaeus claims that 'all that becomes necessarily comes to be under the agency of some cause' (28a4). A reader of the middle dialogues would expect a discussion of the causal role of the Forms to ensue, but it does not. Instead, Timaeus continues:

> Whenever the craftsman (*ho dēmiourgos*, 28a6), looking toward that which is always in the same state and using something of that sort as a paradigm, produces its form and power, everything thus accomplished is necessarily beautiful; where he looks to something that has come to be, using a created paradigm, it will not be beautiful. (28a6−b2)

The cause of becoming Timaeus mentions is thus the craftsman; the Form is the paradigm from which the craftsman works. In 28c, Timaeus restates the same view: he claims again that all becoming has some cause and immediately adds, 'The maker and father of this whole it is both a task to find out and impossible to explain to everyone when found' (28c3−5).

Concerning the passage so far, several points must be made. First, only things that become require causes, not things that are. In other words, an explanation is necessary for the existence of a beautiful sculpture or tree but not for the existence of a Form of Beauty, Sculpture, or Tree. Secondly a cause is required for the cosmos as a whole, as well as for its individual parts. The cosmos, like the things in it, is the object of sensory experience and is a physical thing; therefore it is in the realm of Becoming and therefore it requires a cause for its generation (28b−c).

Thirdly, the cause Plato seeks is the cause of the existence of the cosmos and not just of its having certain characteristics. The cosmos, as we have seen, is one of a class of things that 'become and [are] generated' (*gignomena kai genneta*, 28c1–2). Some scholars have argued that Plato does not believe in a literal creation but holds rather that the world is in a state of perpetual flux.[5] This is in fact a sophisticated response, originating with ancient supporters of Platonism, to problems arising from the doctrine of a literal creation. As a reading of the text, however, it will not do. When Plato claims that the cosmos 'has become' (*gegonen*, 28b7), that it is one of the things that become (28c1) and even that it 'has become, having begun from some starting point' (28b6–7), he might, though with considerable strain, be interpreted as saying that the cosmos has always been in the process of change. When he says that the universe is one of the things that are 'generated' (*genneta*, 28c2), however, he can only taken to assert that it has been created.[6]

When we note this, however, we must be careful to avoid the implications that the cosmos was created in time or that it was created from nothing. Plato rejects both claims. The cosmos was not created out of nothing; it was created from a pre-existent chaos (30a). The cosmos is, in the literal sense of the term, an order; the creation of the order does not imply creation of the stuff from which the order is produced. In this respect, the analogy between the creator of the cosmos and an ordinary craftsman is illuminating; for the ordinary craftsman works on material which he does not himself produce, but which he attempts to 'make something out of' or 'bring some form to'. The cosmos was not created in time, because time comes into being with the cosmos (38b). Time, in Plato's view, is the measure of the regular motion of the heavenly bodies; before there were any heavenly bodies, there was no time (37e). The creation Plato envisions is thus somewhat different from that envisioned in Judaeo-Christian theology.

Fourthly, we must consider the nature of the new causal agent in Plato's account. Plato calls him 'the maker and father' (28c3) of the cosmos; he is usually referred to as the Demiurge, after Plato's comparison of him to a craftsman (*demiourgos*). He is a causal principle not to be found in the theory of the *Phaedo* and the role he plays is that of an efficient or moving cause in the new scheme.[7] It is not clear whether he takes over this role from the Forms in the *Phaedo*, or whether he is an entirely new kind of cause in Plato's theory (see above, p. 14); but in either event the addition of the

Demiurge is a significant modification in Plato's theory of causation. (It is interesting to note that all four Aristotleian causes are to be found in the *Timaeus*. The material cause is the pre-existent chaos from which the cosmos is formed, the efficient cause of the creation of the cosmos is the Demiurge and the formal and final causes are the Forms after which the cosmos is patterned.)

Plato tells us little about the nature of the Demiurge in the *Timaeus*. He says that the Demiurge is good, and therefore not jealous; because of this he is said to have made the cosmos as perfect as possible (29d–30a). He refers to the created works of the Demiurge as 'the things crafted by Reason' (*ta dia nou dedēmiourgēmena*, 47e4): this shows that the Demiurge is identical to or a personification of Reason. This identification is confirmed by the *Philebus*. There (26e) Plato again states that all becoming requires a cause, which he identifies with the maker of the thing that becomes. At 28d–e he says that the universe is a product of Reason, *Nous*, and Reason is again identified as the cause of the universe at 30d–e. This cause Plato lists as one of four categories or classes of things, and at 27b1 he refers to it as 'that which crafts (*dēmiourgoun*) all these things'.

The *Philebus* is not the only dialogue in which the creative work of God or Reason is described by Plato in terms of craftsmanship. We find the analogy at work in *Rep.* VI, 507c and VII, 530a; *Soph.* 265b–c; *Pol.* 270a, and *Laws* X, 903c. It hardly seems accidental that most of these references are to dialogues which post-date the *Parmenides*. The Demiurge, I shall argue, is in fact Plato's response to the problems of separation raised by that dialogue.

In the *Phaedo*, the Forms themselves were cause in virtue of their immanence in things; in the *Timaeus* the possibility of such immanence has been ruled out. Yet the Forms continue to function as the patterns from which the phenomenal world is constructed, despite the fact that they cannot be regarded as intrinsic to the phenomenal order. The separation of the Forms thus requires the principle of the Demiurge in order that the relation between Forms and phenomena can be explained. The explanation, once the existence of the Demiurge is assumed, is simple: the phenomenal world exhibits an order which is derived from the Forms (the principles of that order) because the Demiurge has embodied that order in the phenomenal world. The Demiurge is the agent that puts order in the world by moulding the world in the image of the Forms. The Demiurge is a necessary link between the two worlds, and, as such, he gives Plato a response to the Two-Worlds Argument as well as a new theory of causation.

We saw in Chapter 2 (see above, pp. 80–2) that the assumption of a relation of participation was insufficient to refute the Two-Worlds Argument, since the other arguments of the *Parmenides* had raised doubts about the possibility of such a relation. Some of those doubts have been laid to rest by Plato's denial of the immanence of the Forms; others (most notably the doubt produced by the second version of the Third Man Argument, which is specifically directed against the version of the Theory of Forms employed by Plato in the *Timaeus*) remain. Until these are resolved, the objection of the Two-Worlds Argument cannot be met completely. None the less, the assumption of the Demiurge gives Plato a powerful rejoinder to the argument.

This may be made clear as follows. The relation of participation is treated in the middle dialogues as a given. No attempt is made to explain its nature (cf. *Phdo.* 100d) or to show why we should assume that such a relation exists. Thus, when the coherence of the concept of participation is questioned in the *Parmenides*, Socrates has no way to show that we ought to believe that phenomena do, after all, participate in Forms. The introduction of the Demiurge into the cosmological scheme of the *Timaeus* gives Plato at once a higher principle from which the existence of such a relation can be derived and a plausible interpretation of the nature of that relation. If, in other words, there exists a rational and benevolent deity who created the cosmos, and if there exist Forms which can serve as eternal principles of order, it follows that the deity would embody those principles in so far as possible in that order. If, further, this deity works in the same way that an ordinary craftsman works, we can understand the relation that holds between the model, pattern, plan, or design the craftsman uses in his work and the product of his efforts. In appealing to this analogy we of course do not answer the Third Man Argument, which purports to show that such a relation is unintelligible; but, by appealing to a clear case (that of the ordinary craftsman) where the relation is exhibited, we go a long way toward reducing the force of the Third Man's objection.

Plato responds to the Two-Worlds Argument not by exposing a formal fallacy in the argument but by substituting for the picture presupposed by that argument of totally separate worlds a quite different one. In the picture of the *Timaeus*, the worlds are indeed separate, but related. The relation between them is the pattern-copy relation, which is explained as the result of the creative activity of the Demiurge. For the gods of the Two-Worlds Argument, confined to the realm of Being, Plato substitutes the Demiurge, who serves by his creative efforts as a bridge between the two worlds.

Plato also substitutes a different picture of the soul and its potential for knowledge for that presupposed by the Two-Worlds Argument. This picture is similar to the one employed in the middle dialogues: according to it, the soul can have knowledge of the Forms. What Plato does in the *Timaeus* that is different from what he had done earlier is to portray the soul as constructed from materials which guarantee from the outset that it is capable of knowing the Forms. He describes the construction of the World-Soul, which is the soul of the entire cosmos, as follows:

> Of the indivisible and always unchanging Being and of that again which comes to be divided among bodies he mixed an intermediate Form of Being from both; and from the nature of the Same and that of the Different in the same way he combined the indivisible sort of those things and the sort that is divided among bodies; and taking these three things he mixed them all into one form, putting together by force the nature of the Different and that of the Same, which were hard to blend. (35a1−8)

The composition of the individual souls of human beings is said at 41d to be the same but less pure. The purpose of this elaborate mixture is revealed at 37a−c: the soul, being made of both sorts of Being, Sameness and Difference, is able to recognise these properties both in the case of things that have divided existence (i.e. phenomena, which are spatially distinct) and in the case of things which have undivided being (Forms). This cognition results in the former case in 'firm and true opinions and beliefs' (37b8) and in the latter in 'reason and knowledge' (37c2)

Before I go on to note some objections and limitations to this view of the new theory of causation as a response to the Two-Worlds Argument, let me call attention to some significant features of this portrait of the soul. First, Plato again recognises that there is a sort of being which spatially separated objects have, as he had at *Phdo.* 79a. This shows again that the Being-Becoming dichotomy is not absolute and that things in the category of Becoming (i.e. phenomenal, physical objects) partake of a kind of

Being. Secondly, the distinction between two kinds of Being, Sameness and Difference (which is unparalleled in Plato) both depends on and gives additional support to Plato's recognition that Forms are non-spatial entities. A physical object exists because it is in some place and is the same as itself and different from other physical objects in virtue of spatial relations that hold between them. These sorts of Being, Sameness and Difference cannot possibly apply to Forms, in virtue of their non-spatial nature; thus, Plato is compelled to posit different sorts of Being, Sameness, and Difference for Forms and for physical objects.

Thirdly and most important, the passage contains the claim that Being, Sameness and Difference 'blend' with one another to form the soul. This is a claim, as we saw in Chapter 2 (above, p. 57) that the Socrates of the *Parmenides* would have emphatically denied. According to him, the participants in Forms might partake of opposite Forms, but the opposites themselves (e.g. Sameness and Difference) could not partake of each other. This view may well be the position of Plato in the *Phaedo*. In the *Sophist* Plato gives an argument to show that Being, Sameness and Difference do all blend with one another; and his statement that they do in this passage certainly serves to link the *Timaeus* with the *Sophist* and to distinguish it from the pre-*Parmenides* dialogues.[8]

I have argued that Plato employs his new theory of causation in responding to the Two-Worlds Argument of the *Parmenides*, and I have portrayed that response as the substitution of one cosmological picture for another. That is not all there is to the matter; if it were, Plato would be open to the obvious objection that he has provided no rational basis for preferring one picture to another. He does, in fact, attempt to give arguments for the existence and the rational good-will of the Demiurge. These arguments are among the earliest instances of arguments for the existence and nature of God that are of central importance in philosophical theology. The argument for the existence of the Demiurge is a version of the Cosmological Argument; I have mentioned it above. Everything that becomes must have a cause; the universe has become, therefore the universe has a cause, namely the Demiurge (28a–c). This argument establishes at most that a first cause of Creation exists. Plato in the *Timaeus* takes it for granted that the Demiurge is rational and benevolent (he remarks at 29a that it would be impious to assume that the Demiurge was not good). In the *Laws*, however, he does employ a version of the Argument from Design, arguing from the fact that the motions of the planets are regular to the conclusion that the soul that guides the cosmos is good and rational (X, 897b–899c). The governing soul of the *Laws* may or may not be identical with the Demiurge of the *Timaeus*; however, that may be, and though Plato does not specifically formulate the Argument from Design in the *Timaeus*, it is not unreasonable to assert that Plato uses the detailed account of the rationality of the cosmos that he gives in the *Timaeus* as evidence for the rationality and goodness of its creator.

The argument, then, in favour of the existence of a rational and benevolent creator deity, is as long and elaborate as Parmenides had said a response to the Two-Worlds Argument would have to be. Plato devotes most of Book X of the *Laws* arguing that gods exist, that they are concerned with the affairs of men (one of the points disputed by the Two-Worlds Argument) and that they can't be bribed. He devotes most of the *Timaeus* to displaying the rational order in the cosmos, which as I have noted may be thought to attest to the rationality and benevolence of its creator. Moreover, just as Parmenides had claimed that only an able person would be able to follow the refutation of the Two-Worlds Argument, Timaeus here (28c) notes that it would be impossible to prove to everyone that the Demiurge existed. All of these facts — the length of the arguments, the fact that they do provide a response to the Two-Worlds Argument and Plato's recognition that not everyone will be convinced by them — create the suspicion, if they do not establish beyond all doubt, that the new theory of causation and the theology of the late dialogues constitute precisely the response to the Two-Worlds Argument Parmenides had in mind.

I have argued that the new theory of causation that appears in the *Timaeus* both resolves the difficulty that arises when the Forms, which in the middle dialogues function as causes, are made wholly transcendent, and provides the Platonic response to the Two-Worlds Argument of the *Parmenides*. It is interesting to note that, if what I have claimed is true, the method Plato has employed in defending the existence of separate Forms is exactly that recommended in the *Phaedo*. There Socrates has said that, when a hypothesis such as the existence of Forms is questioned, it should be defended by deducing it from a higher hypothesis (101d–e). Here Plato has tried to exhibit the coherence of the Theory of Forms and the relation of participation by showing that the role of the Forms in the generation of the cosmos and the relation between the cosmos and the Forms are part and parcel of a more comprehensive scheme of explanation than any he has attempted before.

I have relied in my argument on the assumption that Plato is serious in his assertion that the Demiurge exists; without this assumption the new theory of causation would be a fiction. The need for such a theory of causation if the problems of the middle dialogues are to be resolved and Plato's repeated references to the Demiurge in the late dialogues testify to the correctness of this assumption. In spite of this, however, some scholars have interpreted Plato's account of the Demiurge as mythical or symbolic, or have identified the Demiurge with the World-Soul.[9] This interpretation arises largely from the problems that surround Plato's doctrine of a literal creation (if creation is a fiction, it stands to reason that the agent of creation must be also fictional) and is subject to the same criticism — that is, it may be justifiable as a sophisticated response to difficulties that arise when we attempt to take what Plato says seriously; as a report of what Plato says, however, it has no merit. Plato gives no hint that the Demiurge is a symbol of anything, or that the account is a fiction; to the contrary, he treats it as a serious scientific account but one which is not on the level of philosophy in terms of knowledge. As for the distinction between the Demiurge and the World-Soul, Plato could not be clearer: the World-Soul is the creation of the Demiurge and not identical to it. The functions of these two entities are quite different, also: the Demiurge brings the entire cosmos into existence, and mediates between the world of the Forms and the phenomenal world by imposing order on the phenomenal world. The World-Soul, on the other hand, gives the cosmos its life and intelligence (Plato's principle being that an intelligent created thing is superior to an unintelligent one; 30b–c) and maintains the order imposed on it as creation from above. It also is a mediating principle, but it mediates between the two worlds by looking up at the world of Forms from below, as it were, whereas the Demiurge mediates by looking down from above. Both are necessary to Plato's cosmology and it is important that their functions be not conflated.

Although the new theory of causation provides Plato with solutions to problems inherent in the Theory of Forms of the middle dialogues and enables him to portray the totality of existence in a more comprehensive way than previously, it remains somewhat limited in its effectiveness as a response to the Two-Worlds

Argument. First of all, it is no stronger than the arguments used to support it, the Cosmological Argument and the Argument from Design. The strength of these arguments has, of course, been a matter of considerable dispute in philosophical theology. Secondly, although the new theory of causation uses an analogy with the ordinary craftsman that makes plausible the interpretation of participation in terms of the relation between pattern and copy, it does not, as I have noted above, directly answer the objection of the Third Man. Plato must still deal in some way with that troublesome argument if the coherence of the Theory of Forms is to be vindicated. Nowhere in the dialogues does he respond to the argument directly; none the less, the account of the nature of the Forms as paradigms and the account of predication he offers in the *Timaeus* provide the basis for a rejection of the crucial premiss of the Third Man, the self-predication assumption. It is to these themes in the *Timaeus*, therefore, that we must now turn.

### III. The Forms as Paradigms

The *Timaeus* is the only late dialogue wherein Plato explicitly treats the Forms as paradigms. He uses the concept of paradigm more frequently here than in any other dialogue (cf. 28a—c, 29b, 31a, 37c, 38b—c, 38b—c, 39e, and 48e—49a). It is not hard to see why this should be so, in light of the remarks made about the new theory of causation. The *Timaeus* is unique among the late dialogues in taking causation as a central theme (though the subject is also discussed, less thoroughly in the *Philebus*) and, given the nature of the theory of causation Plato adopts here, the treatment of the Forms as paradigms is not merely natural, but required.

In Chapter 1, Sec. III, I argued that when Plato referred in the middle dialogues to the Forms as *paradeigmata*, 'paradigms', he meant that they were standards in the sense of general patterns, not in the sense of perfect exemplars of the characteristics of which they were Forms. This claim is closely related to two others I discussed in Chapter 1: the claim that when Plato says that phenomena resemble Forms he does not mean that they share a property, and the claim that the Forms are not in general self-predicative. Central to all of these claims is the question whether the Forms in general *have* the properties of which they are the Forms; if Forms are standards in that they are general patterns they will not, in general; if they are standards in that they are perfect exemplars, they will. The position of the middle dialogues was confused by the fact that some Forms (e.g. Bed) seemed clearly not to be self-predicative, whereas others (e.g. Beauty) seemed definitely to be, and still others (e.g. Equality) were problematic.

The issue of what sort of standards the paradigm Forms are is crucial to the assessment of the Third Man, for that argument treats the Forms as exemplars rather than patterns. The argument also requires that the relation of resemblance between Forms and phenomena be interpreted as the sharing of a property (see above, p. 73). The evidence of the *Timaeus*, I shall argue below, shows conclusively that both assumptions are false: the Forms are not exemplars, but patterns, and Plato does not treat resemblance always as the sharing of a property. If this can be shown, it will defuse completely the second version of the Third Man Argument.

We have already seen that the causal theory of the *Timaeus* requires the existence of a paradigm and a craftsman for every product brought into existence (28a–c). Since the cosmos is brought into existence by the Demiurge, he must have looked toward the eternal, uncreated paradigm that is always in the same state (28a, 29a). As the Demiurge wished to make the cosmos as good as possible, he gave it reason and soul as well as body and made it a living being (*zōion*, 30b8).

What was the eternal paradigm from which the cosmos, as a living being, was copied? As Timaeus puts the question, 'in the likeness of which of the living beings did the artificer devise it?' (30c3). His answer is that the cosmos is patterned after the Form, Living Being. What is the nature of this Form? Plato's account gives us several pieces of important information about it. First, he rejects the idea that the cosmos could be copied from any pattern which was 'incomplete' or a mere part of some larger whole (30c4–5). Rather, he urges,

> Let us posit that it is of all things most like that of which the other living beings individually and by species are parts. For this contains in itself all the intelligible living beings, embracing them, just as this cosmos unites us and all visible creatures. (30c5–d1)

The cosmos, in other words, is copied from a Form which is a whole and which embraces in itself both the various species of living and their individual members.

As a Form, and as the all-embracing whole which contains all other intelligible living beings, the Form of Living Being must be itself an intelligible object. Is it reasonable to think, in the light of this account, that Plato thought of the Form of Living Being as itself *a* living being, an instance of the genus of which it is the Form? Is the Form itself, like the cosmos patterned after it, a living thing with reason and soul? Such an assumption would be disastrous for Plato's purpose in this passage. As Gregory Vlastos has written:

> he would have absolutely nothing to gain by so thinking of the Form of Animal — it would advance none of the stated purposes for which he postulates the existence of Forms; on the contrary, it would defeat disastrously the chief among them, which is to provide the Creator with an eternal, immutable model; for Plato thinks of all living things as moving, and if the Form of Animal were (an) animal the result would be a contradiction — that which by hypothesis cannot move moves. And the contradiction would be such an obvious one that he could hardly miss it.[10]

Not only are all animals in Plato's mind movable; they are all generable and destructible (including the heavenly bodies, which are in Plato's eyes divine living being, and the other traditional gods; cf. 40b, 41a–b). The Forms, in contrast, are eternally existent and completely unchanging. Nor could any instance of the Form, Living Being, be properly said to embrace or encompass the various species of living being; individual animals are, rather, embraced by the species and genus of which they are members.

This difference between the relation of an individual animal to its species and the relation of the generic Form, Living Being, to the various species of animal is reflected in Plato's use of language. As Vlastos has noted:

> Plato speaks of the Ideal Living Creature which serves the Demiurge as his model as 'containing' the four Kinds — God, Bird, Fish, Land-Animal — which the Demiurge proceeds to create. . . . He says that the four kinds 'are in' the ideal Living Creature . . . Plato says that $F$ 'is in' $x$, not the converse, to express the notion that $x$ is characterized by $F$. So if he had wanted to assert so perverse a proposition as that the Form, Land-Animal, is characterizable as a living creature, he would have said that Living Creature is 'in' Land-Animal, not vice versa.[11]

In addition, we have seen that Plato in the *Timaeus* recognises that Forms are abstract, non-spatial entities. An instance of the Form, Living Being, an individual living being, however, would seem to demand some spatial location if it is to exist. For all these reasons, then, it seems absurd to regard the Form of Living Being as an exemplar of itself. If we take the Form to be the generic pattern of which all actual living beings are instances, however, we find that such an assumption fits perfectly with Plato's description of the Form. Such a pattern would be intelligible, all-embracing and eternally unchanging. Individual living beings may change but the abstract concept of what it is to be a living being does not (at least, not according to Plato).

We need not wonder that Plato refers to the Form itself as 'Living Being'; for like the term 'horse' this term may intelligibly be used to refer either to the natural kind or to some member of that kind. Nor need we be surprised that something which is in Plato's view a living being (the cosmos) is copied from something that is not. Many ordinary instances of craftsmanship are of this nature: houses are built from blueprints, portraits are produced from human models, etc. It is perhaps a cause of some concern that Plato does not distinguish this sort of craftsmanship from the sort where copies are made from originals of the same sort (e.g. paintings from paintings) and largely ignores the difference between the way in which genera embrace species (i.e. by class inclusion) and the way in which species embrace their members (by class membership): but it seems to have been in general characteristic of Greek philosophy to ignore this important distinction.[12]

It is from a general pattern, then, and not from an ideal instance of living being that the Demiurge produces the cosmos. Plato emphasises that the aim of the Demiurge is to make the cosmos resemble its original as much as possible (29a–c, 30c–31a, 37c–38c, 39e). If we understand this claim in its most ordinary sense, it would state that the Demiurge sought to reproduce in the cosmos the features of its original pattern. It seems impossible, however, to make sense of Plato's account if we interpret the resemblance between Form and cosmos in this way.

In the first place, we have the fact that the cosmos, as a living being, is patterned after the Form of Living Being; but we have seen that it is absurd to think of that Form as itself a living being. So in making the cosmos in the image of the Form the Demiurge did not reproduce in it properties which the Form itself had. The

Demiurge does try to capture in the cosmos the comprehensive nature of the Form and thus to reproduce in it a property of the original; but in fact he can only produce in the cosmos a comprehensiveness that is analogous to that of the Form. For the Form of Living Being is able to embrace both the species of living being and their members, as we have seen, whereas the cosmos can only embrace (spatially, rather than conceptually) the members of those species.

Perhaps the most striking instance of a relation that Plato calls a resemblance relation, but which does not involve sharing of properties, occurs at 37c–38c, where Plato discusses the nature of time. He begins by stating that the Demiurge sought to make the cosmos similar to its pattern with respect to the eternity of its existence. The Form of Living Being, however, is strictly eternal (in the sense of existing timelessly), and it is impossible for the cosmos, a generated thing, to be so. The Demiurge therefore made time, a moving image of eternity; and he made the cosmos coextensive with time in duration. Plato concludes:

> Time therefore came to be with the heavens, so that, having come to be together they might be destroyed together also, if ever destruction of these things should come about; and [it was made] after the pattern of the eternal nature, in order that it might be as similar to it as possible; for the pattern exists eternally, whereas it came to be, and is, and will be throughout all time. (38b6–c3)

Thus the cosmos is most similar to its pattern, despite the fact that the pattern exists outside of time altogether whereas the cosmos endures forever in time, and though time and the cosmos are both conceived as in motion, whereas the Form is conceived as absolutely motionless.

There is in fact just one case of resemblance between the cosmos and its paradigm Form that can without question be called the sharing of a property. At 31a–b Timaeus argues that the cosmos must be unique because its pattern is unique. In support of this claim he presents an argument that has been misinterpreted,[13] and which we might do well to consider briefly. On the surface, it may appear that Plato is claiming that the craftsman has to make the cosmos unique if it is to be in the image of its pattern; but this is absurd. It would imply that there could only be one image of a given original, and this would destroy the Theory of Forms; for one of the things which Forms are posited to be is ones over *many*, entities which unify an indefinite plurality of instances of a given kind. Moreover, in the specific case of the Form of Living Being, Plato certainly recognises that there can be many things which exemplify the Form.

Plato's actual argument depends on the comprehensive nature of the Form of Animal itself. The Form that embraces all of the species of living being, Timaeus argues, cannot be one of a pair; for if we hypothesise two ultimate Forms of Living Being, we should be compelled to posit still another embracing them, which would be the genuine Form. Likewise, the cosmos must be unique because it in turn comprehends all the sensible instances of the various species. The argument recalled the Third Bed Argument of *Rep.* X (see above, pp. 23–5), with the important differences that here the Form of Living Being is said to embrace a multiplicity of other Forms, not just a multiplicity of particulars, and that the unity of the Form and of the cosmos are not derived from the nature of the Form *qua* Form but from the particular property of embracing a number of other entities of the same type which both the Form and the cosmos are required to have.

In any case, we can see from these examples that what Plato is willing to call instances of resemblance are in fact quite different from each other. He does use the term for the case where Form and copy share the property of uniqueness; but he also uses it when the two have merely analogous properties (as in the treatment of time) and when the copy has a property (i.e. that of being a living being) of which the Form is the pattern. It seems clear from this that it is false to assume that, when Plato says that Form and phenomenon resemble each other, he must mean that there is some property which both share.

We have seen, then, that the sense of resemblance needed to make the second version of the Third Man Argument work is too narrow to capture Plato's meaning (though this still leaves open the possibility that there may be cases of this sort of resemblance between Form and participant, e.g. in the case of Beauty). We have also seen that when Plato calls Forms 'paradigms' he does not in general mean that they are exemplars. Without these assumptions, the second version of the Third Man cannot be taken as an effective refutation of the Theory of Forms.

## IV. The Receptacle and Self-Predication

If the argument of the last section is correct, we cannot legitimately infer from the facts that Plato calls the Forms 'paradigms' and says they resemble phenomena that the Forms are self-predicative. This breaks the back of the second version of the Third Man Argument, which makes just such an inference. Still, it might be argued that we have not shown that the Forms are *not* in general self-predicating, that the case constructed against self-predication was based in large part on the absurdity that resulted when we assumed that the Form of Living Being was a living being. Fortunately, however, there is more evidence in the *Timaeus* against the self-predication assumption; evidence that shows conclusively, I shall argue, that Plato is not committed to that assumption. This evidence occurs in a passage of the dialogue in which Plato introduces another new ontological principle, the Receptacle. Whereas the Demiurge had been referred to in the *Republic*, the Receptacle is without precedent in the dialogues and its introduction constitutes a major new departure for Plato's metaphysics.

The passage I shall discuss in detail (48e−52d) contains one of the fullest accounts to be found in the dialogues of Plato's ontology. The addition of the Receptacle, as we shall see, enables him to explain more clearly than before the relation between Forms and phenomena. This is not to deny that problems remain when the account is finished: Timaeus says that the nature of the Receptacle itself is 'difficult and obscure' (49a3) and that phenomena, as copies of Forms, are 'modelled from them in some marvellous and hard-to express way' (50c5−6). None the less, the passage marks an important advance in Plato's metaphysical development.

Plato does not introduce the Receptacle for the purpose of clarifying the relation between Forms and phenomena. His purpose, rather, is to explain the nature of Necessity, the force that, together with Reason, creates the cosmos (47e−48a). The discussion of Necessity or the Errant Cause, the random and irrational power that limits the creative efforts of the Demiurge, requires a discussion of the traditional four elements of Greek cosmology: earth, air, fire and water. We must, Timaeus says (48b), determine their condition before the generation of the cosmic order and explain their generation. It turns out that they are not, as others had assumed (e.g. Empedocles) the first principles or 'letters' from which the book of nature is written; they are in fact not even as fundamental as syllables (48b–c). By using the analogy of letters and syllables, Plato implies that the so-called elements are in fact complexes of more elementary constituents. These turn out to be, ultimately, the Receptacle, some primordial traces of the natures of these four 'elements', and some primary geometrical shapes (52d–57d).

In the previous discussion (and indeed in all previous discussions of Platonic metaphysics), only two categories of being had been required: the intelligible pattern (i.e. the Form) and its phenomenal copy (48e–49a). Now, however, Timaeus adds a third category: 'the Receptacle and nurse, as it were, of all Becoming' (49a5–6). In order to explain why this new element of Platonic ontology is necessary, Timaeus brings up the problem of the transmutation of the 'elements'. Which of the four 'elements' has the right to be called 'water' rather than 'fire' or something else? All of the four appear to transmute into one another (49b–c),[14] so that the lump of stuff we call at one moment 'earth' we find later turning into something we call 'water', and so forth. The apparent transmutation of the elements — like Plato's claim that they are not 'letters' but 'syllables' or worse in the grammar of creation — again reveals the need to find an unchanging, elementary underpinning to serve as the substantial base from which these complex, constantly changing 'elements' can be constructed. This substantial base is the Receptacle.

Speaking of the 'elements', Timaeus asks:

Since none of these ever appear to be the same, who would not be ashamed of himself for confidently affirming of any of them that it is 'this', whatever it may be, and not something else? It is not possible, but by far the safest course is for us to propose to speak thus concerning these: whenever we see something coming to be at one time or another,[15] such as fire, to address fire on each occasion[16] not as 'this', but as 'the such';[17] nor to address water as 'this', but always as 'the such'; nor to address anything as if it had any stability, of all the things we indicate by using the words 'that' and 'this', believing that we are pointing out something; for they[18] flee, not awaiting the utterance of 'that' or 'this' or 'to this',[19] or any utterance which indicates that they are stable. But we should not call any of these things by these names;[20] rather, concerning each and all we should call them thus:[21] 'the such, always the same as it is borne about'; and in particular we should call fire 'the such throughout all time',[22] and [we should speak thus concerning] all that has generation. (49c7−e7).

Since the 'elements' lack suitability and permanence, they ought not to be called by terms that carry the implication of stability; and, clearly, Plato believes that 'this' and 'that' are such terms. Thus, he coins another term for all entities of this sort: *to toiouton*, 'the such'. The passage does not explain the meaning of the new term but we may assume that it does not have the implications of permanence that 'this' and 'that' possess.

The scope of *to toiouton* is quite broad. It is not restricted to the four 'elements', but applies to 'all that has generation'. In other words, its scope is the entire category of Becoming. It applies both to individual instances of, e.g., fire (we are to address these as 'the such' on each occasion in which we see them coming to be) and to the totality of such instances or the phenomenal character itself (the such throughout all time). This character is not to be confused with the Form; it is an entity in the category of Becoming (Forms are not brought into the discussion until 51b).[23]

Although Plato makes the distinction between phenomenal character and an instance of it, he does not exploit the distinction in any way; in fact, for the most part, he ignores it. Both the character and its instances are in the category of Becoming. Both are unstable: the instances, because they come into being and cease to be, and the characters, because they are always 'borne about' (*peripheromenon*, 49e5; cf. *pephorēmenon*, 52a6), are always 'entering and exiting' the Receptacle (50c4−5). Such instability is of course an instability of location, not of nature; Plato is not suggesting that the character itself changes its nature.[24]

This passage tells us, then, that everything that is generated, all of the phenomenal world, is to be called not 'this' but 'the such'. Timaeus lists Becoming as one of the three categories in his ontology in a brief summary at 50c−d and describes its nature in detail in the final summary of that ontology at 51e−52d. There he claims that Becoming is homonymous with and like the Form, 'sensible, generated, always borne about, and coming to be in some place and perishing again back out of it' (52a5−7), and the object of opinion. All of these claims except the restriction of Becoming to existence in space were used in the middle dialogues to describe this category of existence; some of the implications of the insistence that phenomena are spatial entities have been discussed above (pp. 91–2). There is no reason to doubt that it is the familiar category of Becoming, then, that is to be characterised as 'the such' rather than as 'this'.

The Receptacle is defined in contrast to Becoming; it has precisely the properties that entities in the category of Becoming lack. Immediately following the passage quoted above, in which Plato claims that we should not call phenomena 'this' or 'that', Timaeus states:

> but that in which each of these things appears, coming be, and from which again it perishes — that alone we should address using the word 'this' and 'that'; but that which is of any nature whatsoever — hot or white or any of the opposites whatsoever, and anything which is derived from them — we ought never to call that by any of these terms. (49e7–50a4)

'This' and 'that' can be applied to the Receptacle because of its complete freedom from essential change, its complete stability. Plato proceeds to make this clear.

Timaeus uses an analogy to expound the contrast between the Receptacle and Becoming. Consider a man moulding a lump of gold continually into different shapes:

> if someone should point to one of them and ask, 'What is it?', by far the safest thing with respect to the truth would be to say that it is gold; concerning the triangle and whatever other shapes came to be, these should not be spoken of as *beings* for they change even as they are spoken of. But if these should be willing to accept from anyone even the term 'the such' with certainty, he should be content. (50a7–b5)

The gold in the example plays the role played by the Receptacle in Plato's ontology; the shapes moulded in it are analogous to Becoming. Plato denies that the shapes are to be referred to as 'beings' (*onta*, 50b3), since they are in constant change. Change, of course, is the mark of Becoming, that by which it is contrasted with Being, in the ontology of the middle dialogues. Plato, in denying that the shapes moulded in the gold are properly called 'beings', implies that the gold (and thus the Receptacle) are properly so called. Both may be called 'beings' because they are, unlike the phenomena and shapes that come to be in them, unchanging.

The gold analogy is misleading in at least one respect, for it implies that the Receptacle is actually modified by the person who moulds it, that it actually becomes in turn triangular, square, round, etc. To assume this would be to assign to the Receptacle the role played by matter in Aristotle's ontology. This is not correct, however.[25] Subsequent passages make it clear that Plato regards the Receptacle as utterly impervious to any true change and as the substratum of change in the sense of a location for it rather than in the sense of a kind of stuff that undergoes it.[26] As Timaeus remarks:

> It must always be called 'the same'; from its own nature it never departs at all — for it always receives all things, and never at any time in any way ever takes on any form similar to the things that enter it; for it is by nature a place for every impression, changed and formed by the things that enter it, and it appears because of them different at different times. (50b6–c4)

Plato thinks of the Receptacle as self-identical and unchanging in that it never loses its essential characteristic of receptiveness. It changes only to the extent that it appears to take on the characteristics of the phenomena that it receives. Plato emphasises the apparent nature of this change by comparing the Receptacle to an odourless perfume base and a smooth surface, which are themselves free from the characteristics imposed on them (50e–51a).

It is this stable, impassive, receptive, characterless Receptacle that supplants in Plato's cosmology the 'elements' of the Presocratics:

> Therefore the mother and Receptacle of visible Becoming and of sensible Becoming in general we ought to call neither earth nor air nor water nor fire, nor anything which comes to be from these nor from which these come to be; but we shall not lie is we call it a certain invisible kind, and amorphous, all-receiving, partaking of the intelligible in some very puzzling and hard-to-grasp way. Insofar as it is possible from what has been said before to arrive at its nature, one would speak of it most correctly as follows: that part of it which is inflamed appears on each occasion as fire; that part which is moistened, as water; and (part appears as) earth and air to the extent that it receives copies of these. (51a4–b6)

The Receptacle plays the role of a substratum, a subject, a substance, of which entities in the category of Becoming are predicated or to which they are attributed. It can be called 'this', unlike the entities predicated of it, because it always remains essentially the same. Its nature is receptiveness; and, though there is a sense in which it does receive properties, a sense covered by Plato's remark that it 'appears' to become them, the properties it receives are like Aristotelian accidents: they do not change the essential nature of that in which they appear.

It is because the Receptacle is all-receptive that it has no definite characteristics of its own. Its nature, one is tempted to say, is that it has no nature. Its complete indefiniteness makes it difficult to comprehend, and Plato remarks that it is 'grasped without sense experience by a certain bastard reasoning, scarcely an object of belief' (52b2). Unlike the copies of Forms that appear in it it cannot be sensed, as it has no definite sensory properties. Unlike the Forms themselves, which are apprehended by a legitimate kind of reasoning, it cannot be defined in terms of any definite characteristics. It is only when we perform the thought experiment of abstracting from every definite qualification that we can understand the nature of the Receptacle.

It is only after the Receptacle has been distinguished from, and described as the substantial underpinning of, Becoming that Plato mentions the Forms, the members of his third ontological category, Being. As in the *Parmenides* and *Philebus*, he asks whether there are any such things at all:

> Is there any such thing as Fire just in itself, or any of the things of which we are always speaking thus: that each of them *is* just in itself? Or do those things at which we look, and all other things which we perceive by the body, alone have this sort of reality, but there is nothing else besides these in any way at any time? Is it in vain on each occasion that we say there is a certain intelligible Form of each thing, and is this nothing but a word? (51b7–c5)

The very fact that Plato raises this question is a sign that the *Timaeus* is a post-*Parmenides* dialogue. In the early and middle dialogues, he does not regard the existence of the Forms as subject to serious philosophical doubt; the *Parmenides* gives us the first indication of this. If the *Timaeus* shows a heightened awareness of this problem, however, it does not reflect a change of Plato's view

on the answer to it. He affirms the existence of the Forms, and on
the basis of a familiar distinction: that between knowledge and
belief. If these two mental states differ, they must have different
objects; and the objects of knowledge are the Forms (51d–e; cf.
*Rep.* V, 477b–478b). The answer is perfunctory and disappointing
in its brevity. Timaeus excuses it on the grounds that a long digression on the existence of Forms would be out of place (51c–d). The
very brevity of the answer, however, is a striking indication of how
little Plato was troubled by the challenge of the *Parmenides*, how
little he thought the critique of his metaphysics in that dialogue
affected the central tenets of that metaphysics.

As we have already seen (above, pp. 90–2), Plato in his final
summary of his ontology describes the Forms and Becoming in
terms that are largely familiar from the middle dialogues, but he
also adds the claim that Forms do not exist, as phenomena do, in
another thing (namely, the Receptacle).[27] The Forms, like the
Receptacle and unlike phenomena, exist in and of themselves; they
depend on nothing else to sustain them. They are, as Aristotle is
fond of saying of them, substances.

It is this fact, this difference between the mode of existence of the
Forms and the mode of existence of phenomena, that indicates the
way in which Plato can escape from the clutches of the Third Man.
For what Plato has done is to describe an ontology in which there
are two kinds of *substances* or independently existing entities, the
Forms and the Receptacle, and one kind of dependently existing
entity, or non-substance, Becoming. The Forms are substances in
that they exist independently as the intelligible essence of things;
the Receptacle is a substance in that it exists independently as the
ultimate substratum or subject of predication. The phenomenal
images reflected in the Receptacle, in contrast, are not substances.
They cannot exist independently of the Receptacle in which they are
imaged or the Forms of which they are images. As Plato puts it:

> for an image, on the once hand, since not even that itself in
> dependence on which[28] it has come to be belongs to it, but it is
> always borne along as the appearance of another, for these
> reasons it is fitting that it should come to be in something else,
> clinging to being in some way, or it would be nothing at all.
> (52c2–5)

In other words, just as the image depends for its essential nature on a principle external to it, namely the Form of which it is an image, so it depends for its existence on another external principle, namely the Receptacle. Although Plato does not say in this passage that phenomenal images of the Forms are accidental properties of the Receptacle, he describes them in the same way that Aristotle describes accidental properties. They depend for their existence on the substance in which they are reflected; they do not alter the essential nature of that substance; they are to be called not 'this' but 'the such'.[29] Given these facts, it seems fair to characterise the phenomenal images which make up the category of Becoming as accidental properties of the Receptacle.

We saw in Chapter 2 that the Third Man Argument required the assumption that the Forms were self-predicative, that they had the properties of which they were the Forms (cf. Sec. IV). We saw in Chapter 1 that it was unlikely that Plato accepted this assumption as a general principle, as applying to all Forms, though he may have accepted it for some (cf. Sec. IV). We distinguished there two claims: (a) that the term, '*F*', must be applicable to the Form of *F*; and (b) that the basis of the application of the term must be the possession by the Form of the property, relation, or kind named by the term (cf. p. 25). I argued that Plato is committed to (a) as a general principle but not (b).

The ontological scheme of the *Timaeus* supports this conclusion. As in earlier dialogues, Plato affirms that Forms bear the names of the properties of which they are Forms. He refers to the Form of Living Being as 'Living Being' (*zōion*), and he points out at 52a5 that phenomenal properties of the Receptacle have the same name as the Forms (the two are 'homonymous', *homōnymon*). Thus, the general term, '*F*', is applicable to the Form of *F* as well as its phenomenal instances. All this licences us to say, however, is that the general term, '*F*', is the name of the Form of *F*, that it refers to the Form; we cannot infer that the term and its correlative property are predicated of the Form. To the extent that Plato's doctrine of the homonymy of Forms and their instances suggests or constitutes a semantic theory, it is a theory of reference, of naming, and not a theory of predication. '*F*' serves as the name of two distant things, the Form of *F* and the phenomenal character of *F* which is present in the Receptacle. Only in the second case can it be plausibly said that '*F*' names a property; in the first case it names a substance.

The fact that '*F*' can function as the name of a property provides Plato with the basis of a doctrine of predication, though he does not explicitly extend his doctrine of homonymy this far. Since the phenomenal images of the Forms may be taken to be accidental properties of the Receptacle, and since the Receptacle, being an independently existing, unchanging, 'this', may be characterised as a substance, it seems reasonable to say that the attribution of a phenomenal property to the Receptacle is a case of the predication of that property and its name to a substance. Thus, 'This is fire', said of a region of space, would be a legitimate case of predication.

'This is Fire', said the Form of Fire, however, would not be a genuine predication, since 'Fire' functions in the case of the Form of Fire not as a name of a property attributed to a substance, but as the name of the substance itself. To call the Form of Fire 'Fire' or the Form of Living Being 'Living Being' is not to predicate something of the Form, but to refer to, designate, denote the Form itself. The application of the general term, '$F$' to the Form of $F$ thus appears to be a case of reference, not a case of predication.

In saying this, I must call attention to the difference between two sorts of reference. The application of 'this' to the Receptacle is not based on the possession by the Receptacle of any concrete characteristics. The only requirement is that the Receptacle be impervious to change, i.e. a substance. This is a case of what I shall call 'pure' reference. In pure reference, something is indicated, but given no definite characterisation. Most cases of reference are not like this. When I say 'The desk is brown' I use the phrase 'the desk' to refer to an object, to which I then attribute the colour brown. Everyone would accept the claim that my attribution of the colour brown to the desk is an instance of predication, for predication is just the attribution of a characteristic to some subject. When I refer to this object as 'the desk', however, I also describe it in a certain way. My reference to it states, implies or presupposes that the object I so designate has the characteristics essential to being a desk. Unlike 'this', 'the desk' cannot be used to refer to things of any description; if the object I refer to as 'the desk' turns out to be a table, my attempt to refer to it goes wrong in some way. I shall call reference of this sort 'descriptive reference'. It is clear that in descriptive reference there is a predicative component; just as in the case of my attribution of the colour brown, so also in my reference to the object as a desk, I assert or at least imply that the object in question has certain characteristics. Plato seems to have recognised the predicative aspect of descriptive reference when he described our

reference to individual instances of fire as attribution of the characteristic, fire, to a portion of the Receptacle — when he treated
descriptive reference in such cases, that is, as predication.

In descriptive, as opposed to pure, reference, we attribute
characteristics to objects in referring to them. Ordinarily, when we
use some general term that names a kind of being, such as 'desk' or
'man', we use this term to refer to an individual that falls under
that kind. In this case (e.g. when we say, 'the man is pale', we
attribute the characteristics essential to an instance of that kind to
the individual we refer to. If it is true that man is a rational animal,
when we use 'the man' to refer to an individual human we attribute
to that individual the characteristic of being a rational animal. This
sort of descriptive reference is the kind that Plato has assimilated to
predication.

We may also use a kind term to refer to the kind itself, rather
than to instances of the kind. 'Man' may name the species *homo
sapiens*, as well as members of that species. Plato recognises this
fact when he notes that Forms and their phenomenal instances are
homonymous. When we refer to the species as 'Man', we mean to
distinguish that species from all other species and genera of things.
At least implicitly, again, we attribute some descriptive content to
the referent of the term. In this case, as in the case of the use of the
term to refer to an individual member of the species, we are not free
to use 'Man', as we are free to use 'this', to refer to things of any
description. One of the many things we assert or imply when we
refer to the species as 'Man' is that it is this species, and no other,
of which all individual humans and only they are members.

Thus, 'man' is a term of descriptive reference rather than pure
reference, whether we use it to refer to Socrates or to *homo sapiens*.
Yet although the term has descriptive implications in both cases,
the implications are not the same. When we use the term to refer to
Socrates, we imply that Socrates has the characteristics a human
being must have. When we use the term to refer to the species, we
imply that it has such characteristics as are necessary to enable it to
include in its extension all the instances of 'man'. We do not
attribute to the species the property of being bipedal or rational,
but the property of embracing all rational or bipedal creatures.

Those who believe that Plato was committed to the self-predication assumption hold that Plato did not see the difference between
the use of, e.g., 'man' to Socrates and its use to refer to the species
*homo sapiens*. It is easy to see why one might think this. Plato does

assume that when we refer to the species we do succeed in picking out something real and something distinct from everything else in the universe. He believes further that the Forms can be described, that they have definite characteristics (this is what makes them intelligible); and, presumably, he must believe that it is in virtue of these characteristics that we are able to refer to them by their appropriate names. In some cases they appear to have those very characteristics that their instances have and, until his introduction of the Receptacle, Plato has had no way to make clear the distinction between the use of a general term to attribute a characteristic to an object and the use of the same term to refer to a kind, property or relation. In the absence of such a device, it is only natural that some scholars have argued that Plato was not attuned to the distinction and that he regarded all uses of general terms as predicative.

The passage we have just examined makes that assumption untenable. For Plato distinguishes clearly between the way the general term, '$F$', applies to the Form of $F$ and the way it applies to various phenomenal instances of $F$. The application of the term to the Form is a case of descriptive reference of the second kind, the kind of reference we make when we use 'Man' as the name of the species *homo sapiens*. The application of the term to phenomenal instances or to the phenomenal character itself is a case of what I have called descriptive reference of the ordinary, first kind, the kind of reference we make when we use 'man' to refer to Socrates. It is an interesting peculiarity of Plato's treatment of this sort of reference that he assimilates it to predication. He does not distinguish between substance terms, such as 'man' or 'fire', and other terms, such as 'large' and 'pale'. Nor does he distinguish between the appearance of substance terms such as 'man' in the referential or subject position and their appearance in the predicative position in a sentence: he draws no distinction between the use of 'man' in 'The man is large' and its use in 'Socrates is a man'. This assimilation of all sorts of terms, in so far as they apply within the phenomenal world, to predicates, is closely related to his assimilation of all sorts of reference in the phenomenal world to the pure reference involved in the assertion of 'this' of the Receptacle. Though we may find Plato's failure to make a number of these distinctions peculiar, it must be admitted that his assimilation of descriptive reference of the first kind to predication only makes clearer his recognition of the difference between the referential

application of '*F*' to the Form of *F* and its predicative application
to the many *F* things.

It is important to note that Plato does not, in this passage,
present an analysis of predication. He does not say that to possess a
property is to image a Form; he does not imply that the only proper
subject of predication is the Receptacle; he does not say that
properties, by their very nature, are confined to the realm of
Becoming. To understand precisely what Plato is saying, we must
remember that the *Timaeus* is a work of cosmology and that part of
its object is to explain how the phenomenal world is composed. His
answer is that it is composed of the Receptacle, a substance, and all
the phenomenal properties that are reflected in it. These
phenomenal properties make up the realm of Becoming and are
described as images of Forms. The Forms of which they are images
are described in turn as independently existing, intelligible
substances to which the appropriate general terms apply primarily
and directly. For those terms that name phenomenal properties
(e.g. terms such as 'green', 'three feet long', and 'animal', terms
which have only physical instantiations or embodiments) — and it
must be remembered that these are the only terms Plato is
specifically concerned with in this part of his cosmological project
— it turns out that the introduction of the Receptacle makes self-
predication not only mandatory but forbidden. To predicate the
properties essential to being a living being of the Form of Living
Being would not be merely absurdly inept and counter-productive,
as indicated in the last section of this chapter; it would be in some
metaphysical sense ill-formed, a violation of the categorial distinctions Plato has drawn.

Let us see why this is so. Consider the putative sentence, 'the
Form of Living Being is a living being'. According to the account
just given, the subject term, 'the Form of Living Being', refers to
an intelligible object, the genus Living Being. The predicate, 'is a
living being', at least if this sentence is read as a case of self-
predication, attributes to the subject a property or set of properties.
Yet these properties are phenomenal properties; they are of such a
nature that they must have a physical embodiment. To predicate
them of an intelligible object is to attempt to attribute an entity in
the category of Becoming to an entity in the category of Being; and
this is not merely absurd, it is specifically ruled out by Plato's claim
that entities in the category of Being neither receive into themselves
things from elsewhere nor themselves go out into another thing

(52a2–3; cf. pp. 90–1 above). The only appropriate subject of which phenomenal properties can be predicated is the Receptacle; the attempt to predicate a phenomenal property of the Form of that property is a category mistake. It violates the principle of the separation of the orders of Being and Becoming, on which Plato has always insisted. Further, according to the account just offered, to be a phenomenal property of the Receptacle is to be an image of a Form. To attribute such a property to the Form itself would be to say that the Form is an image of itself. Yet imaging is by definition a relation between two different objects; nothing could be an image of itself. (Even if a Form could have a property in this way, by being an image of itself, this would not lead to the Third Man; for the Third Man is generated by assuming the truth of the metaphysical claim just mentioned, that no object can be an image of itself, and inferring from self-predication and the analysis of predication in terms of imaging that the Form must be in turn the image of something else.)

If the account of the Receptacle I have given is substantially correct, it shows conclusively that Plato does not accept self-predication as a general principle and that he does not in general view Forms as perfect instances of themselves. I have argued that Plato did not so think of Forms even in the middle dialogues, so the *Timaeus* does not, on my interpretation, represent a change in view on Plato's part concerning these matters. In this respect, the introduction of the Receptacle is a less radical modification of Plato's metaphysics than is the new theory of causality and the introduction of the Demiurge into that metaphysics. The Receptacle is an addition to the ontology of Platonism and in this respect it is a novel contribution; but its value, for our purposes, is that it enables Plato to explain his earlier insights about the relation between Forms and phenomena more clearly than he could before. Plato's earlier account of the Forms, properly interpreted, would have led to the conclusion that the Forms were not perfect exemplars of themselves but general patterns, not individual *F* things but *ho esti F*, 'what *F* is', the essences (*ousiai*) of things rather than instantiations of essences. Yet that earlier account was susceptible to misinterpretation, as the *Parmenides* showed; and only when that misinterpretation had been exposed could Plato's original insights about the Forms be vindicated.

I see the introduction of the Receptacle into the ontology of the *Timaeus* as providing proof that Plato's Theory of Forms is not

in fact susceptible to the Third Man. We cannot, that is, understand the function of the Receptacle as Plato describes it and its
relation to the categories of Being and Becoming, and still hold the
view that Plato was committed to self-predication. I have not
claimed in the case of the Receptacle as I did in the case of the new
theory of causality that Plato introduced this new element in his
ontology for the express purpose of rebutting the Third Man. He
does not. It is indeed possible that Plato did not see the relevance of
this passage to the Third Man. As I noted in Chapter 2, the key
premiss of self-predication is not explicit in the Third Man
Argument; it is possible that Plato did not recognise that the
argument depended on this.

Plato introduces the Receptacle in the course of explaining the
nature of Necessity, which is in turn part of his larger cosmological
project. His aim is to show that the phenomenal world is composed
of two sorts of things, not one, and that one of these is the
substratum of the other. Not only does he not introduce his new
category for the purpose of refuting the Third Man; when the
Receptacle has been introduced and its function explained he does
not go on to point out the relevance of this discussion to the
argument. For all we know for certain, Plato may not have seen the
relevance of this discussion to the argument at all.

None the less, the account of the Receptacle seems to me to give
conclusive proof to the claim that the Theory of Forms is in fact
immune to the Third Man. If this is so, and if this passage enables
Plato to explain clearly a coherent conception of the relation
between Forms and their phenomenal instances in a way that was
not previous possible, we may safely say that Plato's continued
adherence to the Theory of Forms after the *Parmenides* was a
rational course of action. Plato need not have been able to pinpoint
the exact problem with the Third Man to be aware that the
premisses and concealed presuppositions of that argument
seriously misrepresented the Theory of Forms; and he need only
have been aware of the latter point if he was to be justified in
rejecting the argument.

There are two further points which need to be emphasised concerning Plato's account of the nature of the Receptacle and the
relation between Forms and phenomena. As I have noted above,
this account is not an analysis of participation. Although Plato
describes the relation between Form and phenomenal namesake as
one of imaging or resemblance, he does not state that this relation

is constitutive of participation, as had Socrates in the *Parmenides*, in the second version of the Third Man (132d). As the *Sophist* introduces instances of the relation of participation that hold between Form and Form rather than between Form and phenomenon, this is perhaps just as well. It seems best to assume that Plato took the original-image relation to be descriptive of the relation that held between entities in the different orders of reality or between different stages of the divided line (cf. *Rep.* VI, 510a–511a) rather than of participation *per se*.

The fact is that Plato does not attempt to define participation in the dialogues written after the *Parmenides*. Aristotle chides him for this, saying that he was content with 'empty words and poetic metaphors' (*Meta.* A, 991a21–22). It could be argued that this was a strategy Plato adopted as a result of the failure of every attempt to define the concept in the *Parmenides*. As I have argued that the actual arguments of the *Parmenides* do not seriously damage the Theory of Forms as Plato actually held it, I cannot believe that it was on account of them that he refused to define participation. I think it is rather that he realised that participation was a fundamental, primitive concept in his metaphysical scheme, and that it would be a mistake to attempt to analyse this concept into something more basic. Participation, like exemplification, instantiation, predication or class membership in other systems of metaphysics, cannot be analysed or defined because it is the basic concept used to define everything else. The most that can be done is to give some sense to the word by the use of metaphors or analogies that may be familiar. Thus Plato uses the analogy of imitation to give his reader an intuitive idea of the nature of participation, and, as we saw earlier, he attempts to justify his belief that phenomena do participate in Forms by introducing the concept of a craftsman god who creates the imitations of the Forms we find in the phenomenal world. Plato himself seems to have been aware that this falls short of a full explanation; as I noted above, he notes that phenomena are copied from Forms 'in some marvellous and hard-to-express way' (50c5–6; cf. p. 108 above).

The second point, again one which I have touched upon, is that Plato's analysis only concerns phenomenal properties, things that belong necessarily to the realm of Becoming. By showing that Forms cannot partake of these properties, Plato shows that he is not committed to self-predication as a general principle. Not every property is such that only phenomena can have it, however; if it were, there could be nothing in common between the realms of Being and Becoming, and the problem of the two worlds would again arise. In fact, the most likely cases of self-predication from the middle dialogues (e.g. the case of Beauty) concerned those properties which do not seem to require a phenomenal instantiation. Only a phenomenal object could be green, but an abstract concept could be beautiful, one, real, self-identical, etc. It is for these properties that the problem of self-predication remains a problem; but this problem is addressed not in the *Timaeus* but in the *Sophist*, to which I shall turn in the next chapter.

In this chapter I have argued that the metaphysics of the *Timaeus* responds with a high degree of success to the challenges raised in the *Parmenides*. The coherence of the Theory of Forms is vindicated against the arguments of that dialogue. This is not to say that the Theory is correct or that no other problems remain for Plato to deal with. Many remain; only a few does he deal with successfully. None the less, if my account is correct, the introduction of the Demiurge and the new account of causation, the way in which Plato describes the paradigmatic function of the Forms and the relation of resemblance between them and phenomena, and his account of the nature of Forms, phenomena and the Receptacle all combine to render the criticisms of the *Parmenides* impotent against the fundamental principles of Platonic metaphysics.

## Notes

1. As is well known, Taylor defends the thesis that the *Timaeus* is Plato's representation of an amalgam of fifth-century Pythagoreanism and Emedoclean biology. Cf. Cornford (1937), pp. vi–ix, for a critique of this view, which has won little support.

2. It is easy to see why Socrates, who is present during Timaeus' discourse, cannot serve as Plato's spokesman here. As the historical Socrates had no interest in natural science (cf. *Apol.* 19c–d, and Aristotle, *Metaph.* A, 987b1–2), he could hardly be put forth as the expositor of an elaborate cosmology.

3. It cannot be the conversation of the *Republic* itself that is referred to; the chronology, content, and cast of characters are all different. (Cf. Cornford, 1937, pp. 4–5). Still, the association of the *Timaeus* with the political doctrines of the *Republic* is unavoidable. Owen (1953), pp. 329–36, makes much of this connection; but his interpretation of the political philosophy of the dialogues he discusses seems to me to be quite wrong (cf. Prior 1975), pp. 103–15, for a detailed discussion of this claim); and, if the *Timaeus* is linked with the *Republic* on this point, it is equally certainly linked with the late dialogues on several points, as the argument of the chapter will show.

4. E.g. Cornford (1937), pp. 28–32. Sayre, pp. 240–1 and ff., takes the

extreme view that the entire dialogue is fictional; he states, quite surprisingly, that 'most commentators should be prepared to accept' this judgement (240). Sayre ignores both Gregory Vlastos' discussion of the epistemological status of the cosmology of the *Timaeus* (1939; cf. esp. pp. 380–3), in which the scientific status of the cosmology is defended, and Ross's remark that Plato reserves the language of probability and a 'likely story' for the cosmology of the dialogue alone, not for its metaphysics (p. 127). I believe that Vlastos and Ross are correct and that the metaphysics of the *Timaeus, pace* Sayre, can be treated in the same manner and given the same weight as that of the *Phaedo, Sophist, Parmenides* and *Philebus*.

5. Cherniss (1944), Cornford (1937) and Taylor among modern students of Plato adhere to this view; so did most ancient interpreters, incuding Proclus and Xenocrates. For references, cf. Cornford (1937), pp. 25–6; and Vlastos (1939), pp. 383–5 and (1964), pp. 401–2.

6. Aristotle and Plutarch, among the ancients, held that Plato in the *Timaeus* presented a literal doctrine of creation. This view has been ably defended in recent years by Vlastos (1939 and 1964); Hackforth (1959) and Robinson, pp. 64–5, agree with his conclusions.

7. Solmsen (1942), p. 181, makes this point.

8. I do not think that the parallel can be used to establish the temporal priority of one of these dialogues to the other (cf. Ch. 4, Sec. IV below). On this point I agree with Owen (1953), pp. 327–8; unlike Owen, however, I find the parallel striking and significant and believe that it is indicative of rough contemporaneity of composition of the two dialogues.

9. The issue is played out on the same lines as the dispute mentioned in n. 5 and n. 6 above; cf. eg. Cornford (1937), p. 37, for a statement of this view.

10. Vlastos (1971b), p. 262.

11. Vlastos (1970), pp. 303–4.

12. The distinction does not seem to have been discovered until Frege. As Vlastos (1970) shows, Plato fails to recognise the difference between class inclusion and class membership (or the analogous relations among Forms) even in the *Sophist*. For a classic example of Aristotle's failure to make the distinction, cf. *Cat.* 5, 2a36–2b1.

13. E.g. by Keyt. Parry's reply also seems to misinterpret, though in a different way from Keyt, the nature of the Form of Living Being.

14. As Plato explains at 54b–c, only three of the four 'elements' really transmute into each other; 'appearance' is in this respect misleading.

15. As Lee (1967), p. 14, notes, the translation proposed by Cherniss (1954), p. 114 ('at different times in different places'), is unwarranted. In my translation of this difficult passage I have in general preferred the traditional reading of Cornford (1937) and others to the radically different version proposed by Cherniss (1954) and followed, with reservations, by others, including Lee (1967), Mills (1968), p. 153 and Fujisawa, p. 53, n. 61.

My rejection of Cherniss' reading is based on philosophical rather than textual grounds. It is well known that Cherniss' reading commits Plato to a fourfold division of entities (Form, Receptacle, immanent character or property and instance of property), whereas Plato insists (51e–52b) on a threefold division (cf. Mills, 1968, pp. 153–154, 170). Moreover, Cherniss claims it as a consequence of his interpretation that 'phenomena cannot be distinctively denominated, because no part of the phenomenal flux is distinguishable from any other' (1954, p. 128). The phenomenal characters can be named but not their instances.

There are three things to be said against this position. First, as we shall see below, Plato ignores the distinction between property and instance on which Cherniss trades. Secondly, Plato shows at 51b that he has no difficulty naming instances of properties as well as the properties themselves. Thirdly and finally, if the phenomenal flux were, as Cherniss suggests, the night in which all cats are grey, there would be no such thing as right opinion, at least as concerns particulars; and the philosopher-king would have no right to rule, since his claim to power is based on his ability to make superior judgements within the confines of the cave, as a result of his acquaintance with the Forms (cf. *Rep.* VII, 520b–d).

16. *Hekastote* (49d5–6) parallels *aei* (49d4, 7) and contrasts with *mēde . . . pote* (49d7). Cherniss (1954), p. 115, finds this redundant, but I doubt that Plato would have so regarded it, given his delight in pleonasm and parallel construction.

17. Alex Mourelatos has pointed out to me that this use of *to toiouton* is demonstrative. This is quite natural in Greek but there is no parallel use of 'such' in English. Hence the awkwardness of the translation.

18. Cherniss (1954), p. 117, thinks that the subject of *pheugei* (49e2) is *touto*. Lee (1967), p. 6, thinks that the subject is 'simply one of those individual things which we so often point at and talk about'. Without wishing to limit the things to individuals, as does Lee, I agree with his interpretation. There is no grammatical problem with taking *hosa* (49d7) as the antecedent of *pheugei*, as neuter plural subjects taking singular verbs.

19. Many commentators have noted the difficulty of giving a sense to the phase, *kai tēn tōide* (49e3), and some have simply not translated it. I take it that Plato's point is that any inflection of *tode*, and not just the nominative singular, expresses or implies stability; thus he includes a dative singular as an example. The sense of the phrase is of secondary importance.

20. The reading of Cornford (1937), p. 179. Taylor, p. 318, notes a parallel with 50a4 which supports this reading.

21. Cherniss (1954), pp. 120–3, places heavy emphasis on the meaning of *houtō* and chides those translators who omit it. I have rendered it 'thus', and have altered the Greek word order so that it refers to a phrase which follows it (as 'thus' does in English) instead of a phrase which precedes it (as *houtō* does in Greek). I take it that the adverb modifies *kalein* and refers to the phrase *to de toiouton . . . homoion* (49e5), which specifies how phenomena are to be addressed.

22. With Gulley, p. 54, I take it that *to toiouton* is predicated of 'fire' and not the reverse.

23. The instance of fire Plato treats here as he treats Tallness in Simmias in the *Phaedo*; the totality of fire parallels what he there he calls 'Tallness in us' (102d7). Thus far the two dialogues are similar; for an important difference between them, see above, Ch. 1, n. 5, final paragraph.

24. As Cherniss (1954) notes, pp. 128–30.

25. As Cornford (1937) notes, p. 181.

26. Arthur Millman has pointed out to me that there are numerous parallels between Plato's analysis of material objects and Descartes'. Plato makes space, rather than Aristotelian matter, the substratum of things; Descartes makes extension the essence of material substance. Both attempt to explain the properties of material things in terms of their mathematical characteristics; thus, both may be said to have a programme of making physics into a mathematical science. Aristotle sides with the empiricists in objecting to this approach to science.

27. Charles Kahn has pointed out to me that this claim is also made at *Sym.* 211a8–9. As the view that the Forms do not exist in another thing is at odds with the view of the *Phaedo* that the Forms are immanent causes, I take the *Symposium* passage as further evidence of a conflict in the middle dialogues between the transcendence and immanence of the Forms.

27. Charles Kahn has pointed out to me that this claim is also made at *Sym.* 211a8–9. As the view that the Forms do not exist in another thing is at odds with the view of the *Phaedo* that the Forms are immanent causes, I take the *Symposium* passage as further evidence of a conflict in the middle dialogues between the transcendence and immanence of the Forms.

28. Cornford (1937) discusses the phrase, *eph'hōi*, in a note (pp. 370–1, n. 4) but fails to consider this sense of *epi* with the dative, which is well attested in Liddell, Scott, and Jones, s. v. *epi*, B. 1. g.

29. The contrast between 'this' and 'such' is paralleled at the verbal level by Aristotle's solution to the Third Man (given in *De Soph. El.* 178b36–39), and it is tempting here to see a Platonic influence on Aristotle. The verbal parallel conceals deep differences in their respective ontologies, however. Aristotle calls individuals in the world of Becoming 'thisses' whereas Plato would call them 'suches'. Matter, the closest Aristotelian correlate to Platonic space, is not for Aristotle a 'this', as space is for Plato. Aristotelian natural kinds, which are the closest correlates in his ontology to Platonic Forms, are 'suches', whereas Forms are substances in Plato and thus at least more 'this'-like than 'such'-like.

30. If Plato had observed the Quinean distinction (Quine, pp. 118–19) between abstract singular terms, such as 'roundness', and general terms, such as 'round', he would have been able to say that, strictly speaking, the Form and its phenomenal counterparts were *not* homonymous. He could have said that the Form, as an abstract object, was the referent of 'roundness', whereas the instance and its phenomenal character were called 'round'. Plato does not seem to be aware of this distinction here or in general, though he draws it himself on one occasion, at *Tht.* 182a–b. The result of his failure to observe the distinction here is that he must make the distinction between Form and instance or participant on ontological, rather than semantic, grounds.

# 4 THE *SOPHIST*

In the preceding chapters of this book I have defended the traditional view that the *Timaeus* is one of Plato's latest dialogues, in the face of the revisionist position that the dialogue was written in Plato's middle period, before the *Parmenides*. In laying out my view of the place of the *Timaeus* in Plato's works I have attempted to show that the dialogue contains a metaphysical position that is insusceptible to the criticisms of the *Parmenides* and that represents an advance over the metaphysical of the middle dialogues in its comprehensiveness and clarity. This substantive position on the development of Plato's metaphysics coheres with the evidence pertaining to stylometry and the ancient interpretive tradition of the *Timaeus* presented in the Appendix; I hope that these three factors together suffice to show that the *Timaeus* is indeed a late dialogue.

Determining the place of the *Timaeus* within the late group of Platonic dialogues is more difficult than establishing its membership in that group, for the simple reason that more evidence (and in particular more stylistic evidence) bears on the former question than the latter. The evidence of style discussed in the Appendix points unequivocally to a late placement of the *Timaeus*, but the statistics concerning Plato's prose rhythms suggest that the *Timaeus* may have been the first dialogue written in the late period. This is the view of Brandwood, and I have followed him in adopting it also.[1]

It is a consequence of this somewhat conjectural placement that the *Timaeus* was composed before the *Sophist*; and I have therefore placed the *Sophist* after the *Timaeus* in this work. This relative ordering of the two dialogues raises anew the possibility that Plato radically revised his metaphysics after the *Timaeus*. Even if the metaphysics of the *Timaeus* has successfully met the objections of the *Parmenides*, it has not been shown to be ultimately satisfactory in Plato's eyes. New objections to the Being-Becoming distinction in particular are raised in the *Sophist*, and those who favour a revisionist conception of Plato's development have argued that the positive views which Plato expounds in response to those objections and elsewhere in the dialogue show that Plato has greatly changed his metaphysics and perhaps even his concept of the nature of philosophy.[2]

I shall not be concerned to deny that the metaphysics of the *Sophist* differs somewhat from that of the *Timaeus* and earlier Platonic dialogues. In view of the fact that I regard the *Sophist* as the later of the two dialogues, I shall treat these differences as developments in Plato's views. I am concerned to deny, however, that the metaphysics of the *Sophist* presents any radical new departure in Plato's thinking. In this chapter I shall attempt to show that the developments of Plato's views that we find in the *Sophist* are natural outgrowths of the metaphysics of the earlier dialogues. The genuine advances made in the *Sophist* are couched in the language of the Theory of Forms and probably would have been impossible for Plato to make without that theory. Plato is not less committed to the Theory of Forms or to be the general enterprise of metaphysics in the *Sophist* than previously; his positions in the *Sophist* are best understood as extensions of the Theory of Forms, rather than as departures from it.

As in previous chapters, I shall attempt to general exposition of the dialogue beyond that required to place the passage I deal with in context. I shall examine two passages in depth. The first of these, 248a–249d, contains a powerful critique of the Being-Becoming distinction and leads, some have thought, to Plato's abandonment of that distinction. If it could be shown that this was the case, it would prove that the *Sophist* differed substantively from the *Timaeus*; I shall argue, however, that the discrepancies between the *Sophist* and other dialogues on this point are verbal rather than substantive. The second passage I shall discuss is 251a–259d, which contains Plato's account of Being and Not-Being. I shall examine 255e–256e in particular detail. My aims will be to show that this passage does not contain, as some have thought, evidence for a new conception of philosophy or for a new Theory of Forms; rather, it exhibits Plato putting familiar concepts to an important new use. I shall also argue that the *Sophist* contains no evidence of the abandonment of the view that the Forms are paradigms; rather, it contains evidence that the metaphysical scheme of original and image is still part of Plato's thought. To establish this point I shall look briefly at two additional passages of the dialogue: 232a–236c and 264c–268d, which contain Plato's final definition of the sophist. I shall not, however, give these passages the detailed scrutiny I shall give to the first two. I shall conclude with some remarks on the general character of the development of Plato's metaphysics, as I have tried to describe it in the book as a whole.

## I. The Critique of the Friends of the Forms (248a–249d)

The *Sophist* is, on its face, a search for the definition of the sophist. It is manifestly a sequel to the *Theaetetus* (216a) and contains the same characters as that dialogue (Socrates, Theaetetus, Theodorus). In addition, a fourth character, an unnamed Eleatic Stranger, is introduced with high praise by Theodorus (216a–c). Socrates and Theodorus play little part in the dialogue itself, which is carried on by the Stranger with the help of Theaetetus. There is no reason to doubt that Stranger, like Socrates in the earlier dialogues, Timaeus in the *Timaeus*, and the Athenian Stranger in the *Laws*, is the spokesman for Plato.[3] The Stranger, it should be noted, does not share Socrates' passion for conversation; he agrees to engage in dialogue with Theaetetus only on condition that he prove tractable and not troublesome (217d). Theaetetus is so obliging that the Stranger wonders at 236d whether he has begun to assent from habit. This remark indicates Theaetetus' minimal contribution to the advancement of the dialectic (in contrast to his role in the *Theaetetus*) and highlights the fact that the dialogue is, like the *Timaeus*, in fact a treatise or essay, although its nature is in this case disguised by the conversational format.

Seven attempts are made to define the sophist. The method used is that of collection and division, the method of dialectic most prominent in the later dialogues (it is used in the *Statesman* also and mentioned in the *Phaedrus*, at 265d–e, and in the *Philebus*, at 16b ff.). The seventh definition describes the sophist as the maker of false images; this definition raises the problem of falsity and not-being and is the occasion of a long digression (236c–264b) which constitutes the metaphysical core of the dialogue. The discussion of the problem of falsity links the *Sophist* thematically, as it has been linked dramatically, with the *Theaetetus*. That dialogue had raised the problem of how false belief could be possible. It had seemed that there could be no such thing, for to have a false belief is to believe *what is not* (*Tht.* 188d): and this is not to think at all (189a). Anyone who thinks must think something that *is*; thus, thinking what is not is impossible (189b). The *Theaetetus* had explored several avenues of escape from this dilemma (189b–200c): but none had proved satisfactory.

It had seemed that the possibility of false belief depended on the being of that which is not; but Parmenides had explicitly ruled this out, stating that 'never shall they prove in any way that things that are not are' (237a8). It is this prohibition that the Stranger attacks in the *Sophist* (cf. 241d–242a), substituting a new conception of not-being for the view of Parmenides that not-being is the contrary of being, and thereby showing that there is a sense in which that which is not is. Aided by this new account of not-being, he is able to show how false statements and false beliefs are possible and thus how the sophist can be defined.

The metaphysical section of the dialogue begins with a lengthy statement of the *aporiai*, the perplexities or problems, involved with the concepts of being and not-being. In the first part of this section (237b–241c) the Stranger focuses on not-being; in the second (242b–251a), he shows that equal difficulties beset the explication of being. The statement of problems concludes with the hope that, since both being and not-being are equally problematic, the clarification of one will provide the clarification of the other (251e–252a).

The first passage with which we shall be concerned occurs in the second part of this aporetic section. In showing the problems that attach to the concept of being, Plato has undertaken a survey of the views of his predecessors on the subject. First he has examined the opinions of 'those who give an exact account' (246e6) of being and not-being (i.e., those who state that some specific number of things exist); now he goes on to deal with those who approach the question in a different way.

These people he describes as members of two perpetually warring camps. On one side are the 'giants', the proponents of materialism, who maintain that only what is tangible is real (246a–b); on the other side are the 'gods', who 'press by force the view that the true realities are certain intelligible and bodiless Forms' (246b7–8). These latter are described later in the dialogue as 'Friends of the Forms' (248a4).

The Stranger tried to reform the members of both camps. The giants are more easily handled (246e–248a). They accept, it is said, the existence of mortal living creatures, which are ensouled bodies; thus they must accept the existence of souls. Souls may be wise or foolish, just or unjust; and they can only be so by possessing the appropriate characteristics. Thus, the materialists are forced to accept the existence of such characteristics, also. Yet souls and characteristics such as justice are not material things; they are invisible and intangible. Therefore the giants must accept the existence of some immaterial things. In the light of this, the Stranger proposes that instead of their criterion of tangibility they accept power (*dunamis*, 247e4) as the criterion of being: on this criterion, anything exists if it had the power to affect or be affected by another thing, for however brief a moment, even if only on one occasion (247d–e). Theaetetus accepts this proposal on behalf of the materialists, but the Stranger warns that 'later it may perhaps appear different to us and to them' (247e7–248a1).

At this point the materialist position has been suitably modified, so the Stranger turns to the Friends of the Forms. These people speak of Being and Becoming as separate and distinct and say we have communion with Becoming via bodily sensation, but with Being via reasoning of the soul. They maintain further that Being is unchanging and Becoming in constant flux (248a). This view is manifestly the view put forth by Plato in the *Phaedo*, *Republic*, and *Timaeus* (cf. Ch. 1, Sec. V; Ch. 3, Sec. I); it is fantastic to suppose that Plato has anything in mind in this passage but that earlier view.[4] We may therefore take it that Plato here, as earlier in the *Parmenides*, has set out to criticise his own metaphysics.

The Friends of the Forms are more resistent to reformation than the materialists; they reject the Stranger's first two attempts to argue them out of their position. First, the Stranger invokes the criterion of being he has just got the materialists to accept. He points out that, when our bodily senses commune with bodies in the external world, they either experience or produce some effect of some power. If being is power, therefore, the entities that cause our sensory experience must exist (248b). Not surprisingly, the Friends of the Forms reject the criterion of being as power; they say that power is a mark, not of Being, but of Becoming (248c).[5]

Thwarted in his opening gambit, the Stranger then raises a similar question about our knowledge of the Forms. Isn't the communion of the soul with the Forms an action or the experience of an effect (248d)? Theaetetus and the Stranger agree that the Friends of the Forms would have to deny this: for, 'if knowing is acting on something, it follows that the thing known is necessarily acted upon' (248d10–e1). If a Form were acted upon, it would thus be changed or moved (*kineisthai*, e3); but Forms are by definition changeless.

It is entirely consistent with Plato's earlier position that its proponents should reject both the Stranger's criterion of Being as power and his suggestion that to know a Form is to act on it. Readers of this section of the dialogue are apt to feel that the criterion and the suggestion should not be rejected, perhaps because they seem plausible or correct. It is important to bear three facts in mind when considering the exchange just described, however. First, it occurs in an aporetic section of the dialogue; the Stranger's purpose (and Plato's) is not to put forth metaphysical doctrine at this point, but to raise problems. The criterion of being is put forward tentatively, as subject to later revision; and, however attractive the criterion and the suggestion that knowing is acting upon something may appear, they disappear from the dialogue at this point and play no role in the constructive section of the dialogue that follows. Secondly, we must remember that the Friends of the Forms are expounding genuine Platonic doctrine. This doctrine is about to be revised but we may assume that Plato wanted to make the least change possible in it that would accommodate his latest insights. What better way could there be to indicate what revision was required than to show proponents of the earlier view (albeit imaginary ones) in dialectical combat with the proponent of the new? Most important, however, is the third point. The passage just discussed proves that the Stranger's criterion of being and the claim that to know is to act upon something are incompatible with the claims that the soul knows the forms and that the Forms are unchanging. It will become clear in the following that the Stranger wishes to retain both of the latter claims; thus he must reject the claims that knowledge is power and that to know is to act upon something.

The Friends of the Forms have survived two waves of the Stranger's attack, but the 'great third wave' engulfs them. With a note of impatience, the Stranger asks:

> What then, by Zeus? Shall we be so easily persuaded that truly motion and life and soul and intelligence are not present in the altogether real, that it neither lives nor thinks, but is standing unmoved, reverend and holy, not having mind? (248e6–249a2)

There must be a place in 'the altogether real' (the realm of Being) for intelligence; this implies life, which in turn implies soul (249a);

and these in turn imply change or motion:

> *Str*: But certainly, if it has mind and life and soul, being ensouled will it stand entirely immobile?
> *Tht*: All these things appear to me to be unreasonable.
> *Str*: Then we must agree that motion and the moved are real things. (249a9–b3)

As in the case of the argument with the materialists and elsewhere in Plato, the confusion that *F*-ness exists is taken to follow immediately from the premiss that *F* things exist.

In the next several lines, the Stranger sums up the argument. On the one hand, if all of reality were motionless, there would be no place in it for mind (*nous*). On the other hand, if everything were in motion, mind would have no place either. For there could be no constancy without rest, and objects that are constant are required if there is to be mind or knowledge. Thus,

> For the philosopher and for one who honors all these things [knowledge, intelligence, and mind; cf. 249c7–8] especially, as it seems, it is necessary for these reasons to accept neither the view of those who say on behalf of the One or the many Forms that the whole of reality is stationary, nor hear at all those who say that being is everywhere in motion; but, following the wish of children, he must say that being and the whole is 'both' — whatever things are unmoved and whatever are moved. (249c10–d4)

What is the view propounded here by the Stranger? Several answers have been put forth by scholars; at least two of these seem to be simply incompatible with the text itself. First, some scholars have thought that the argument shows that the intelligible world itself, i.e. the Forms, must have life, soul, mind and motion.[6] This cannot be correct. If there is to be mind, there must be some appropriate objects for mind to apprehend; and, as 249b–c shows, these must be unchanging. The only unchanging objects Plato has ever accepted are Forms;[7] hence, these unchanging objects of knowledge must be Platonic Forms. Since the Forms are unchanging, both in terms of the demands of the argument and in terms of traditional Platonic doctrine, they cannot possess motion, and thus, life, soul and mind. The living soul or mind that knows the Forms must be something that populates the realm of being in addition to those Forms. Thus, the passage affirms rather than denies the standard Platonic position that the Forms are unchanging objects of knowledge.[8]

Other scholars have held that the Friends of the Forms are only compelled to accept the existence of souls in addition to Forms, and not the entire realm of Becoming.[9] It is true that the Stranger argues specifically about the existence of living things, souls and minds (249a); but this is a matter of strategy on his part. He is employing specific Platonic doctrines to procure the assent of the Friends to the reality of change. The Friends of the Forms have long accepted a close kinship between the Forms and the soul (cf. e.g. *Phdo.*, 78b–80b); more recently, in the *Timaeus*, they have given a central place in the Platonic ontology to a craftsman deity who is described at 47e4 and in the *Philebus* at 28d–e and 30d–e as divine mind or reason (*nous*; cf. above, p. 96). Thus the Stranger is able to trade on the fact that soul and mind are important entities for a Platonist, though they do not seem to have a place within the Being-Becoming dichotomy, as Plato has hitherto described it. Being has always been described as the realm of the Forms, and Becoming as the realm of phenomena; if mind and soul are not phenomenal, they are equally not Forms, since they undergo change. Because the Friends of the Forms are unwilling to relegate the soul and mind to the realm of Becoming, they are forced to include them in the realm of Being: and, in so doing, they are forced to reject motionlessness as a criterion of membership in that realm.

Had Plato said no more than this, it would be possible to argue that he expands reality only enough to include mind and soul in addition to the Forms. In sweeping away the criterion of change-lessness, however, the Stranger goes further: he concludes that 'motion and the moved are real things' (249b3), and that 'being and the whole is "both" — whatever things are unmoved and whatever are moved' (249d3–4). Since motionlessness is no longer a necessary condition for inclusion in the realm of Being, there is no reason to deny that *all* moving things, including the members of the realm of Becoming, are real. This is the Stranger's position, and the Friends of the Forms do not dissent from it. To argue that *some* changing things, e.g. soul and mind, are real, but that others are not, would in these circumstances be special pleading, and the Friends of the Forms are wise not to engage in it.

The position reached at this point seems to be this: the criterion of being as power and the claim that knowing is acting on something have been rejected by the Friends of the Forms. These people do accept, however, the reality of things in motion, however, and in so doing reject their previously held that reality is motionless. There remain two categories of things: those that are absolutely changeless (the Forms) and those that change (everything else, including soul and mind as well as the previous members of the class of Becoming); but no longer can the Friends of the Forms speak only of the former category as Being. Instead of the dichotomy between things that are and things that become, we have a new dichotomy between things at rest and things in motion, with both sorts of thing now included in the category of Being or Reality (cf. also *Laws* X, 893b–c).

Two questions remain to be answered about this new position. First of all, just how new is it? Secondly, is it Platonic doctrine: or does it turn out to be, like the Stranger's proposed criterion of being, a view accepted by a character in the dialogue but not by Plato?

In assessing the novelty of the scheme, we should first note that there remain two categories of things, just as there always have been for Plato; now, however, in referring to only one category as Being, he so refers to both. In lieu of his earlier labelling of the classes, he calls one category Rest and the other Motion (a distinction that is carried over to the positive metaphysical section of the dialogue). Secondly, the membership of the new class of Rest remains exactly what the membership of the old class of Being had been: the Forms. Thus, there still exists in Plato's ontology a contrast between the motionless Forms and everything else.

The second category *is* substantively modified. In addition to the previously accepted members of the class of Becoming, soul and mind are added to the class of Motion. In making this change, however, Plato does not add any new entities to his ontology (as he did in adding the Receptacle — curiously absent from the discussion here — to his ontology in the *Timaeus*); he merely locates in his ontology two previously unplaced entities. Given that these entities undergo change, there is no place they could be put other than the erstwhile category of Becoming, now renamed the category of Motion.

It is likely that the renaming of the two categories was intended to remove some of the negative connotations of Becoming which are to be found in the earlier dialogues. If such exalted Platonic principles as soul and mind are to be placed along with phenomena in a single class, this class cannot be so denigrated as the class of Becoming is in the *Phaedo* and *Republic*. It should be pointed out in this connection, however, that Plato had to a large extent removed those negative connotations himself in the *Timaeus* by assigning to the phenomenal world the attributes of life, soul, reason, completeness, unity and everlastingness (cf. p. 92 above). The phenomenal world, so described, is hardly the same in value as Plato had regarded it earlier; yet Plato had in the *Timaeus* placed it in the category of Becoming (28b–c). Thus, if the inclusion of soul and mind with the phenomenal world and its parts in the category of Motion represents a change in attitude toward things that move, it is a change that had already taken place in the *Timaeus*.

It seems, then, that the new categories of Rest and Motion do not differ, except in name, from the implicit ontology of the earlier Platonic dialogues. Still, it may be objected, the *Sophist* differs from the earlier dialogues, including the *Timaeus*, in granting Being, reality, to the class of things in motion. This is true; but, again, the change is not so great as it sounds. Although Plato has in the past described the classes of Being and Becoming as mutually exclusive (cf. *Tim*. 27d–28a), he has also described both classes as *real* (cf. *Phdo*. 79a, *Tim*. 35a). The reason for this ambiguity seems to lie in the fact that the Greeks, having no separate term for existence, used the verb 'to be' and its relatives sometimes to make existential claims and sometimes to make claims of other sorts, including the claim that something was enduring.[10] When 'being' is used in the latter sense, the thing that is said to be is said to be lasting and is contrasted properly with things that are ephemeral. When 'being' is used existentially, however, it is used to state that something exists or is real, and such a thing is properly contrasted not with the ephemeral but with the unreal, non-existent or illusory.

Plato, in contrasting Being and Becoming, had never intended to convey the claim that phenomena do not exist; he was contrasting the eternal Forms with their ephemeral counterparts. In this use of 'Being' the existential implications of the term are not relevant. In saying that both Forms and phenomena are real, however, he was claiming that both exist. Plato's earlier contrast between Being and Becoming emphasised the durative aspect of 'being', and neglected the existential aspect. The revision of this doctrine into a contrast between Rest and Motion, both embraced by Being, neglects the durative aspect of 'being' and emphasises the existential. The difference between the two views is not substantive, but terminological. Plato has always described phenomena as real, actual or existent, but ephemeral, and Forms as real and unchanging. The Being-Becoming distinction and the new distinction Rest and Motion merely pick up different aspects of a constant view; it is not the case that a new view is substituted for the old.

Thus, the discussion of *Sophist* 248a–249d contains no radical modification of Platonic metaphysics. The entities discussed — Forms, phenomena, mind and soul — are familiar components of Plato's ontology and they are described in familiar ways. What is really modified in this passage is the criterion of being Plato had accepted in earlier dialogues; and this modification represents not a new view of the nature of reality but a shift of emphasis from one aspect of this ambiguous concept to another. The shift is significant but hardly constitutes the abandonment of Plato's earlier doctrines. Plato has found, not a new view, but a new and different way of describing an old one.

If this is the case, it gives us the answer to our second question, whether the new view is genuine Platonic doctrine. If it is simply familiar Platonic doctrine in new verbal packaging, it must be genuine. This conclusion is reinforced by the fact that the three classes of Being, Rest and Motion figure prominently in the constructive section of the dialogue that follows this aporetic one. There are, however, considerations which may lead us to wonder how important a change this passage contains, even at the verbal level.

Aristotle testifies that Plato held the view that sensible things were in a spate of flux and could not be known 'even in his later years' (*Metaph.* A. 6, 987a34–b1). His testimony conflicts with any interpretation of 248a–249d that would make the change in Platonic doctrine more than verbal; however, as Aristotle describes only the substance of Plato's views and not the terminology in which they were expressed, he is of no help in determining whether Plato adhered to the new terminology he adopts in this passage.

The evidence of the other late dialogues shows no general abandonment of even the language of the Being-Becoming distinction. We have already seen that the *Timaeus* employs this language freely, but this has been taken as an argument that the *Timaeus* must be earlier than the *Sophist*.[11] Brandwood placed the *Philebus* after the *Sophist*, however,[12] and the *Philebus* (59a) contrasts eternal being with that which comes into being in much the same way as does the *Timaeus*.[13] One could, of course, argue that the *Philebus* was written before the *Sophist*: but it would take great ingenuity to make the same claim about the *Statesman*, since that dialogue is clearly the sequel to the *Sophist*. In the *Statesman*, at 293e3, we find Plato denying that constitutions other than the ideal, correct one he has just described are 'really real'. As Gregory Vlastos has pointed out, he cannot mean by this that they do not exist: 'the constitutions which are said not to be really real are precisely the existing ones — those which, to Plato's disgust, clutter up the political may of Greece.'[14] Instead, he is using 'real' in one of the ways he had used the term in the Being-Becoming distinction: to distinguish what is genuine or perfect from what is an imperfect imitation.

Even in other late dialogues, then, Plato continues to invoke the Being-Becoming distinction in its old, familiar language. We have seen that the discussion of 248a–249d does not lead to a new doctrine, but merely emphasises one aspect of standard Platonic doctrine; now it appears that even the linguistic repackaging of that doctrine represents no permanent change in Plato's vocabulary. If, as I have argued, the substantive position underlying the verbal transformation of this passage is essentially the same, this should not surprise us. For Plato was by his own admission a person who thought it in poor taste to be overly concerned about words. (*Tht.* 184c).

In light of the exegesis of the passage just presented — Aristotle's testimony — and the passages cited from the later dialogues, it seems clear that *Soph.* 248a–249d presents no radical revision of Platonic ontology. Even the verbal changes adopted in this passage do not seem to be adhered to outside the *Sophist* itself; it therefore seems likely that, in proposing them, Plato was not changing his mind about some fundamental principle, but pursuing a more limited purpose. What this purpose was can best be seen by considering the passage in its proper context. We must recall that the section of the dialogue in which the passage occurs is aporetic; Plato's purpose is to indicate that all previous conceptions of being and not-being are inadequate. Accordingly, he must find something wrong with his own earlier view; if it should turn out to be unproblematic, there would be no need to proceed with the dialogue. He raises, in fact, a genuine problem with his use of 'being' in the Being-Becoming distinction and proposes a revision of that distinction that leaves it substantially intact (and, incidentally, bequeaths it to be succeeding constructive section of the dialogue), while bringing out, by a verbal change, a neglected aspect of Plato's own view. The modification of Platonic doctrine is undertaken to suit the dialectical purposes of the dialogue: and this is no less the case when, after having established in this passage the conclusion that Being is the sum of Rest and Motion, Plato has the Stranger establish what is apparently the exact opposite conclusion: that Being is a distinct third nature, outside both Motion and Rest and in its own nature neither moving nor resting.[15] Thus, although the criticism of the Theory of Forms contained in the passage is legitimate and the revision well taken, Plato was motivated to criticise and revise his view by the constraints of the dialogue he was engaged in writing; in the other late dialogues, when his purposes were different, he had no difficulty returning to the substance and the language of a doctrine he had found to be essentially sound and useful.

## II. Plato's Account of Being and Not-Being (251a–259d)

Following the aporetic section of the dialogue, in which the problems inherent to any account of being and not-being are described and in which Plato put forth the critique of his own position discussed above, there is a constructive section, in which Plato presents a solution to the problem of not-being. Plato's own account of the relation between being and not-being occurs between pages 251a and 259d of the dialogue; from 259d–264b Plato applies the lessons of the account to the problems of false statement and false belief. Both of these passages are constructive in character and doubtless present Platonic doctrine. I shall focus in this section on the first passage, summarising the second only briefly.

Plato scholars — especially those who hold the radical revisionist view of Plato's development — have seen in this account of being and not-being a considerable departure from Plato's earlier views; some have also found in it a redefinition of philosophy. The passage indicates, they have thought, Plato's abandonment of metaphysics in favour of conceptual analysis or the philosophy of language (see above, n. 2, p. 165). I shall argue that, although Plato makes a genuine conceptual breakthrough in his account of being and not-being and adopts a position which differs in substance from his own earlier views, this breakthrough is made with the aid of the familiar apparatus of the Theory of Forms and represents an extension of that theory rather than an abandonment of it in favour of something else. To establish these points, I shall first present a description of the content of the passage itself; then I shall offer an interpretation of the passage described.

The Stranger opens this section of the dialogue with the question how one thing can have many names. This question had not arisen explicitly in the aporetic section of the dialogue, though some of the dilemmas raised in that section point towards it; and, in general, the constructive section of the dialogue does not rely heavily on points made in the aporetic section, though Plato does, as I noted earlier, retain the three classes of Being, Rest and Motion from that section.

The question would seem at first glance to be a linguistic one, but the Stranger is concerned with the attribution of properties to things as well as names:

> In naming a man I suppose we say many things, attributing to him colors and shapes and sizes and evils and excellences, and in all these cases and thousands of others we say that he is not only 'a man', but also 'good', and countless other things . . . (251a8–b2)

This practice is objectionable to a group of people the Stranger describes as 'the young and those among the aged who have come to learning late in life' (251b5–6).[16] These people that we must not call a man 'good', but only speak of good as 'good' and only man as 'man' (251b8–c2). In other words, they wish to limit all cases of prediction to self-prediction or perhaps identity.[17] The Stranger proposes to deal with these 'late-learners' and with all others as well who have ever spoken on the subject of being (251c8–d1), including all the philosophers previously discussed.

He does so by raising three questions:

> Whether we are to attach Being neither to Motion nor Rest not to anything else, but to treat these thus in our discussions as unmixed and impossible to have a share of one another? Or are we to collect all into the same category as able to have communion with one another? Or are some able, others not? (251d5–9)

The reader will note that the questions pertain not to the individual members of the categories of Rest and Motion, but to those categories themselves and to the concept of Being as well; this is clear, at least in the case of Being, from the fact that the Stranger asks whether we can attach it to Motion and Rest, whether we can treat it as a predicate. Plato does not always observe the distinction between concept and object, or that between a class and members of the class, in the ensuing discussion — a failure which results in a certain level of ambiguity.[18] To the extent that it is safe to invoke these distinctions on his behalf, however, it may be said that Plato's concern in the passage is with the concepts or classes of Being, Rest and Motion, and not with individual members of those classes or objects falling under those concepts. As Plato later in the passage identifies these concepts or classes with Forms, I have capitalised their names to indicate that the questions concern the Forms of Being, Rest and Motion.

The first two proposed alternatives are quickly rejected. If nothing participants in anything else, 'Motion and Rest will in no way participate in Being' (251e9); thus, neither of them will exist (252a2). As the Stranger points out, this alternative overturns all theories, including those that say that everything is in motion or everything is at rest; for both camps assert that everything is really in the state they champion. The view is in fact self-refuting, for its proponents must make use of the combinations they reject even to state their rejection of combination (251b–c). As for the second alternative, Theaetetus states that even he can put an end to it: for if everything could combine with everything else, then 'Motion itself would stand entirely still and Rest itself would move' (252d6–7), a result the Stranger and he agree is impossible.

The third possibility, that some things will blend and others will not, remains. We need grammatical knowledge to determine which letters combine with which and musical knowledge to determine which notes can combine; the situation is the same in the other arts (253a–b). Therefore some sort of knowledge, and in fact the greatest sort, as Theaetetus suggests at 253c4–5, is needed to determine which Kinds[19] can combine. This knowledge of the proper combinations among Kinds or Forms (cf. *eidos*, 253d1) turns out, not surprisingly, to be dialectic (253d2–3). The man who is able to discern the one Form (*idean*, d5) in many and the many embraced by one is the philosopher (253e); and the Stranger remarks that in searching for the sophist they have come upon the knowledge of free men (253c7–9). He contrasts the philosopher and sophist as follows:

> The one runs away into the darkness of not-being, laying hold of it by practice, and because of the place is hard to understand; . . . The philosopher, on the other hand, always keeps close to the Form of Being, and because of the brightness of the place is not at all easy to see; for the eyes of the souls of the many are unable to endure looking at the divine. (254a4–b1)

No one familiar with the metaphysics of the middle dialogues can fail to see the allusion to it contained in this passage. The portrayal of the philosopher as a free man, his science as the greatest science, its concern the relations between Forms, the use of spatial metaphors and metaphors of light and darkness to describe the difference between the philosopher and the sophist — all these points echo the doctrines of the *Phaedo* and *Republic* and in particular the analogies of the Sun and the Cave. Also, in portraying the realms of being and not-being as far removed from one another, as in fact polar opposites, Plato recalls the contrast between and not-being offered in *Rep.* V, 475e ff., where being was portrayed as the object of knowledge and not-being as the object of ignorance. These allusions must be international on Plato's part; and they create two distinct expectations. The first, that the metaphysical apparatus of the middle dialogues will be used in the succeeding discussion, is fulfilled. The second, that the doctrine of the essential contrariety between being and not-being, a doctrine which Plato had inherited from *Parmenides*, will be maintained, is emphatically not fulfilled; it turns out to be the central accomplishment of Plato's new analysis of not-being that this contrariety, so freely recalled here, must be rejected.

The Stranger at this point restates in full the hypothesis of the selective combination of Forms: Some Kinds can combine with one another, some cannot; some combine with only a few others, some with many and some with all (254b–c). He hopes to use this hypothesis to attain clarity about being and not-being; to do so he selects a few of the 'most important' or 'greatest' (*megistōn*, 254c3; cf. *Megista*, d4) Forms (*eidōn*, c2) or Kinds (*genōn*, d4) for discussion. The purpose of the selection is to avoid the confusion that might result from trying to cover every Form.

The most important of the Kinds so far discussed are Being itself,

Rest and Motion. The latter two are mutually imcompatible but Being mixes with both, since they both exist (254d). Each of these Forms is different from the others and the same as itself. This raises the question whether Sameness and Difference are additional Kinds; an intricate argument succeeds in showing that they are, by showing that they are not identical to Being, Rest or Motion (254e–255e).[20] Sameness and Difference, like Being, can mix with anything; in this all three are unlike Rest and Motion, which are restricted to mutually exclusive domains.

With the five Forms thus distinguished, the Stranger uses them as examples in his account of being and not-being. The Form he discusses first is Motion; it is in fact the only example he deals with in any detail. As he has repeatedly insisted, Motion and Rest are mutually incompatible; thus, Motion 'is altogether different from Rest' (255e11–12) and 'is not Rest' (e14) 'in any way' (e15). By his emphasis on the total separation of Motion and Rest the Stranger wishes to exclude both the possibility that Motion and Rest are identical and the possibility that Motion participates in Rest (cf. 256b6–9).[21]

Motion is related differently, however, to Being, Sameness and Difference. In the case of Rest, we could say that Motion simply 'is not' Rest; in these cases, we must say both that 'it is' and that 'it is not' the other Form. Consider first the relation between Motion and Sameness. On the one hand, Motion is different from Sameness (256a3), and thus 'is not' the same (a5). On the other hand, it 'is' the same, since everything participates in Sameness (a7–8). As the Stranger spells matters out:

> The Motion is the same and not the same, we must agree and not be vexed. For when we call it 'the same' and 'not the same' we do not speak in the same way; but when [we call it] 'the same', we speak thus because of its participation in Sameness with respect to itself; but when [we call it] 'not the same', because of its communion with Difference, because of which it has, being separated from Sameness, come to be not that but different, so that it may be called again in turn 'not the same'. (256a10–b4).

In the same manner, Motion 'is and is not' different; it partakes of Difference with respect to Difference and thus 'is not' different; but it also is different from Sameness and thus partakes of Difference (256c). Finally, as Motion has proved to be different from

Rest, Sameness and Difference, it must be different from Being, since it was agreed that the Forms were five in number (256d11–12). Therefore, since Motion is different from Being, it 'really is not Being' (d8); yet it equally 'is' real, since it participates in Being (d8–9).

At this point the analysis is generalised. Necessarily, not-being *is* (256d11), since Motion and all the other Kinds 'are not' by virtue of participating in Difference from Being. By the same token, they all 'are' because they participate in Being. This only explains the use of 'is' and 'is not' that relates other Forms to the Form of Being: Plato goes on to generalise the account even further. 'Concerning each of the Forms, being is many, and not-being unlimited in number' (256e5–6), 'the Stranger remarks; this cannot mean that each Form has many existences or participates many times in the Form of Being; but rather, that each Form *is* many things, participates in many Forms, and that it *is not* many others or participates in difference with respect to them. By means of this extension of the concepts of being and not-being, the Stranger is now able to state the respect in which even the Form of Being itself 'is not':

> *Str*: Therefore even Being itself must be called different from the others.
> *Tht*: Necessarily.
> *Str*: Then Being also, on our account, is not in as many respects as there are the other things. For not being those, it is however itself one, and again is not this indefinite number of other things. (257a1–6)

As in the argument with the materialists discussed earlier, the Stranger takes the existence of things which have some properties and not others to be proof of the existence of being and not-being. The reality of not-being, of course, is what the Stranger had originally set out to establish. He has done this by showing that what is not is not the contrary of being, as Parmenides had assumed, but only what is different from the Form of Being (257b). What has made this conceptual breakthrough possible is the analysis of negation as difference; as the Stranger states:

> Then we shall not agree, whenever it is said that negation signifies an opposite, but [we shall admit] only this much, that the 'not', when placed before, indicates something different from

the following words, or rather from the things to which the
words uttered after the negative refer. (257b9–c3)

The Stranger goes on to compare Difference with Knowledge.
Both are divided into parts (just as there is Knowledge of Beauty or
of Justice, so there if Difference from Beauty or from Justice),
each of which exists as much as do the parts of Being (257c–258c).
The Stranger at this point brings the discussion back to
Parmenides' prohibition of not-being, which, he says, has now
been transcended (258c–e). The passage concludes with a recapitu-
lation of the results of the explication of the blending of the Forms,
which emphasises again that both Being and Not-Being (i.e. Difference) are and are not (258e–259b). The Stranger challenges
those who disagree with the analysis given to produce a better one,
and not merely to object with trivial puzzles (259b–d).

At this point the section we are concerned with ends and the discussion turns to the specific issue of saying what is not, or the
application of not-being to the sphere of discourse. The sophist
denies that not-being in discourse, that is, falsity, is possible. To
rebut this claim, the Stranger divides statements into their
component parts, which he labels 'nouns' and 'verbs'. Both of
these elements name things (nouns name performers of actions,
verbs their actions); when a noun and verb are combined, a simple
statement is produced. It if necessary that the object named by the
noun should exist; otherwise the statement would not be about anything. The verb which is attached to the noun may, however,
denote an action that the agent does not perform. That is, although
both the agent Theaetetus and the action of flying exist, Theaetetus
does not fly. The statement 'Theaetetus flies' accordingly asserts of
Theaetetus that he performs an action which is in fact different
from those actions which he does perform; and, in this sense, not-
being or falsity is possible in the realm of discourse. As the Stranger
defines thinking as internal discourse, it is easy for him to extend
the analysis of falsity from statement to thought or judgement
(259d–264b). With the completion of the analysis, the Stranger is
able to return to the problem of defining the sophist, which I shall
discuss briefly in the next section.

Having reviewed the content of the constructive portion of the
dialogue and the content of 251a–259d in some detail, we must
now attempt to understand it. As I have noted above, a number of
scholars have seen in Plato's treatment of Being a radical departure

in his thought. The primary reason for this seems to be that it has seemed to almost everyone who has written on the *Sophist* in recent years that Plato's concern in this passage is with the verb 'to be' and that his singular accomplishment is to disambiguate different senses or uses of the verb, such as the 'is' of identity, the existential 'is' and the 'is' of predication. There has been disagreement, to be sure, concerning which senses or uses of the verb Plato succeeds in disambiguating: but in their general description of Plato's project scholars (even those as different in their overall approach to Plato as Cornford and Owen) have been in remarkable agreement.[22] If their account of this passage is correct, it is at least arguable that the *Sophist* represents a shift in Plato's interest from the metaphysical concerns that dominate the middle dialogues and the *Timaeus* to philosophy of language and the problems of reference, prediction, and truth that have been central to analytic philosophy in this century. The *Sophist*, regarded in this light, has a curiously contemporary look which other Platonic dialogues appear to lack.

This implication of a radial shift in Plato's thought is not drawn by all those who have characterised his enterprise in the *Sophist* as the disambiguation of senses of the verb 'to be'. The reason is that not all scholars and philosophers see the philosophy of language as divorced from metaphysics. It is undeniable that Plato in the *Sophist* is concerned with problems of reference, predication and truth, and that his doctrines anticipate in some ways those of contemporary analytical philosophy; but these undeniable facts show no departure from Plato's earlier interests. Questions of reference, predication and truth have always been relevant to the Theory of Forms, as I have tried to show in earlier chapters of this work; thus it should not surprise us if Plato, as I shall argue he does, uses the apparatus of the Theory of Forms in dealing with them here.

As to the relation between philosophy of language and metaphysics, it must be said that, although the techniques of linguistic philosophy appeared to their proponents in the 1940s and 1950s to be a means of escape from the problems of traditional metaphysics and although programme of logical positivism promised the complete elimination of metaphysics, most philosophers of language in the analytical tradition have seen their enterprise as inextricably connected with that branch of metaphysics known as ontology; they have seen the theory of language, that is, as inseparable from the theory of reality. This view of the relation of language and metaphysics is no more characteristic of Russell and Quine, however, than it is of Plato. When he addresses in the *Sophist* problems in the philosophy of language, he is not abandoning metaphysics but engaging in it.

The implication drawn by radical revisionists from the content of the *Sophist* is not the only misrepresentation of Plato derived from this passage, however. The description of Plato's project shared by revisionists and conservative interpreters of Plato also seems to me to be incorrect. Plato is not concerned in the *Sophist* with the disambiguation of the verb 'to be'. He is not trying to show that a number of apparently identical occurrences of that verb have in fact different analyses; on the contrary, he is attempting to show that a bewildering variety of statements of different sorts have in fact the same analysis. It is a feature of this analysis that *esti*, the Greek verb 'to be' in its third person singular present tense form, is univocal in meaning rather than ambiguous and that it is the linguistic correlate of the metaphysical relation of participation.

This point can be proved by considering three of the statements Plato gives an analysis of in the passage. Let us consider first the statements 'Motion is the same' and 'Motion is not the same'. As we would analyse these statements, with the distinctions between statements of identity, predication and existence ready-made for us, they turn out to be identity statements which appear to have the term on the right of the identity sign omitted or understood. Plato, in contrast, treats both as statements of the grammatical of logical form, '$F$-ness participates in $G$-ness':

Motion is the same = Motion participates in Sameness with
   respect to itself (256b1)
Motion is not the same = Motion participates in Difference with
   respect to Sameness (256b2–4)

There are three points of interest concerning Plato's analysis of these two statements. The first is that the analysis does contain the recognition of an ambiguity (the Stranger remarks, 'when we call it "the same" and "not the same" we do not speak in the same way,' 256a11–12); but it is not, as Plato's interpreters have alleged, an ambiguity in the verb 'to be'. The verb 'to be' is so far from Plato's mind in his treatment of these statements that it does not even appear in them as copula when they are analysed (256a11–b4) but must be understood by the reader. The ambiguity Plato mentions is in the expression, 'the same'. In the affirmative statement, 'the same' is the main predicate term, denoting the Form in which Motion is said to participate; in the negative statement, it is the object of a prepositional phrase modifying the main predicate, a phrase which limits or defines the respect in which Motion is said to participate in another Form, namely Difference.

Secondly, the analysis Plato gives of these two identity statements is the same in form as that which he has previously given of statements of predication. In the *Phaedo*, we recall, Plato had explained the attribution of beauty and of the term 'beautiful' to something on the basis of that thing's participation in the Form of Beauty (100c, 102b). He had also in the *Phaedo* used the more complex terminology invoked here to explain that one thing could participate in a Form in relation to another thing (the example of the *Phaedo* is that of Simmias participating in Tallness with respect to Soctrates but in Shortness with respect to Phaedo; 102b–d). It can hardly be accidental that the analysis of predication given in the *Phaedo* is presented in the same terms as the analysis of identity offered in the *Sophist*. It is difficult to find a comparable analysis of predication in the *Sophist*, incidentally, because the putative case of predication Plato does analyse (i.e. 'Motion is at rest', analysed as 'Motion participates in Rest' at 256b6–7) is not a genuine predication at all but rather a statement of class inclusion. Plato appears to think of it as a case of predication, however; at least, he treats it indifferently from the genuine cases of predication that occur in the *Phaedo*; so we may perhaps take it as evidence that his analysis of predication has not changed from that dialogue.

The third point of interest is this. Plato translates both the affirmative and the negative statements into the same schema, '*F*-ness participates in *G*-ness'. This translation enables him to take an obstensibly negative statement and turn it into an affirmative one. Once the statement is analysed in Plato's manner, we no longer need to understand it, or the verb in it, as negative. We do not have to treat the statement as a claim that something is not the case, nor as a claim that some subject does not have some property — the claims that Parmenides found unintelligible and which have given rise in later thought to such problematic entities as negative facts and possible, but non-actual, states of affairs. We can, rather, understand the ostensibly negative statement as an affirmative one, as the statement that the subject does participate in a specific Form, namely the Form of Difference. Plato's breakthrough in understanding negation, regarding in this light consisted in his discovery that negative statements could be regarded as affirmations of difference.[23]

What we have seen so far is that Plato's analysis of both affirmation and negative identity statements conforms to the analysis he had offered in the *Phaedo* of predications. Far from disambiguating an 'is' of identity from the 'is' of predication, Plato has assimulated both to the relation of participation (a point which can be seen clearly by consulting the chart below, p. 151). How does he handle the 'is' of existence? The issue had been most controversial; for even among those who agree that Plato distinguishes the 'is' of identity from some other use, there is not agreement on whether he succeeds in recognising the existential 'is'. Part of the problem stems from the fact, mentioned above (p. 136), that the Greeks had no distinct word for 'exists'. As they had to rely on 'is' in statements of existence as well as in identity statements and predications, we must decide from context whether a statement such as 'Motion is' is in fact an existential claim or a truncated predication or identity statement.

It is undeniable, and is agreed by all parties to this dispute, that there are instances of *esti* in Plato that are best translated by 'exists'.[24] It does not follow from this, of course, that Plato distinguished the existential 'is' from some other use; it only shows that Plato, like everyone else, needed on occasion to make existential claims. To show that Plato distinguishes the 'is' of existence from some other use, one would have to show that he treats the verb differently in his analysis of existential and predicative or identity statements. I shall argue that, just as he fails to distinguish an 'is' of identity from the 'is' of predication, Plato does not distinguish an existential 'is' from some other sense or use. On the contrary, the 'is' he employs to make existential statements is the same linguistic correlate of the relation of participation we have met already.

In spite of disagreements about the proper translations of certain statements in this passage of Plato where *esti* is used absolutely (i.e. without expressed linguistic complement), there seems to be no reason to deny that 'Motion is' (256a1) is an existential statement. This statement is a direct descendent of the outcome of 251e–252a, where it was stated that the Motion and Rest would not *be* unless the Forms could combine. That passage, moreover, reflected the concern of 247a–249d that Being should not be denied to Motion.

In all of these passages it seems most natural to regard Plato as making the existential claim that Motion exists when he relates Motion to Being.

It would appear at first sight that the 'is' in 'Motion is' has one of the properties of the 'is' of existence which is not shared by the 'is' of identity or the 'is' of predication. The 'is' in 'Motion is' appears to be used absolutely, to be grammatically complete, to be, like 'exists', a one-place predicate, rather than a two-place predicate, such as the copula or identity sign. This appearance is deceiving, however. At 256a1 Plato analyses 'Motion is' as 'Motion participates in Being'; at 256d9, he gives the same analysis for 'Motion is real' (*hē kinēsis estin on*). As the two statements are given the same analysis, we may assume that they are the same in meaning and that therefore the 'is' of the first statement is elliptical for the 'is real' of the second. Thus, although the 'is' in the first statement appears to be complete, it can in fact take the grammatical complement 'real (the participle *on*). The existential statement, 'Motion is', therefore, is treated as equivalent to 'Motion is real' and is analysed as 'Motion participates in Being'.[25] This analysis has the same form as the analysis of the statements of identity and predication we discussed earlier: *F*-ness participates in *G*-ness.

In the case of each kind of statement he discusses, then, Plato gives an analysis of the same sort. According to this analysis, the subject term names a Form (in the examples we have discussed, the Form of Motion); and this Form is said to participate in another Form which is named in the predicate. In some cases, the participation of one Form in another is qualified with respect to a third Form; but the fundamental character of the analysis remains the same. (The analysis could easily be modified to cover cases where the subject is not a Form, but a phenomenal thing, such as those discussed in the *Phaedo*; however, as Plato's purpose in this passage is to show how Forms blend with one another, he confines his treatment to statements about Forms.) As in every case we find the subject term of the statement correlated with a Form and the predicate term likewise correlated with another Form, so in every case do we find the 'is' of the statement to be analysed correlated with the relation of participation referred to in the analysis, as the following chart makes clear:

I. Existential Statements

*analysandum:* Motion        is        (real).

*analysans:*    Motion participates in Being.

II. Identity Statements

A. Affirmative

*analysandum:* Motion        is        the same (as itself).

*analysans:*    Motion participates in Sameness (with respect to itself).

B. Negative

*analysandum:* Motion        is        not the same.

*analysans:*    Motion participates in Difference with respect to Sameness.

III. (Grammatically) Predicative Statements

*analysandum:* Motion        is        resting.

*analysans:*    Motion participates in Rest.

Plato's analysis of these statements shows clearly that his purpose is not the disambiguation of *esti*, but (as he himself notes at 257b9–c3, quoted above, pp. 144–5) the redefinition of 'not'. Nor is the analysis of 'not' engaged in for the purpose of revealing an ambiguity; the only meaning offered for 'not' is 'different from'. As I have noted above, the only term that is disambiguated in the course of Plato's treatment of these statements is 'the same' (cf. pp. 147–8). Plato's analysis does indeed point out the differences between statements of identity, statements of predication and existential statements; but it does so without attributing to these statements analyses of differing logical form. As we have seen, the underlying form of all these statements is, in Plato's eyes, the same: *F*-ness participates in *G*-ness.

The fact that Plato's aim in his analysis of these different statements is not the discovery of ambiguity does not make his analysis any the less an exercise in the philosophy of language; but the terms in which the analysis is carried out make it impossible for us to divorce this exercise in the philosophy of language from metaphysics. The tools of the analysis are the Forms and the relation of participation; what Plato attempts to show is that the linguistic entities and relations found in these different statements are to be understood in terms of the ontological entities and relations

152                                                *The* Sophist

contained in the Theory of Forms. Plato is not interested in translating one sort of statement ('ordinary Greek') into another sort ('philosophical Greek'); he is interested in connecting statements of whatever sort with the states of affairs they represent.

That the 'linguistic analysis' carried out in this passage of the *Sophist* is as metaphysical as any earlier discussion we have examined is shown by the striking parallels, both linguistic and doctrinal, between this passage and those previously dealt with. On the linguistic level, we should note three things. First, the entities employed as the referents of the subject and predicate terms in the statements analysed are repeatedly referred to as 'Forms'. The term *eidos* is used at 253d1, 254e2, 256e5, 258c2, and 258d6; we find *idea* 253d5, 254a9, and 255e5. Plato also calls these entities *genē*, or 'Kinds', as noted above (p. 141); but this does not signal either a new conception of Form or a different sort of entity altogether, as some scholars have thought.[26] In the *Parmenides*, as we have seen (cf. above, p. 57), Plato had used both *genos* and *eidos* to denote the Forms in stating the Theory of Forms of the middle dialogues. Secondly, the verbal parallels are not confined to the references to 'Forms'. The vocabulary in terms of which Plato describes 'participation' is the same as that he had used in the middle dialogues: *metechein*, *koinōnein*, and *metalambanein* (cf. e.g. *Phdo*. 100c–d and 102b).[27] Thirdly, when Plato introduces his analyses of the statements discussed above, he uses the same word, *dia*, 'because of', which he had used to introduce his analysis of causation in the *Phaedo* (101a; cf. *Soph*. 256a1, 7, b1, 2). In both cases the Forms and participation are brought in not just to reformulate certain statements, but to explain their truth conditions.[28]

When these three linguistic parallels are added to the parallels mentioned earlier between the analysis of predication in the *Phaedo* and the analysis of identity in the *Sophist* (cf. p. 148) and between the description of the philosopher and the sophist and the doctrines of the *Phaedo* and *Republic* (cf. p. 142), it seems impossible to deny that the theory of the *Sophist* is couched in the vocabulary of the metaphysics of the earlier dialogues. Now when a philosopher (especially one who, like Plato, is a master stylist) uses in a passage terminology which we have come to associate with one of his philosophical doctrines and gives us no hint that he is using that terminology for some novel purpose, we are surely entitled to infer that the philosopher is in that passage employing the doctrine normally expressed by that terminology. In the absence of evidence to the contrary, it would simply be special pleading to suggest that all of the parallels between this passage of the *Sophist* and earlier dialogues are merely verbal, that Plato is using the language of Platonic metaphysics to make some totally different point. On the basis of these verbal parallels alone, then, it would be safe to assume that Plato's analysis of the statements discussed above is carried out in terms of the Forms and the relation of participation.

There is no need, however, to rely solely on the linguistic evidence provided in the passage, persuasive though that is. For the substance of the Theory of Forms, and not just the language, has been brought up for discussion before in this dialogue, in the passage discussed in Section I of this chapter. In that section we saw that, although the Forms came in for some judicious criticism, in the end the reality of Forms as unchanging objects of knowledge, distinguished in virtue of their motionlessness from all other things, was vindicated (cf. above, pp. 133 ff.) Since the Forms, essentially under the same description they were given in the middle dialogues, have passed this earlier test, there seems to be no reason to doubt that they are employed by Plato here in his explanation of not-being.

The conclusion we have so far reached is that the constructive account of being and not-being Plato offers in this section of the dialogue is expressed not only in terms of the language of the Theory of Forms, but in terms of the Theory itself. The fact that Plato invokes this metaphysical doctrine in a dialogue as late as the *Sophist* is additional evidence, if any were required, that he did not abandon it in light of the critique of the *Parmenides* (or that of the *Sophist* itself). In fact, Plato may well have regarded his success in using the Theory of Forms to explain the problem of not-being as the ultimate confirmation of the truth, or at least the theoretical value, of that theory. Thus, our passage testifies, not to any radical change in Plato's philosophy, but to the continuity in his thought. None the less, it would be unwise to neglect the truly important developments contained in this passage merely because these developments are based on, and expressed in terms of, doctrines advanced in earlier works.

In the first place, it should be noted that Plato's doctrine of the relation between being and not-being is a major advance, not merely over his own earlier view (expressed in *Rep.* V), but over the entire earlier history of Greek philosophy. Every Greek philosopher since Parmenides, including Plato himself, had accepted the

claim that being and not-being were contraries. This doctrine had
produced severe problems for Greek philosophy concerning the
possibility of false statement and belief, the reality of motion and
change, and the intelligibility of the cosmos, which no one had
succeeded in solving. Plato, in showing that these problems were
based on a false understanding of the relation between being and
not-being, effectively removed the major stumbling block in Greek
thought. In this respect, at least, the high status of the *Sophist*
among proponents of linguistic analysis is completely justified; for
Plato did just what the method of linguistic analysis promises to
do: by means of the analysis of the concept of not-being he made a
philosophical problem disappear. The liberating effect of this bit of
philosophical therapy on later thought (in particular on the thought
of Aristotle) can scarcely be overestimated.

Secondly, Plato in this passage asserts for the first time that
Forms participate in one another. From the early dialogues on,
Plato had maintained that the Forms stood in various relations to
one another, such as contrariety and inclusion (cf. above, p. 44); he
had seen the realm of Forms as a systematic whole and not as a
collection of unrelated objects. He had also maintained that Forms
possessed certain properties, such as being, unity, intelligibility,
eternality, immobility, etc.; but he had offered up to this point no
explanation of what it meant for a Form to possess a property. He
had, of course, explained the possession of property by a
phenomenon in terms of that phenomenon's participation in a
Form (cf. *Phdo.* 110c); but participation had been, until the
*Sophist*, a relation that held between Forms and phenomena only,
not among Forms themselves.

In the *Sophist*, Plato states that Forms as well as phenomena
may participate in one another. This enables him to give the same
sort of explanation of the possession of properties by Forms that he
had earlier given of the possession of properties by phenomena,
and thus to extend again the explanatory power of the Theory of
Forms. As with any theoretical advance, however, this extension of
the Theory of Forms raises new questions, none of which Plato
definitively answers.

In the first place, it seems reasonable to assume that the relation
of participation that Plato posits among Forms is the same relation
that he had earlier posited between Forms and phenomena. This is
reasonable in the light of two facts: the first that, as we have seen,
he uses the same terms for both relations (cf. p. 152): and the

second that both relations serve the primary purpose of explaining the attribution of properties to things. If it is true, however, that the relation is the same in both cases, this has consequences for our understanding of participation. The nature of participation was one of the major unresolved problems of the middle dialogues, and a problem on which the critique of the *Parmenides* focused. Plato had, in the *Timaeus*, offered no analysis of this crucial notion but had remarked on the difficulty of expressing the relation between Forms and phenomena (cf. above, p. 108). Although Plato had offered no definitive analysis of participation, however, he had repeatedly used the relation of imaging that holds between an original and its copy to illuminate the concept — and this in the *Timaeus* no less than in the middle dialogues, despite the fact that imaging, as an analysis of participation, had been criticised in the *Parmenides* in the second version of the Third Man Argument.

Imaging, or the original-copy relation, has therefore been up to this point a prime candidate for the analysis of participation. If participation holds among Forms, however, this analysis is no longer tenable. Imaging is, as Plato uses it, essentially a relation between entities of different ontological types; therefore Forms, being of a single type, cannot be said to be images of one another. The metaphysical baggage carried by the relation of imaging is simply out of place in the description of the participation of the Form of Being in the Form of Sameness; we must therefore seek some other interpretation of this relation, one sufficiently general to include both the relation among Forms and that between Forms and phenomena.

Regrettably, no such interpretation is forthcoming in Plato. Indeed, he does not seem to be aware of this consequence of the extension of the relation of participation to include relations among Forms. The suspicion arises that no explication of participation is possible in terms of Platonic metaphysics. Perhaps participation is, and ought to be regarded as, a primitive concept; perhaps participation is simply the relation that grounds predication and has no more intuitive content than does the notion of predication itself. We shall see in the next section that Plato continues in the *Sophist* to regard the relation of original to image as a useful explication of the relation between entities of different ontological types; but he does not put forth this relation as an analysis of participation. (Strictly speaking, of course, the only place where the original-image relation was suggested as an analysis of participation was the *Parmenides*; Plato is more cautious elsewhere, including the *Timaeus*.)

There is a second problem raised, at least indirectly, by the extension of participation to the realm of the Forms. This is the problem of self-predication. I have argued in earlier chapters that Plato was never committed to self-predication as a general principle; none the less, there have always been Forms that seemed to be straightforwardly self-predicative: Beauty was beautiful, Unity single, etc. This passage of the *Sophist* confirms this fact, in affirming that Being is (257a), that everything (including, presumably Sameness) is the same as itself (256a), and that everything other than Being (including, presumably, Difference) is different from Being (256d−e). In the case of Sameness, Plato seems to affirm not merely self-predication but self-participation,[29] for he says that 'everything participates in Sameness' (256a7−8).

If the Forms are, at least in some cases, self-predicative and perhaps even self-participative, how are we to avoid the regress of the Third Man in these cases? As I noted in discussing the Third Man (above, p. 66), the argument depends on two suppressed premisses, self-predication and non-identity. I argued in Chapter 3 that Plato rejected self-predication for Forms of phenomenal properties, where self-predication would produce an absurd and incoherent theory (pp. 115 ff.); however, no such absurdity results from assuming that Forms possess the properties of which they are Forms, when those properties are not restricted to phenomenal instantiations (as are, e.g., red and large), but may also be possessed by non-phenomenal, non-spatial, abstract objects (cf. pp. 122−3 above). Such properties are being, sameness and difference; thus, they may be meaningfully predicated of their respective Forms, provided the Third Man can be avoided.

As Plato accepts the self-predication assumption for these Forms, it seems he can only avoid the Third Man by rejecting the non-identity assumption. As I have noted, these premisses are not explicit in the Third Man Argument, and Plato may well not have been aware of them as such. None the less, just as there are indications in the *Timaeus* that Plato rejects self-predication for most properties, there is some indication in the *Sophist* that he rejects non-identity for those Forms for which he accepts self-predication. The indication is little more than a hint, and its exact meaning is unclear, but it is important none the less.

The reader will recall that Plato in 256d−e establishes that all the

Forms other than Being 'are not' in that they are different from Being, and 'are' in that they participate in Being. Obviously, the same account will not work for Being itself, since it is not different from itself and cannot 'not-be' in the sense that other Forms can. Thus, the Form of Being must be said not to be in some other way; and the Stranger accordingly remarks that it 'is not' by virtue of being different from (participating in Difference with respect to) all the other things, whereas it 'is' in that 'it is . . . itself one' (*hen . . . auto estin*, 257a5).

As I mentioned, the exact meaning of this phrase is not clear. From the fact that the word 'one' occurs in it, it could be assumed that the being of Being was grounded in its unity, its participation, that is, in the Form of Unity. Although a Neoplatonist might find this interpretation attractive, as it would ground even Being in the One, it seems unlikely to me that this is Plato's point. Rather, it seems that Plato is emphasising the fact that, whereas Being is said *not* to be in relation to the 'indefinite number of other things' (257a6), it is said to be in relation to just one thing, namely itself (cf. Cornford's translation: 'it *is* its single self'). If this is correct, Plato is saying that the source of the being of Being is just Being itself; and this claim contradicts the non-identity assumption, which asserts that, if something has a characteristic (e.g. being), it must derive that characteristic from something other than itself. Whether Plato regards the statement above as meaning that the Form of Being participates in itself or as meaning that the Form is identical to itself, it is clear that he regards the Form of Being itself as the ultimate ground for the self-predicative statement, 'Being is'.

I have argued that the constructive section of the *Sophist*, the account of being and not-being, represents not an abandonment or radical modification of Platonic metaphysics, but the employment of that metaphysics in a new area. I have argued that the metaphysical apparatus of the Forms and participation is essentially changed from the middle dialogues, and that the genuine advances made in this passage occur because Plato uses this apparatus to solve an important metaphysical problem (the problem of not-being) and to explain an important feature of his own metaphysical view (the possession of properties by Forms). These advances make the interpretation of participation in terms of imaging impossible and raise anew the problem of self-predication and the Third Man; but these developments do not cause Plato to alter the view that Form are eternal objects of knowledge which undergo no change, a

view he has always held. We have not yet determined the effect of
these advances on the view that the Forms are paradigms, however;
and this was an important part of Plato's concept of Form in the
middle dialogues and the *Timaeus*. This is the question we must
consider in the next section.

### III. Paradeigmatism in the *Sophist*

As we have seen (cf. Ch. 1, Sec. III; Ch. 3, Sec. III), Plato treats
the Forms in the early and middle dialogues and in the *Timaeus* as
paradigms, as intelligible standards which are imitated by their
phenomenal participants. This interpretation of the Forms is
criticised in the *Parmenides* (cf. pp. 71–5); and Owen, who found
this criticism a sound objection to the view that Forms are paradigms, used this fact to support his claim that the *Timaeus* was
written before the *Parmenides*.[30] The criticism of the *Parmenides*,
the second version of the Third Man Argument, relies on the
implicit claim that the Forms are self-predicative and the explicit
one that Forms and the phenomena that resemble them share a
property. As I have attempted, in my discussions of the paradigmatic role of the Forms, to separate the claim that the Forms are
paradigms from the matter of self-predication and to refute the
contention that Plato regards resemblance in terms of sharing a
property, I reject the claim that the Third Man shows paradeigmatism to be untenable. There is no reason to think that Plato
abandoned the view that the Forms are paradigms (by which I
understand him to mean 'patterns' of an abstract sort rather than
perfect instances or 'exemplars' of the properties of which they are
Forms) after the *Parmenides*, or to think that the *Timaeus*, where
paradeigmatism is prominent, is a middle dialogue.

If my argument is sound, we should expect to find Plato treating
the Forms as paradigms in the other late dialogues; but he does not
do so. As I note in the Appendix, the *Seventh Letter*, which must
date from this period, speaks of the relation of original to image,
which is part and parcel of the view that the Forms are paradigms,
in much the same manner as do the middle dialogues and the
*Timaeus*; but the late dialogues themselves (other than the
*Timaeus*) do not exploit this conception of the Forms.[31]

It would be wrong to infer from the absence of evidence on this
point that Plato at some date in his career abandoned paradeig-

matism; we should require stronger evidence than silence for this claim. There is, moreover, some indirect evidence in the *Sophist* that the metaphysics of original and image, which is central to paradeigmatism, is still intact. For Plato relies heavily on the relation between original and image in defining the sophist.

The seventh definition of the sophist (232a–236c; 264c–268d) describes him as an illusionist (cf. *thaumatopoiōn*, 235b5, and *thaumatopoiois*, *Rep.* VII, 514b5) and image-maker. Images are divided into two classes: likenesses (*eikones*), which accurately reproduce the dimension of the model (*paradeigma*), and appearances (*phantasmata*), which do not (235d–236c). The art of appearance-making (*phantastikē*) is characterised by a general disregard for the truth, in the interest of opinion (236a). This characterisation of appearance-making leads to the problem of falsity and not-being, which occasions the long digression in the middle of the dialogue. When the process of defining the sophist by division is resumed at 264c, the Stranger divides all art into two categories: acquisitive and productive (265a). Productive art is divided into two sorts: divine and human (265b). Both sorts of art produce both originals and images (265e–266a). The originals of divine production include animals, plants, and inanimate bodies; the images, dreams, shadows and reflections (266b–c; cf. 265c). Human production makes such originals as houses and such images as paintings (266c).

In all of this discussion we have the familiar language of original and image, paradigm and likeness. Yet these terms are used, not to explicate the Theory of Forms, or to distinguish the Forms from phenomena, but to distinguish two sorts of thing within the phenomenal world. Things treated as images in the *Timaeus* (animals and plants) are here treated as originals, and Plato is willing to talk about the reality or truth of such things (cf. 236a). One might suspect that this change in the use of these concepts marked a change in Plato's metaphysics; but in fact it does not. The points made here have been made earlier, in the *Republic* (cf. pp. 41–2 above). In the account of the Divided Line (*Rep.* VI, 509d–511e), he states that the lowest division of the line contains images (*eikones*, 509e1) and that these include shadows and reflections. The second section contains 'that of which [the thing in the first class] is a likeness' (510a5) — the whole class of animals, plants and human artefacts. These two sections are both in the lower half of the Line, which represents the visible world (509d8).

The upper portion of the Line, representing the intelligible, is divided into Forms grasped by means of images (third section) and Forms grasped without the aid of images (fourth and highest section). In the third section, the investigator makes use of the originals of the second section, but treats them as images of still higher originals (Forms):

> And in all cases it is thus: these things themselves, which they sculpt and draw, of which there are shadows and images in the water, these they use in turn as images, seeking to see those things which one cannot see otherwise than with the understanding. (510e1−511a1; cf. 510b4−5)

Thus, Forms stand to phenomena in the same relation as phenomena to their shadows, reflections, etc.: as originals to images. As the epistemological corollary of this scheme is the principle, 'as the opinable to the knowable, so the likeness to that of which is a likeness' (510a9−10), it follows that phenomenal originals stand *relative to their images* as objects of knowledge to objects of opinion. In other words, phenomena can be spoken of as 'known' within the context of the lower half of the Line. One and the same distinction thus serves both to divide the sensible world from the intelligible and to make two subdivisions in the sensible world.

Thus, the account of image-making and the definition of the sophist are in full harmony with the metaphysics of the *Republic*, and indeed contain verbal echoes of that dialogue. As noted above, Plato uses the term *thaumatopoios*, 'illusionist', both in *Soph.* 235b to define the sophist and in *Rep.* VII, 514b (the Allegory of the Cave) to denote the people who carry the images projected on the wall of the cave for viewing by the prisoners. It is not far-fetched to assume that these 'illusionists' of the *Republic* allegory are precisely the sophists of this dialogue and their companions the demagogic politicians for whom Plato had so much contempt: for he certainly regarded the occupation of both as the delusion of the public.

Plato in defining the sophist confines his account to the lower half of the Line because it is in the lowest division of the Line that he wishes to locate the sophist. Thus, there is no occasion in this account for the relation between Forms and phenomena to arise. Likewise, when he discusses dialectic in the treatment of being and not-being, he confines himself entirely to the upper half of the

Line, for his concern there is to exhibit some of the relations that
hold among Forms. Again, there is no occasion for a discussion of
the relation between Forms and phenomena. In terms of the
Divided Line, the sophist and the philosopher are placed at
opposite extremes; the sophist, in the lowest section, is concerned
totally with illusion, whereas the philosopher, in the highest
section, is concerned solely with the ultimate reality, the Forms.
This is just what we should expect, given the account of the relation
between the sophist and philosopher quoted earlier (p. 142). Thus,
it is hardly surprising that the paradigmatic role of the Forms is not
mentioned in the *Sophist*. The absence of this doctrine does not
reflect the abandonment of the doctrine, but its irrelevance to the
discussion of the dialogue.

It could be argued that Plato's use of the original-image relation
shows that he did not accept the second version of the Third Man as
a valid objection to the Theory of Forms. For, as Cherniss has
pointed out, 'that argument . . . is in fact much more than a refutation of the doctrine of paradeigmatic ideas. If it were valid, it
would be a general proof that nothing can be a likeness or image of
anything whatever . . .'[32] That is, any purported case of
resemblance, whether it involves Forms or not, generates an
infinite series of objects in resemblance relations, according to the
argument. If Plato recognised that the argument applied to more
than the Forms, his use of the original-image relation in the *Sophist*
would show that he did not accept its critique of that relation as a
valid one. In any case, the evidence of the *Sophist* shows that Plato
did not give up the view that at least some objects are related to
each other as originals and images; that he retained, in other words,
at least some part of the metaphysics of paradeigmatism found in
the *Republic*.

## IV. The *Timaeus* and the *Sophist*; the Development of Plato's Metaphysics

I noted at the outset of this chapter that it was easier to group the
*Timaeus* and *Sophist* together as members of a late group of
dialogues than to determine their position relative to one another.
This seems to me to be no less the case when the doctrines of the
two dialogues are compared than when the stylistic evidence is considered. Both dialogues contain doctrinal advances from the middle

dialogues, and both seem to be in some sense responses to the *Parmenides*. I argued in Chapter 3 that the introduction of the Demiurge and the Receptacle in the *Timaeus* were responses to the critique of the Theory of Forms in the *Parmenides*. The *Sophist* does not respond directly to that critique, but the doctrine of the blending of the Forms seems to contradict the claim of Socrates in that dialogue that opposite Forms could not be predicted of each other (cf. Ch. 2, Sec. I).

One of the arguments that the *Timaeus* was a middle dialogue was based on the claim that its metaphysics resembled the metaphysics of the middle dialogues. I have argued that, though the metaphysics of the *Timaeus* goes beyond anything in the middle dialogues, there is a fundamental continuity between the two in several key doctrines. In this chapter I have attempted to show that the same is true of the *Sophist*. The advances of the *Sophist* have seemed to some to be so revolutionary that the dialogue must be late; but I have argued that this view is in fact a misreading of the dialogue based on a rather parochial conception of the nature of philosophy. We ought to be extremely sceptical of any attempt to order the dialogues on the basis of the 'modernity' or sophistication of their doctrines, remembering both the variety of orders of the dialogues that existed before the advent of stylometry (see the Appendix, Sec. II) and the fact that, whereas this generation of Plato scholars has anointed the *Sophist* Plato's deepest and most mature metaphysical treatise, both the ancient interpreters and the generation of scholars that immediately preceded the current one reached the same conclusion about the *Timaeus*. Just as the *Sophist* has seemed to many contemporary Plato scholars to be an anticipation of the work of Wittgenstein and Austin, or perhaps of Frege and Russell, the *Timaeus* seemed to some scholars and philosophers of a half century ago to be an anticipation of process philosophy; before which, of course, it was hailed as an anticipation of German Idealism, and so on back to Neoplatonism.[33]

I have adopted the view that the *Timaeus* is chronologically the earlier of the two dialogues. The evidence I based this on was stylistic, not doctrinal. The *Sophist* does seem to go beyond the *Timaeus* in its modification of the Being-Becoming doctrine; but, as I have argued, this modification is verbal rather than substantive, and Plato reverts to the familiar Being-Becoming dichotomy in other late dialogues, including the *Statesman*, which is the successor to the *Sophist*. Thus. there seems little basis here for assigning temporal priority to one dialogue or the other.

There is no hint in the *Timaeus* of the revolutionary account of being and not-being given in the *Sophist*; but there is an apparent allusion to the blending of Forms at *Tim*. 35a. There is no reference in the *Sophist* to the Receptacle, despite the fact that this entity is surely relevant to the discussion of the problems related to being and not-being; but there is a reference to the Demiurge at *Soph*. 265b–c. Any attempt to order the two dialogues on the basis of such clues quickly runs afoul of the fact — noted by Owen in his discussion of Cornford's attempt to establish the priority of the *Sophist* to the *Timaeus* — that 'such arguments for dating can cut both ways'.[34]

I believe that the uncertainty concerning the relative order of the *Sophist* and *Timaeus* stems from a fact too often overlooked by scholars who, like myself, are concerned to plot the course of Plato's development. The fact I have in mind is this: it is possible to find divergences and inconsistencies in doctrine between any two Platonic dialogues, however close they may be to each other in date of composition. It is even possible to find doctrinal inconsistencies within a single dialogue. The attempt to eliminate these inconsistencies by placing the dialogues in a strict chronological order is doomed to failure, because, for any order imaginable, a doctrine transcended or surpassed by another is sure to recur in a dialogue that must, for one reason or another, postdate its alleged transcendence. This fact by itself shows the futility of attempting to order the dialogues on the basis of doctrinal development and in particular to separate the metaphysical dialogues from the 'critical' dialogues by removing the *Timaeus* from the late group.

The fact is that the development of Plato's thought is not a neat, one-dimensional progression from one position to another. There are reasons for this, I think, but they certainly do not include the reason that Plato was too dense to appreciate the inconsistencies or difficulties in his various doctrines. One reason seems to be that his metaphysics was rooted in a great number of independent interests. Plato wanted to establish a theory of knowledge, a theory that explained the generation and nature of the cosmos, an aesthetic theory, a theory of political and ethical value, a theory of the soul, and a philosophy that exhibited the rationality and divinity of the world-order. The Theory of Forms was remarkably suited for all these purposes, and its development was doubtless what enabled Plato to solve the problems involved in all of the theories mentioned above in such a systematic way. None the less, conflicts were probably inevitable in the development of this theory, because the very features of the Forms that made them well suited to be, for instance, objects of knowledge, made them ill-suited for other purposes (e.g. the explanation of the composition of phenomena). These conflicts could only be recognised in the course of delineation of the various roles of the Forms and could only be alleviated once recognised.

As Plato's metaphysics was a response to numerous independent and occasionally conflicting aims, so it was a response to specific problems that arose in particular dialogues. We view Plato as a systematic philosopher and it is undeniable that, in some sense, he was. There are certain strains of thought that characterise Plato's work in every period: belief in the Forms, acceptance of some distinction between Forms and their participants, belief in the existence of the soul, the care of which is supposed to be a (if not the) primary purpose of human existence, belief in the objectivity of value and belief in the rationality of the universe. None the less, Plato was also (and perhaps more importantly) committed to dialectic, to philosophical argument. Plato wrote dialogues — that is, records of real or invented philosophical conversations. These dialogues each focus on a specific problem; and, though the constants in Plato's thought limit the scope of the discussion and often provide the solution to the problem, that solution is always worked out in the context of the problem and the interlocutors. Some writers have carried the recognition of this point too far and have denied that there is any distinctively Platonic philosophy, seeing in each dialogue a philosophical drama that is complete and self-contained. To see only this aspect of Plato's thought is to miss the very real systematic interconnections which pervade all the dialogues, connections I have tried to make plain in this work. To see only the systematic elements in the dialogue is, however, to make a mistake equally grave: it is to forget that the doctrines of the dialogues are always developed in the context of a dialectical confrontation between different individuals over a specific problem. If Plato is a systematic philosopher, he is not a philosopher who develops a system for its own sake. His system is a response to genuine philosophical problems, and those problems determine to a great extent the way in which Plato's response to them is worked out, just as the systematic aspects of his thought determine which problems he will take to be real and how he will solve them.

This reciprocal relation between Plato's systematic and his dialectical concerns doubtless explains many of the minor inconsistencies or differences of emphasis that occur in the dialogues of every period. When Plato brings in the Theory of Forms to explain the creation of the cosmos, he is likely to let the nature of the problem he is dealing with dictate the way in which the theory will be developed in response to that problem, and which aspects of it are to be emphasised. When his concern is negation and the problem of not-being, he is apt to develop the same doctrine in different ways, emphasising different aspects of it and thereby creating for the interpreter the problem of unifying these aspects into a single view. It is this fact about the way in which Plato wrote, and not some temporal development in his thinking, that makes the *Timaeus* and *Sophist* appear in some respects quite different from one another.

I have here emphasised the problem-oriented aspect of Plato's thought because this feature of it is often ignored by Plato scholars, and because it serves as a valuable antidote to the desire to over-systematise Plato's thought. I do not believe that this aspect of his thought conflicts with the claims that there is considerable continuity in Plato's thought, and at the same time considerable development. It has been my purpose in the body of this book to emphasise the latter two points, against the largely implicit foil of those who would deny any continuity or any development. I do not claim to have refuted those two extreme views; nor do I think a conclusive refutation of them is possible. I do claim to have provided a more plausible alternative than either, however; and I hope that the reader, even if he has been unable to agree with all the details of my account, will concur with its general outlines.

## Notes

1. Brandwood (1958), pp. 399–402; (1976), pp. xvi–xviii.
2. The remark of Owen (1971, p. 223), 'Platonists who doubt that they are Spectators of Being must settle for the knowledge that they are investigators of the verb "to be",' suggests that Plato saw some difference between metaphysics or ontology and philosophy of language and in the *Sophist* opted for the latter enterprise rather than the former. One of the claims I shall be concerned to deny in this chapter is the claim that Plato's philosophy of language in the *Sophist* is divorced from his ontology.

There is no doubt, I think, that Owen is what I have called a 'radical revisionist' (see the Introduction) in the sense that he regards the metaphysics of the late dialogues as importantly different from that of the middle in at least two respects: the Forms in the late dialogues are no longer paradigms, and the Being-Becoming distinction is abandoned by Plato (see Owen (1953), pp. 321–2, 338). I have the impression from his written works that he was sympathetic to the view that Plato's very conception of philosophy changed in the later dialogues: that linguistic or conceptual analysis replaced metaphysics as the central task of philosophy. On the one occasion when I was able to discuss Owen's views with him in person, however, he responded to my charge that his view of Plato's development 'multiplied Platos beyond necessity' by stating that 'there was but one Plato, and he was a metaphysician'. This statement seems to me to be as much at odds with the views he stated in Owen (1953) as with the more radical view that Plato's very conception of philosophy changed in the late dialogues; indeed, it seems to be an appropriate motto for unitarians. Owen's view on Plato development, beyond the claims in his written work, remains therefore somewhat of a mystery to me; but I hope I do not overstate the case when I say that either of the 'radical revisionist' alternatives stated above could with some plausibility be attributed to him, based on his writings.

3. It is generally thought that Plato chooses an Eleatic philosopher as his spokesman to acknowledge his debt to Parmenides. This seems reasonable, provided we note that Plato's metaphysics is at most a refined and sophisticated descendant of Parmenides', and owes more to Socrates' influence than Parmenides'.

4. For a discussion of the alternatives that have been proposed, cf. Ross, pp. 105–7, and Guthrie (1978), pp. 141–2, n. 3.

5. Cf. Guthrie (1978), pp. 139–40. Guthrie discusses the view that the criterion of Being might be Plato's own and rejects it for reasons similar to mine.

6. This view of Zeller and de Vogel is discussed and criticised by Cherniss (1944), pp. 452–3, n. 397; by Ross, p. 110; and by Seligman, pp. 39–40.

7. Vlastos (1970), p. 277.

8. Ibid., pp. 309–17.

9. Cf. e.g. Cherniss (1957), p. 352, and Guthrie (1978), pp. 144–5.

10. Kahn, pp. 254–7.

11. Owen (1953), pp. 322–5.

12. Brandwood (1976), p. xvii.

13. Vlastos (1954), p. 247, n. 4. Cf. Ch. 1, n. 30.

14. Vlastos (1965a), p. 47.

15. Actually, no such consequence follows, for although Being might be neither in motion nor at rest by virtue of its own nature — i.e. *qua* Being — it must be at rest *qua* Form. Plato does not develop the distinction necessary to escape the dilemma, however, and one can only speculate as to whether his bewilderment here is genuine or whether he is merely attempting to heighten the sense of paradox inherent in the problem of being.

16. Scholars have assumed that Plato is referring to Antisthenes, but the objection of Cornford (1953), p. 254, that 'we know so little of Antisthenes that the reference cannot be taken as certain', is well taken. Apparently the view is in any case fairly widespread, since it is attributed to both young and old.

17. Crombie, p. 251, says that Plato thought that 'is' should really assert the identity of subject and predicate. The idea that Plato held such an identity model of predication is not only without textual basis, but is strongly contradicted by this passage, in which Plato pours contempt on those who adhere to this point of view. As my analysis of the subsequent passage will indicate, I believe it would be more accurate to say that Plato holds a predicative model of identity.

18. Cf. Vlastos (1970).

19. Plato here, as he did in the *Parmenides* (cf. above, p. 57), uses the word *genos*, 'kind', interchangeably with *eidos* and *idea* to denote Forms. This interchangeable use shows that Plato did not, as some scholars have thought, have

something different from Forms in mind when he speaks of 'kinds'. (For references to this view, see n. 26 below.)

20. The details of the argument do not concern us, except for one point. At 255c12–d7 the Stranger distinguishes Being from Difference on the grounds that some things are said to be 'in themselves' (*auta kath' hauta*, c12–13), whereas other things are said to be 'relative to other things' (*pros alla*, c13). He does not specify — and it is impossible to determine from the text — what things are said to be in themselves and what things relative to something else, but the distinction seems to parallel the distinction between self-existent Forms and dependent phenomena made at *Tim.* 51e–52d. If so, this would be a doctrinal link between the two dialogues.

21. Many scholars think that this passage is a recantation of the earlier claim that Motion and Rest are incompatible, but Vlastos (1970), pp. 283–94, has shown that this is not the case.

22. For the alternatives, cf. Cornford (1935), p. 296; Ackrill, p. 222; Owen (1971), pp. 223–5; Frede, pp. 29–37; and Vlastos (1970), pp. 288–9, n. 44, and 295, n. 54.

23. Of course this analysis has a weakness, for there is no way to say that something does not exist, or does not participate in a Form, rather than that it is in some way different from that Form. Plato's failure to notice this problem, despite the difficulty he has in expressing the claim that Motion and Rest are incompatible (255e11–14, 256b6–7), is further evidence that he did not recognise different senses of 'is' or different sentence-frames for existential, predicative and identity statements; if he had recognised these differences in affirmative statements, he could hardly have failed to make similar distinctions among negative ones.

24. Even Owen, who denies that Plato sets off an existential sense of 'is' from other senses, admits this; cf. (1971), p. 248.

25. Ackrill, pp. 212–13, assumed that the 'is' in 'motion is' (256a1) meant 'participates in being', and thus was existential; and that the 'is' of 'Motion is not the same' (256a10) must mean the identity sign. These assumptions ignore the following facts: (a) that 'Motion is' is elliptical for 'Motion is real' (256d8–9); (b) that both statements use *metechei*, 'participates in', in their analyses, presumably with the same meaning it has in predicative statements; (c) that the 'not' in 256a10 is correlated with the Form of Difference (cf. 257b9–c3), and that Form is the predicative complement of *metechei*. In the light of these facts it seems preferable to regard the 'is' of each statement as correlated with *metechei*, rather than to assign it different senses in the different cases.

26. E.g. Ketchum and Teloh (cf. Teloh, pp. 11–12 and 172).

27. Ackrill, pp. 219–21, has refuted Cornford's contention that these terms denote not participation, but a different, symmetrical relation.

28. As Ackrill notes (p. 211–12), the *dia* does not introduce what we would call a causal explanation, but an analysis of their meaning (what Aristotle might call a statement of their 'formal cause').

29. For a discussion of the difficulties involved in the various resolutions of this issue, cf. Vlastos (1969).

30. Owen (1953), pp. 318–22.

31. It was once commonly thought that a passage in the *Statesman* (285d–286a) contained a clear reference to the view that Forms are paradigms. Owen (1973) has cast doubt on this contention, and despite Guthrie's response (1978, pp. 177–80) I am inclined to regard the reference as uncertain.

32. Cherniss (1957), p. 374.

33. Cf. Allen (1965), p. xii.

34. Owen (1953), p. 327.

## APPENDIX: THE DOCTRINAL MATURITY AND CHRONOLOGICAL POSITION OF THE *TIMAEUS*

The aim of any treatment of Plato's thought in terms of its development must be to distinguish the mature formulations of that thought from chronologically earlier versions — to separate the oak from the acorn, so to speak. It is to be expected that Plato's most mature and developed thought should be found in his latest writings; therefore, any discussion of Plato's development must be based on a determination, however provisional, of the chronological order of the dialogues.

Since the advent of stylometry, there has been widespread agreement among scholars concerning the relative chronological placement of most of the dialogues. For instance, all the parties to the dispute over the nature of Plato's development would agree that the *Euthyphro* is an early dialogue; that the *Phaedo* and *Republic* are dialogues dating to Plato's middle period, and that the *Phaedo* is the earlier of the two; that the *Parmenides* post-dates the *Republic*, and that the *Sophist* is among Plato's latest works. This agreement, it should be noted, is the result of the stylometric investigations; before stylometry, almost all scholars would have placed the *Republic* after the *Sophist*.[1]

It is the *Timaeus* about which disagreement exists. The traditional view, confirmed by stylometric studies, is that the *Timaeus* is a late dialogue. Owen, as I noted in the Introduction, challenged this assumption in 1953, in the cause of radical revisionism. In his attempt to prove that the *Timaeus* was in fact a middle period dialogue, he challenged the consensus of scholars on two points: the maturity of the metaphysics of the *Timaeus* and the stylometric evidence for its lateness. (There were, as I also noted in the Introduction, other facets to Owen's argument, which I am not concerned with here.)

The account I have offered of Plato's development is based on the assumption that the *Timaeus* was written after the *Parmenides*, rather than before it, as Owen claims. I hope that the plausibility of the account itself lends some weight to this contention; however, my ordering of the dialogues is based in part on the claim that the external evidence supports the conclusion of tradition and stylometry, rather than Owen. In this Appendix I offer some of that evidence in favour of the late placement of the *Timaeus*. The evidence I consider is of two sorts. The first comes from the ancient interpretive tradition, which has much to say about the *Timaeus* in particular and the character of Plato's mature thought in general. This evidence I hope will show that the metaphysics of the *Timaeus* is representative of what the ancients regarded as Plato's mature views. The second sort of evidence is that of stylometry itself. This evidence shows that the *Timaeus* is chronologically late, that it is in fact among the last six dialogues Plato wrote. I defend the validity of this evidence against the criticisms of Owen and argue that the stylometric evidence, when combined with the evidence of the ancient interpretive tradition, gives great weight to the traditional placement of the *Timaeus* among the late dialogues.

## I. The Ancient Interpretive Tradition

There exists an extensive interpretive tradition for the *Timaeus*; in fact, the *Timaeus* was the work of ancient philosophy most studied and commented on in the ancient world itself. In addition to studies specifically devoted to the *Timaeus*, there is considerable testimony concerning Plato's mature metaphysical views. All of this evidence supports the claims that the *Timaeus* is a work of Plato's maturity and that it expounds metaphysical doctrines Plato did not subsequently abandon.

In assessing the evidentiary weight of the interpretive tradition, we should bear several points in mind. First, the evidence is of unequal value. That which springs from the Academy during Plato's lifetime, or which comes from writers whom we may assume had first-hand knowledge of Plato's views, is incomparably superior to which is later and based on second-hand testimony. Secondly, the evidence which post-dates the period in which all of Plato's works were available for study, in particular the evidence of the early Middle Ages in Europe, is of virtually no weight. The *Timaeus* was the only dialogue studied seriously in the early Middle Ages because it was virtually the only one preserved in that period, for reasons of historical accident and its resemblance to Christian doctrine. Thus, we can ascribe no importance to the fact that medieval Christian thinkers relied on it for their understanding of Platonism. Thirdly, we must distinguish the interpretations of the content of the dialogue which arose in the ancient world from the way in which the dialogue was regarded by all its interpreters. There was wide disagreement among the ancients, as there is today, as to what Plato meant in the *Timaeus*, and many of the claims of the ancient interpreters would strike a modern reader as fanciful and as having little to do with what the text states. There was unanimity, on the other hand, on the question of the dialogue's importance and seriousness as philosophical world and on the question of its centrality for the interpretation of Plato. We can accept their unanimous verdict on the latter matters without accepting their contradictory claims on the former.

In light of the points mentioned above, I shall consider the ancient testimony that pertains to the *Timaeus* and to Plato's metaphysics under three headings. First, I shall discuss the *Seventh Letter*; secondly, the testimony of Aristotle; and thirdly, the post-Aristotelian interpreters of Plato. None of this testimony bears directly on the narrow chronological question, on the relative place on the *Timaeus* in the order of Plato's dialogues; it bears rather on the related questions of the doctrinal maturity of the dialogue, the nature of Plato's mature metaphysical views and the existence or non-existence of a radical change in those views.

## *The* Seventh Letter

The first testimony we must consider is that of the *Seventh Platonic Letter*. I include this among the external sources of evidence about Plato's philosophy because there is some doubt as to its authorship. It may have been written by Plato himself, in which case its testimony would be of even greater weight than I allow. Even if it did not come directly from Plato's own hand, however, its aim of defending Plato's actions in Syracuse and its detailed account of Plato's acts and motives indicate that it was composed in the Academy by a writer who was both interested in defending Plato and capable of doing so on the basis of a close familiarity with his life and thought, The *Letter* cannot be earlier than 354 BC, since it must have been written after Dion's death in that year; thus it must date to the last seven years of Plato's life. (Even if Plato did not write the letter himself, it is most unlikely that it was composed after his death in 347, since the need for a defence of Plato's actions would have diminished greatly as the time from Dion's death increased.)[2]

The author of the *Letter* criticises Dionysius the younger for having presumed to write a book on the principles of reality. The opinions in the book, he states, were those of Dionysius, not of Plato (341b); Plato would not commit his own thoughts on these matters to writing, for they cannot be given verbal expression as can other subjects. Knowledge of such things can only be imparted by a kind of illumination of the pupil's mind, which is the result of long association with the teacher (341c–d).

There are three things necessary for the knowledge of any real being, says the author: the name of the thing, the definition and the image (*eidōlon*, 342b2). All of these, and the knowledge they produce on occasion, are distinct from the thing itself (342c–d). As an example of these distinctions he uses the circle. The image of the circle is 'what we draw or rub out, what is turned and destroyed; of which the Circle itself, to which all these refer, suffers nothing, since it is different' (342c1–4).

The point of these distinctions is that names, definitions and images are all potentially misleading representations of the thing itself; thus, no one who was aware of the thing itself would attempt to communicate it to another by means of these alone. Since one who writes a book is attempting to do just that, it is clear from the very fact that he does so that he does not understand the nature of reality (342e–344d).

Although not every point in this passage has a parallel in the dialogues, the following seems clear. The author is drawing a contrast between real being and its various representations, both linguistic and phenomenal. The thing itself is both real and knowable (*ho dē gnōston te kai alēthōs estin on*, 342b1) — a remark which echoes *Rep.* V, 477a3. In addition to the circle, the author mentions straight and spherical shapes, colours, goodness, beauty, justice, manufactured and natural substances, living beings, dispositions of the soul, actions and passions as being in the same condition (342d); for each of them there is an object itself and a variety of representations. Now this list contains the sorts of things for which Plato postulates Forms in the dialogues; this, and the attribution to these objects of truth or reality and intelligibility, should convince us that the 'real beings' the author refers to are Platonic Forms.

When the author gives the circle that is drawn and rubbed out as an example of an image of genuine reality, he is following the doctrine of the *Republic* (VI, 510b–e), where the square that geometers draw is said to be an image of the Square itself (cf. also

*Phaedo* 74a−75b, *Timaeus* 28c−29b, 30c−d). When he says that such an image, which is itself a sensible object, is necessary for the apprehension of the object itself (342a), he is following the doctrine of recollection in the *Phaedo* (74a−b, 75a−b). Likewise, when he insists on the deceptiveness of sensory experience (343b−d), he is again echoing the *Phaedo* (65a−66a). Finally, when he contrasts the image with its original in that the image is created and destroyed, whereas the object itself is not, he is invoking one of the most basic distinctions between Being and Becoming (i.e. between Forms and phenomena) that Plato draws in the dialogues (cf. *Phdo.* 78b−80b and *Tim.* 27d−28a).

In summary, we find in this passage of the *Seventh Letter* a contrast between Platonic Forms and phenomena which corresponds to the contrast between Being and Becoming, as it is presented in the middle dialogues and the *Timaeus*. We also find the claim that phenomena are images of Forms, which again is a feature of the middle dialogues and the *Timaeus*. These are precisely the doctrines which Owen thinks must relegate the *Timaeus* to Plato's middle period. Yet, as noted above, the *Letter* could not have been written until well into the latest period of Plato's life. If the *Letter* was written by Plato, it provides clear and incontrovertible proof that he adhered to the doctrines mentioned above quite late in life. Indeed, since Plato would be writing in the *Letter*, as he does not in the dialogues, in his own person, we could well consider the evidentiary value of the Letter to be even greater than that of the dialogues. If, on the other hand, the *Letter* was written by someone in the Academy close to Plato, someone familiar enough with Plato's thoughts on Syracusan politics to write about them in detail (and this is the only plausible alternative to Plato's authorship of the *Letter*), it shows that such a person thought it appropriate to attribute the metaphysical doctrines mentioned above to Plato at this stage of his life. It seems hardly likely that one so well versed in Plato's political motives would get his philosophical views as wrong as — on Owen's view of Plato's development — he must have done. Thus, even on the worst plausible estimation of the *Letter*'s evidentiary value, it provides strong support for the persistence of the Being-Becoming distinction and the view that phenomena are images of Forms in Plato's old age.

### Aristotle

The testimony of Aristotle on these matters is even more direct.

Aristotle was a member of the Academy during the last 20 years of Plato's life; and, though his credibility as a reporter of Plato's thought has been repeatedly attacked,[3] it remains scarcely plausible that he was unfamiliar with the latest stage of Plato's thought. Indeed, Aristotle provides us with information about Plato's oral teaching that is unavailable elsewhere, and he certainly acquired this information directly from Plato.

When Aristotle says things about Plato that do not agree with the evidence of the dialogues, we must remember (a) that Aristotle had an unexcelled opportunity to hear anything that Plato may have said to his students but refrained from committing to writing (and the *Seventh Letter* provides ample evidence that Plato thought oral conversation a means of imparting knowledge to students superior to the written word), and (b) that Aristotle often reshapes recognisable Platonic doctrines by presenting them in terms of his own philosophical vocabulary. He rarely simply reports the thought of Plato or of any other philosopher; he diagnoses, interprets and criticises as well. Scholars differ on the value of this reportage *cum* interpretation; but whatever its value, it seems unnecessary to attribute the occasional anomalies of Aristotle's account of Plato to any vindictiveness or deceit on his part, rather than to the factors mentioned above.

Aristotle refers to the *Timaeus* more often than to any other dialogue. To a degree, this is a reflection of his own methods and interests. It was his procedure to introduce a subject by canvassing the views of his predecessors; and the physical and biological sciences were the topics on which he wrote most extensively. As the *Timaeus* was Plato's only work on these sciences, it was naturally the work Aristotle turned to in citing Plato's views. When this has been admitted, however, Aristotle's frequent references to the *Timaeus* remain significant. His discussions of the dialogue show an intimate familiarity with it that indicates long study. It is at least likely that the period in which this study took place was during Aristotle's tenure in the Academy. Whenever he studied the *Timaeus*, however, it is certain from his treatment of it that he regarded the dialogue as the source of Plato's mature views on physics, biology and cosmology.

Nearly all of Aristotle's specific references to the *Timaeus* concern scientific matters and not the metaphysical issues with which we are concerned. Aristotle's discussions of Plato's metaphysics are more general and rarely refer to or quote specific dialogues. The doctrines he attributes to Plato, however, include the doctrines of the *Timaeus*; and what he says about them has significance for our inquiry.

According to Aristotle, Plato's Forms differed from the ethical universals which Socrates sought in that they were separate from Phenomena (*Metaphysics* M. 4, 1078b–32). The reason Plato separated the Forms was that, like Socrates, he believed that Forms were the objects of definition, but that 'it was impossible for the common definition to be of any of the sensible things, for they were always changing' (*Meta.* A. 6, 987b6-7). This Heraclitean view that sensible things were in constant flux, and the consequence that there is no knowledge of them, Aristotle claims, Plato picked up as a youth by virtue of his association with the radical Heraclitean Cratylus (*Meta.* A. 6, 987a32–34).

Aristotle presents these doctrines as the motivating principles for the Theory of Forms:

> The belief concerning the Forms followed for its proponents from their being persuaded of the truth of the Heraclitean doctrines that all of the sensible things were constantly 'flowing', so that if there were knowledge and thought of anything, it would have to be of some other natures which were enduring, in contrast to the sensible things; for there is no knowledge of things in flux. (*Meta.* M. 4, 1078b12–17)

Now the claims that sensible things are constantly changing and that they are consequently unfit to be objects of knowledge are the central features of the doctrine of Being and Becoming (cf. *Phdo.* 78b-80b, *Rep.* V, 479a–e, *Tim.* 27d–28a). Aristotle not only presents them as the rationale for the Theory of Forms, however; he states that Plato accepted these claims *even later in his life* (*Meta.* A. 6, 987a34–b1). The clear sense of this remark is that Plato never abandoned the view that sensible things were in constant flux and, in consequence, unknowable; presumably he also never gave up the view that the Forms were separate from the phenomenal world, which he thought followed from those claims.

Thus, according to Aristotle, the doctrine of Being and Becoming (or at least a central portion of it) was of crucial importance to the development of the Theory of Forms and remained a part of Plato's metaphysics even in his later years. The separation of Forms from their participants was the object of much of Aristotle's criticism of the Theory of Forms (cf. *Meta.* A. 9, 991a8–20), and he clearly regarded it as a key characteristic of the theory. If Plato ever modified the theory to eliminate this separation, in light of the arguments of the *Parmenides*, Aristotle seems unaware of that fact. Aristotle also presents the Third Man Argument as an objection to at least some of the arguments for Plato's Forms (*Meta.* A. 9, 990b17) and dismisses the view that Forms are *paradeigmata*, paradigms, as 'empty words and poetic metaphors' (*Meta.* A. 9, 991a21–22).

In short, the Theory of Forms, as Aristotle discusses it, is the view that there exist objects that are separate from their participants, which are sometimes referred to as 'paradigms', and which are subject to criticism via the Third Man Argument. Now this characterisation is precisely the one that Owen believes applies to the Theory of Forms as Plato presents it in the *Timaeus* but which he believes Plato altered in his later years. Yet Aristotle states these as features of the Theory of Forms without qualification, not as features of a version of the theory Plato later recanted. Only two conclusions seem possible; either Aristotle was unaware of any such modification in the Theory as Owen suggests, or he deliberately misrepresented Plato on these matters. If, as I believe, the former conclusion is more plausible than the latter, it makes the claim that such a modification took place under Aristotle's very nose, but without his knowledge, most unlikely.

These conclusions cannot be dismissed as being the result of any indifference to chronological considerations on Aristotle's part. As we have seen, his remarks about the doctrine of Being and Becoming indicate that he was concerned with matters of chronology; furthermore, he makes a chronological distinction in the development of the Theory of Forms itself. In introducing his critique of the Theory in *Metaphysics* M. 4, he writes:

> But concerning the Forms, first the belief concerning the Form itself must be investigated, attaching nothing concerning the nature of numbers, but as those first saying that there were Forms accepted it from the beginning. (1078b9–12)

It is clear from this passage that Aristotle believed that the Forms were not at the inception of the theory associated with numbers. Now in none of the dialogues is there an explicit identification of Forms with numbers; so the fact that Aristotle attributes such an identification to a later stage of the Theory's development does not help us to order the dialogues. (If any dialogue gives credibility to Aristotle's claim that the Forms were later associated with numbers, however, it is certainly the *Timaeus*; for in that dialogue, at 52d–55c, the imposition of order on the phenomenal world is described in mathematical terms.)[4] Still, it is significant that Aristotle *does* note a distinction between the Theory of Forms as first conceived and the theory as later developed, and the distinction is *not* the one Owen postulates.

All in all, then, the picture of the Theory of Forms Aristotle presents is inconsistent with Owen's hypothesis of a radical revision of the theory following the composition of the *Parmenides*. Aristotle's testimony indicates that: (1) Plato maintained the Being-Becoming distinction in his later years; (2) he held that the Forms were separate phenomena; (3) he called the Forms 'paradigms'; (4) he had no answer to the Third Man Argument; and (5) the earlier Theory of Forms differs from the later only in that it does not, as the later does, identify Forms with numbers. The interpretation of the Theory of Forms I shall present is, in contrast with Owen's, consistent with Aristotle's testimony[5] and has the advantage that it does not require Aristotle to be either dishonest or obtuse in his representation of Plato.

## The Later Tradition

The *Seventh Letter* and Aristotle's account of Plato's metaphysics give us the strongest evidence we possess of the maturity of the doctrines of the *Timaeus*. In themselves they should be sufficient to convince an impartial observer that no change in Plato's metaphysics of the sort Owen proposes took place. The later interpretive tradition is fully in accord with this claim, also; and, though its evidentiary weight is less than that of the *Seventh Letter* or Aristotle's testimony, it deserves brief mention.[6]

It is a measure of the respect with which the *Timaeus* was regarded in the ancient world that it was the subject of virtually continuous discussion from Plato's time to well into the Middle Ages. Not only Academics and Neoplatonists, but Stoics (Posidonius), Neopythagoreans (Numenius), Jewish theologians (Philo) and Christian theologians (Justin, Clement, Origen, Boethius, Basil, Gregory Nazianzen) draw on it in formulating their own views. There seem to have been full-scale commentaries on the dialogue by Crantor, Porphyry, Proclus and Calcidius (it was through the latter's Latin translation and commentary on a portion of the dialogue that it was transmitted to the medieval world). In addition, such figures in the history of Platonism as Eudorus, Severus, Atticus, Plotinus, Amelius, Theodorus, Plutarch of Athens, Plutarch of Chaeronea and Iamblichus commented on specific passages, often extensively.

Even this litany does not give a full picture of the estimation ancient writers had of the importance the *Timaeus* had for the philosophy of Plato. More revealing perhaps is the remark of a modern scholar that the *Timaeus* and *Parmenides* were 'the two dialogues which Iamblichus regarded as containing the whole of Plato's philosophy'.[7] Further, the influence of the *Timaeus* on the thought of Plotinus is shown by the fact that he cites it more often than any other dialogue.[8]

This evidence shows that no work was more important than the *Timaeus* in the history of the development of Platonism in the ancient world. The dialogue was constantly discussed because interpreters saw in it the mature expression of Plato's views on a variety of subjects, including metaphysics. Doubtless its popularity was due in part to the fact that it was a treatise on cosmology, which was of great interest to ancient philosophers. There is to my knowledge, however, no evidence that any ancient writer thought that the metaphysics of the dialogue was something other than Plato's own ultimate position.[9] Indeed, the Neoplatonists, who took over into their own philosophy the metaphysical doctrines Owen wishes to confine to Plato's middle period, believed that the objections Owen finds telling were in fact captious.

As I noted above, the evidentiary weight of the universally high esteem of the *Timaeus* in antiquity is less than the weight of the Aristotelian testimony. This is because later writers did not have Aristotle's opportunity to converse with Plato and discern at first hand tne nature of his thought, and because, even more than Aristotle, later writers were interested in seeing the *Timaeus* in terms of their own metaphysical and cosmological views. It is well known that the attempts of the Neoplatonists in particular to derive their own doctrines from Plato's text often led to interpretations of Plato that are, to say the least, eccentric; and it is perhaps for this reason that recent critics of Owen's view have largely ignored the ancient tradition.

For all that, though, the weight of this evidence is not insignificant. For the ancient interpreters of Plato did work in a tradition, and that tradition traces its roots back to the Academy of Plato's day. It would not have been possible for all of the interpreters mentioned above to take the doctrines of the *Timaeus* as mature Platonism had there been evidence to the contrary. The unanimity of Plato's ancient interpreters on the importance and representativeness of this dialogue shows that the ancient world knew of no such revision of Platonic metaphysics as Owen imagines. It is barely possible that such a revision took place, unbeknownst to all; but if so it was one of the best-kept secrets in the ancient world.

## II. Stylometry

If the above argument is correct, it shows that the ancient world was unanimous in the judgement that the *Timaeus* contained Plato's ultimate views on both cosmology and metaphysics. It was for this reason, perhaps, that the dialogue was held by almost everyone down to Owen's time to be one of Plato's last works.

There is, however, no direct connection between maturity of doctrine and lateness of date. The *Timaeus* might, for all we know from the above information, have been written at the time of the *Republic*, provided only that Plato's thought did not change on significant points after that. In other words, the above evidence shows that the ancients regarded the *Timaeus* as philosophically mature, not as chronologically late. They saw no difference, in fact, between what Owen calls the 'middle' period Platonism of the *Republic*, *Phaedo* and *Symposium* and the 'later' Platonism of the *Parmenides* and *Sophist*. Both groups of dialogues presented to the ancient interpreters, and particularly to the Neoplatonists, a uniform, consistent and authentically Platonic metaphysics.

This is of course in itself important in relation to Owen's attempt to redate the *Timaeus*, for it argues against the existence of a distinction in doctrine on which Owen relies for his case. None the less, it is to modern evidence pertaining to Plato's style, rather than to the ancient interpretive tradition, that we must turn to determine the relative dating of the dialogue. This evidence, I shall argue, is as clear and one-sided in support of a late date for the *Timaeus* as the historical evidence is in favour of the maturity of its doctrines.

As noted in the Introduction, serious study of Plato's stule in relation to the problem of the chronology of the dialogues began with the work of Lewis Campbell in the last third of the nineteenth century. Before this period, it is no exaggeration to say that chaos reigned in scholarship on Platonic chronology. This is due to the fact that, aside from the evidence of style, there is little objective evidence on the basis of which the dialogues can be dated. In the absence of such evidence, scholars used subjective considerations in ordering the dialogues. To mention but two examples: Schleiermacher, one of the earliest scholars concerned with this issue, produced an ordering in which the more dogmatic works succeeded the more critical dialogues. In this he was doubtless influenced by the Hegelian view that criticism leads to dogmatism, which is taken to be the higher form of philosophy. (Owen, of course, would place the 'dogmatic' *Republic* and *Timaeus* before the 'critical' *Sophist* and *Parmenides*; and, like Schleiermacher, he was doubtless influenced in his decision by the philosophical views then current about the relative merits of dogmatism and criticism.) This assumption produced a chronology in which the *Phaedrus* came first, the *Parmenides* soon after, the *Sophist* and *Statesman* before the *Symposium*, and the *Republic* among the latest works.[10]

Munk first aired the theory, later revived by Burnet and Taylor, that Plato's dialogues were designed to present a biography of Socrates. He applied this theory to the chronological question by arranging the dialogues according to their dramatic dates, thus placing the *Parmenides* first and the *Phaedo* last.[11] As Lutoslawski remarked:

Such conclusions illustrate the uselessness of all generalizations, leading to a fictitious solution of the problem of Platonic chronology by a single ingenious hypothesis. The true genetic method should include a careful study of detail, with many parallel comparisons between every dialogue and those immediately preceding or immediately following.[12]

Campbell and his successors brought considerable order out of this chaos. Campbell undertook the first serious study of the details of Plato's style in the course of producing an edition of the *Sophist* and *Statesman*. He was interested in showing that these dialogues were in fact written by Plato (a fact not generally agreed on at the time he produced his edition)[13] and in determining with which other dialogues they had the closest relation. Campbell mentioned a variety of stylistic features of these dialogues in his study; but he reached his conclusions (that the *Sophist* and *Statesman* were indeed authentic, and that they were among Plato's latest works) primarily on the basis of a comparative study of the vocabulary of these dialogues. Noting an unusually high number of rare words in these dialogues, Campbell compared the vocabulary of the *Sophist* and *Statesman* with the vocabulary of the Platonic dialogues generally considered late (the *Timaeus*, *Critias*, and *Laws*). It turned out that the *Sophist* and *Statesman* shared a high number of these rare words with these dialogues alone; from these facts Campbell inferred that they were written at approximately the same time.[14]

Campbell's work did not receive the immediate attention of scholars; rather, in the last years of the nineteenth century, other scholars undertook studies similar to Campbell's, using other stylistic criteria than vocabulary, without the benefit of knowledge of Campbell's research. Blass discovered that Plato avoids hiatus (the occurrence of a vowel at the end of one word followed by the occurrence of a vowel at the beginning of the next word) in just the six dialogues (*Timaeus*, *Critias*, *Philebus*, *Sophist*, *Statesman*, *Laws*) Campbell concluded were Plato's last; his discovery was later confirmed by Janell.[15] Ritter found 45 linguistic features distinctive of Plato's later style in the *Laws*; it turned out that the dialogues containing the highest number of these features were the five Campbell had grouped with the *Laws* as forming the late group.[16] Lutoslawski collected the results of these and other studies, weighted the value of each proposed stylistic indicator, and produced numerical coefficients of the 'relative affinity' of each of the dialogues to the late group, and of each member of the late group to the *Laws*.

According to Guthrie, Lutoslawski's 'claim to determine the order of the dialogues with mathematical exactitude was somewhat overdone and led to criticism'.[17] None the less, the conclusion reached by virtually all investigators of Plato's style, that the six dialogues mentioned above were the last six Plato wrote, was nearly universally accepted by Plato scholars. Consider these comments:

> As to the authenticity of Plato's works and their chronological sequence, there are, in general, hardly any serious differences of opinion. Thus, if it no longer is permissible to constantly rearrange the order of the dialogues on the basis of an alleged development of Plato's thought or doctrines, we owe this result to the achievements of linguistic studies that began with

Lewis Campbell in 1867.[18]

That there is nothing personal or subjective in the use of these methods is proved by the fact that different scholars working quite independently have reached substantially the same results. Further, the results arrived at accord very well with such information as we get from other sources. . . . In particular, they give a very reasonable picture of the philosophical development.[19]

. . . while the views of scholars about the order of the early dialogues are for the most part based on subjective theories about the probable development of Plato's thought, their views about the order of the late dialogues are in the main based on the sure ground of the stylometric tests initiated by Lewis Campbell.[20]

As can be clearly seen from these remarks, the first two scholars (Friedländer and Field) take it that stylometry established the order of all the dialogues beyond serious doubt. The third (Ross), noting the wide divergence among scholars on the order of the earlier dialogues, gives his unqualified support only to their unanimous consensus on the ordering of the late works. All, however, contrast the objectivity and certainty of the stylometric studies with the subjectivity and uncertainty of orderings based on other (including philosophical) considerations.

In light of the widespread agreement on these matters, it is surprising that Owen's attack on the late date of the *Timaeus* should have had the effect of undermining scholarly confidence in the objectivity and certainty of stylometry and of giving at least some credence to an alternative theory based on just those subjective considerations of philosophical development that scholars had rejected. Yet this has been the effect of Owen's attack; and, even though his proposals to redate the *Timaeus* depended for its persuasiveness on a general attack on the methods and results of traditional stylometric studies, some scholars have seen fit to accept the stylometric method in general while rejecting or at least admitting doubt about the conclusions of the method with respect to the *Timaeus*. Thus, Guthrie has written that 'the stylometric method has undoubtedly proved itself',[21] and that 'the *Timaeus* was universally considered one of the latest [dialogues] until G. E. L. Owen's attempt to redate it in 1953, since when it has been the subject of lively dispute'.[22]

Guthrie's position is untenable. If stylometry has indeed 'proved itself', it has done so in the matter of the group of late dialogues, a group which includes the *Timaeus*. It was the first and greatest accomplishment of this method to establish the existence of this group, the style of which 'differs greatly from that in the preceding works, the change being sudden and abrupt'.[23] The most important single criterion for distinguishing this group from earlier dialogues is Plato's avoidance of hiatus in just these six dialogues; but this most valuable of stylometric indicators does not help at all with the grouping of the earlier dialogues. Accordingly, it is with the ordering of the early and middle dialogues, and not with the late ones, that the stylometric method is on its shakiest ground.[24]

As I shall indicate below, there is no stylometric evidence against the placement of the *Timaeus* among Plato's last six dialogues. Since the best stylometric evidence agues for such a placement, it is inconsistent to accept the results of stylometric investigation for the ordering of other dialogues but reject those results in the case of the *Timaeus*. One must either reject the results of stylometry in general or accept the late placement of the *Timaeus* which they support.[25]

Owen attempted to undermine the evidence for a late *Timaeus* while using other stylistic evidence to support his view that the dialogue dated to Plato's middle period. His attack on those studies that support a late *Timaeus* fails to discredit them, however; moreover, the evidence he cites on behalf of an earlier dating of the dialogue gives no support to the claim, which is crucial for Owen's view of Plato's development, that the *Timaeus* was written before the *Parmenides* and *Theaetetus*.

Let us consider first Owen's critique of the evidence for a late dating of the *Timaeus*. He raises the following objections:

(1) Campbell relied for his investigation of Plato's vocabulary on Ast's *Lexicon Platonicum*, which is incomplete.

(2) Campbell made 'uncritical deductions' from the occurrences of rare and unique words.

(3) Campbell assumed that the *Timaeus* and *Critias* were, along with the *Laws*, Plato's latest works.

(4) Lutoslawski assumed that a stylistically uniform *Laws* was Plato's last work.

(5) Lutoslawski's principle that only equal amounts of text should be compared was at odds with, and rendered invalid, his own investigation.

(6) Campbell and Lutoslawski got some strange results from

their methods which they themselves rejected.

(7) The uniqueness of the 'technical range' of the *Timaeus* precludes the mechanical use of its vocabulary as a test for dating.

(8) Hiatus avoidance is not an automatic test for lateness, since stylometrists place the *Phaedrus* (in which hiatus is sometimes avoided) before the *Theaetetus* (in which it is not).

(9) Plato may well have avoided hiatus in a '*tour de force* of style' such as the *Timaeus*, and only later adopted this stylistic trait in more conversational dialogues.

(10) The frequency of hesitant replies, investigated by Ritter, is not a neutral index of style, for it depends on the aim and method of particular dialogues.

(11) The Phraedrus shows that Plato can adopt 'late' traits in the speeches, but avoid their use in the dialogue proper, which indicates that these traits were under his conscious control, to be used or not as context indicated.[26]

I shall deal with these objections in succession. Campbell's reliance on Ast (1, above) does not seem to have produced much inaccuracy in his results (perhaps because the *Lexicon* approaches completeness more closely in the case of rare words than in the case of common ones). I compared the first four of Campbell's lists of rare words[27] with Brandwood's *Word Index to Plato*, which *is* complete. Allowing for disparities between Campbell and Brandwood on the authenticity of certain dialogues, the individuation of words (Brandwood lists adjectival and adverbial forms along with nouns as single words) and manuscript variants, I could discover but one error among the approximately 160 words on Campbell's lists. *Agonistikē*, which Campbell states is confined to the *Sophist* and *Laws*, is also found at *Meno* 75c9. Interestingly enough, though, the error is Campbell's and not Ast's: Ast lists the *Meno* occurrence and every other parallel found in Brandwood but not in Campbell.

Campbell did not make 'uncritical deductions', as Owen charges (2). Owen himself notes (cf. 6) that Campbell used discretion in dealing with some of his own results; and we have already seen (above, n. 14) that Brandwood approves of Campbell's methods, which included the judicious evaluation of his own findings. Owen's remark (cf. 7 above) makes it sound as though Campbell counted the rare words in a dialogue, and placed it later if it had more of these than other dialogues. Campbell did list the words that appeared only in the *Sophist* and *Statesman* and enumerated the words unique to the *Timaeus* and to the *Laws*;[28] but the heart of his study was a comparison between the vocabulary of the *Sophist* and *Statesman* and that of the *Timaeus*, *Critias* and *Laws*. Campbell includes in his list words from the *Timaeus* only when they are also found in the *Sophist* and *Statesman*. The rare words of the *Timaeus* that are due to its 'technical range' would not be found also in the *Sophist* and *Statesman*; so there is no need to worry that vocabulary tests favour the *Timaeus* over the *Sophist* or *Statesman* on that score. (This should lay to rest Owen's point 7 as well as 2.)[29]

Campbell did assume that the *Timaeus* and *Critias* were, with the *Laws*, Plato's latest works. The lateness of the *Timaeus* had much greater acceptance in his time than did the lateness of the *Sophist* and *Statesman*; therefore Campbell argued for the lateness of those on the basis of their stylistic similarity to his assumed last three. Even this assumption, however, does not destroy the evidentiary value of Campbell's study for *our* question, which is the date of the *Timaeus*. For since Campbell's methods were basically comparative, and since his comparisons showed the similarity in vocabulary between the *Sophist*, *Statesman*, *Timaeus*, *Critias* and *Laws*, this argues for grouping all of these dialogues together.

Lutoslawski (Owen's point 4) assumed that the *Laws* was Plato's last work; indeed, every student of Plato's style seems to have assumed this in attempting to determine the membership of the last group of Platonic dialogues. In so doing, stylometrists have found simply followed the best external evidence available on the dating of the dialogues; in this case, the testimony of Aristotle (*Politics* II. 6, 1264b26) that the *Laws* is later than the *Republic*, and that of Diogenes Laertius and Olympiodorus that the *Laws* was left by Plato on wax tablets and published by Philip of Opus after Plato's death.[30] Stylometry had to make *some* initial assumption as to which dialogue or dialogues were late, and the credentials of the *Laws* are better than those of any other. As to the question of stylistic uniformity, on the crucial matters of hiatus avoidance and prose-rhythm, studies have shown that the *Laws is* uniform.[31] If Brandwood is correct (see n. 17 above), there is much to criticise about Lutoslawski's methods; but his assumption of a stylistically uniform, late *Laws* is scarcely the place to begin.

Lutoslawski did claim that only equal units of text should be compared. In the matter of vocabulary studies such as those of Campbell, he is surely correct, for the opportunity for a given word to appear is greater in a long section of text than in a short one.

Lutoslawski's stricture does not, however, apply to those studies where the key figures pertain to the *relative frequency* of certain stylistic phenomena rather than the absolute number of occurrences. It does not matter that the *Laws* is much longer than the *Timaeus* if we are examining the frequency of occurrence of hiatus, or of certain prose-rhythms, or the proportion of certain reply formulas to the total. If only the portion of text surveyed is long enough to keep the possibility of statistical error low, we may compare it in this respect to any text of equal or greater length. It may be that Lutoslawski's failure to observe his own principle affected the validity of *his* study, but it did not discredit others because it does not apply to them.[32]

Campbell and Lutoslawski did, as Owen charges (6), obtain some peculiar results when applying their methods. Campbell, more cautious than Lutoslawski, showed admirable discretion in not concluding from the relative infrequency of rare words in them that the *Philebus* and *Parmenides* were early or middle dialogues. Yet the fact that a method must be applied judiciously is hardly a criticism of the method. Campbell was able to see the limitations in his approach as well as its strengths (as Lutoslawski, if Brandwood is correct, was unable to do). All subsequent studies confirmed the conclusions of which Campbell was confident and showed that his concern about others was well taken.

Despite Owen's denial, the avoidance of hiatus in the dialogues *is* an automatic test for lateness. Owen's error on this point was in assuming that stylometry required the ordering of dialogues in proportion to their declining frequency of hiatus; but this is not correct. It is not important that the *Phaedrus* contains only 23.9 hiatus per page, whereas the *Parmenides* contains 44.1 per page. What *is* important, as Cherniss has pointed out in replying to this argument of Owen's, is that the last six dialogues show an incidence of hiatus much lower than any of the others, varying between 6.71 per page (in *Laws* V) to 0.44 per page (in the *Statesman*).[33] It is this sharp distinction in style between the six dialogues of Campbell's late group and the others, a distinction described by Brandwood as 'sudden and abrupt' (see above, p. 182), that stylometrists have seen as proof of the late composition of these six.

There is no doubt that Plato in these dialogues avoided hiatus as a conscious choice. It is therefore possible, as Owen claims, that he may have adopted the device in the *Timaeus*, dropped it, and then readopted it later (see his point 9). Though this is possible, however, there is no evidence in favour of this hypothesis; and such evidence as there is rather tells against it. For Owen's explanation of Plato's avoidance in the *Timaeus* is that

> the *Timaeus* is essentially an essay, a 'conscious *tour de force* of style' (Shorey) where the carelessness of conversation has no place; it may well have been a later decision to adopt such ornaments in writings which make serious use of the dialogue form.[34]

Unfortunately for Owen's hypothesis, however, the first ten pages of the *Timaeus* make as serious use of the dialogue form as many other dialogues, and the 'carelessness of conversation' (which is always the result of art and not of any genuine carelessness on Plato's part) does have a place in them; yet Plato avoids hiatus there no less than later in the 'essay' portion of the dialogue. Furthermore, if Plato had adopted hiatus avoidance for an essay and stylistic *tour de force* such as the *Timaeus*, what made him decide later to avoid it in works such as the *Philebus* which, whatever, there philosophical merits, are definitely not stylistic masterworks? (Owen's explanation is that this signals 'a new period of assurance' in Plato's thought; but it is hard to see how this would be relevant to the adoption of a single stylistic trait: why didn't Plato adopt *all* of the stylistic traits of the *Timaeus* when his confidence returned, instead of only one?)

The same sort of consideration argues for the neutrality of the criterion of relative frequency of various reply formulas, used by Ritter, as for that of hiatus avoidance — namely that these formulas, despite Owen's claim to the contrary, do not seem to be connected in any obvious way to the content of the dialogues. Just as Plato avoids hiatus in essays like the *Timaeus* and dialogues like the *Sophist*, in works Owen would call critical as well as those he would call dogmatic, so the reply formulas used by Ritter successfully separated the 'dogmatic' *Republic* from the 'dogmatic' *Laws* and placed the *Republic* with the 'critical' *Parmenides* and *Theaetetus*.[35]

Owen's last criticism concerns the *Phaedrus*. He states that Plato uses 'late' characteristics in the speeches, and 'earlier' features of style in the rest of the dialogue. Actually, the situation is even more complex. I noted above that hiatus is rarer in the *Phaedrus* than in other dialogues that precede the final group of six, though not nearly as rare as in those works. It turns out that the frequency of hiatus varies within the dialogue; only in this case the passages that show the greatest avoidance of hiatus are not to be found in the speeches but in the rest of the dialogue.[36] So here is one 'late' trait that varies in the opposite manner to those mentioned by Owen.

The *Phaedrus*, then, remains something of a puzzle. Why is it that some passages contain one late features, whereas others contain different ones? Owen's explanation, 'that, when Plato was still writing dialogue having very close affinities with the *Republic* and Theaetetus, he could write uninterrupted prose having equal affinities with *Timaeus*',[37] cannot be correct as it stands; for, at least as concerns the avoidance of hiatus, it is the dialogue that resembles the *Timaeus* and the uninterrupted prose that resembles the *Republic*. We should expect that a stylistic change that resulted (as Owen thinks this does) from a conscious decision would be more uniform.

Campbell has suggested that in the *Phaedrus* Plato is toying with features that he only later adopts as part of his normal style, that he is both fascinated with and amused by these 'late' traits.[38] This might explain why he does not consistently adhere to these traits throughout the dialogue; another possibility might be that he revised the dialogue at different times, with different stylistic mannerisms in mind.[39] It is likely, I think, that the *Phaedrus* is an intermediate dialogue, a 'proving ground' where Plato experiments with the style that becomes characteristic of his work in later dialogues; I do not think, however, that the failure of stylometry to solve this riddle casts much doubt on the solutions it has reached to other problems, in particular the membership of the final group of dialogues.

Owen's critique of the stylometric evidence for a late *Timaeus* ought not, then, to undermine our confidence in the membership of the *Timaeus* among the last six dialogues. Owen's arguments do not invalidate the major studies of Campbell, Ritter and Janell on Plato's vocabulary, reply formulas and avoidance of hiatus. The most remarkable thing about these studies is the mutual support they give to the existence of this group of late dialogues, though the kinds of evidence with which they deal are quite different. Owen's critique does not deal with this important feature of the stylometric evidence and therefore cannot diminish or destroy it.

In support of his own position Owen cited the studies of Plato's prose-rhythms done by Kaluscha and Billig. According to Owen, Billig found that 'the *Timaeus* has nothing to do with the rhythms of the *Sophist* digression, the *Politicus*, the *Philedus*, and the *Laws*. Rhythm puts its composition earlier than that of all these works.' And in this he confirmed Kaluscha's earlier study in the same field.[40]

Owen argued that prose-rhythm was a more neutral criterion of style than hiatus avoidance because it does not reflect, as hiatus avoidance does, a conscious decision on the part of the writer. Therefore he saw fit to reject the stylometric evidence of hiatus avoidance and accept that concerning prose-rhythm.

Cherniss criticised the two studies of Plato's prose-rhythms on which Owen relied, but Brandwood has argued that the methods of these studies are sound and their data significant.[41] Accordingly, he has accepted the conclusion they reached, that the *Timaeus* was written before the central portion of the *Sophist* and before the *Statesman*, *Philebus* and *Laws*.

Brandwood's support of Billig and Kaluscha lends no weight, however, to Owen's view that the *Timaeus* is a middle dialogue. There are in fact two things wrong with Owen's use of these studies of Plato's prose-rhythms. The first is that it is not clear that prose-rhythm is a more 'neutral' criterion than those used by other stylometrists. As Skemp has noted:

> Owen thinks the paeon *clausula* [one of the rhythms investigated by Billig and Kaluscha] a better criterion, because it is unconscious, than hiatus-avoidance . . . But Aristotle tells us in the *Rhetoric* (iii 8, 1409a2) of such *clausulae: enchrōnto men apo Thrasymachou arxamenoi*. [They began to use it in Thrasymachus' time.] Use of the *clausula* may well have been as conscious as avoidance of hiatus.[42]

Owen's insistence on unconsciousness as a necessary condition of neutrality is in any event too strong; a stylistic trait has the requisite neutrality if it is independent of the content of the dialogue, whether it is chosen consciously or not. We have seen that Owen's arguments fail to establish that hiatus avoidance, similarity in vocabulary and the use of certain reply formulas lack this neutrality.

The second and more serious problem with Owen's use of these studies is that they give absolutely no support to his claim that the

*Timaeus* was written in Plato's middle period. They show only that it was written before other dialogues of the late group, not that it was written before the *Theaetetus* and *Parmenides*. Yet Owen's argument requires that the *Timaeus* be earlier than these two dialogues, and in particular that the metaphysics of the *Timaeus* be refuted by arguments contained in them and subsequently abandoned.

The proper conclusion to be drawn from the sum total of stylometric evidence is that the *Timaeus* is a member of the latest group of Platonic dialogues but that it was written first of the dialogues of that group. This was in fact the conclusion drawn by Billig, who states:

> I shall speak about the Sophist, the Politicus, the Philebus, and the Timaeus. These dialogues all bear the unmistakable features that belong to the later phases of Plato's career, and there is no possibility of drawing chronological inferences within this group on this score.[43]

It is also the conclusion reached by Brandwood.[44] This is especially important, I believe, because Brandwood's stylometric research is the only study of its sort undertaken after, and partially in response to, Owen's attack on the late date of the *Timaeus*. Brandwood's thorough and careful review of past stylometric investigations and his own research into Plato's prose-rhythms support the validity of the various criteria used to establish the existence of a late group of dialogues, including the *Timaeus*, as well as the validity of the criterion of prose-rhythm as a device for ordering the dialogues *within the late group*.

In brief, then, all of the major studies of Plato's style undertaken for the purpose of determining which dialogues were Plato's latest either presuppose or provide evidence in favour of a late date for the *Timaeus*. The most recent investigator of these studies has found this conclusion a sound one. It is not weakened by Owen's arguments against stylometry; nor does the evidence cited by Owen in defence of his own view conflict with it. It is conceivable that, as Owen claims, Plato adopted all of the features of his late style while writing the *Timaeus*, then returned to the style of the middle dialogues for the *Theaetetus* and *Parmenides*, and finally readopted the style of the *Timaeus* for the other dialogues of the late group. This contention has little to recommend it beyond its conceivability, however; surely it is simpler to assume that Plato adopted these features at the outset of his late period and did not subsequently abandon them.

The order of the dialogues established by stylometry conflicts with that defended by Owen. Moreover, it indicates that his views about Plato's metaphysical development are false. If, as stylometric evidence indicates, the *Timaeus* was written after the *Parmenides*, this shows that Plato did not give up the view that the Forms are paradigms as a result of the critique of that view in the *Parmenides*. This is one of the contentions for which I have argued in this work. I have presented an account of Plato's metaphysics according to which the *Parmenides* does not occasion a radical modification in Plato's Theory of Forms. On my account the metaphysics of the *Timaeus* is not a product of Plato's middle period, later revised in light of the critique of the *Parmenides*; it constitutes, rather, along with the metaphysics of the *Sophist*, part of Plato's late metaphysics, developed in response to that critique. In the body of this work I have attempted to show by interpretation of the text and philosophical argument that this account of Plato's metaphysics is a coherent and plausible one. In the Appendix I have supplemented this interpretation and argument with the testimony of the philosophical tradition and the evidence of stylometry. Both conflict with the account of Plato's development offered by radical revisionism, but both are in harmony with my account. I take this to be further reason to prefer my account to that of the revisionists.

## Notes

1. Brandwood (1958), p. 5. For a summary of the variety of views on the order of the dialogues that existed before the advent of stylometry, see Brandwood (1958), pp. 3–5 and Lutoslawski, pp. 35–63.

2. I cannot accept, and indeed find no plausibility in, the extreme position of Edelstein, which denies to the author of the letter accurate knowledge of Plato's political motivations and philosophical views. As Solmsen (1969) points out, 'if we do not insist on Plato's approaching his topics always from the same angle and making exactly the same points about them, E.'s objections to the content of the Letter lose most of their force' (p. 31). Many of Edelstein's objection to the content of the letter, including his claims that it is historically and philosophically inaccurate, are dealt with satisfactorily, I believe, by Morrow (the first edition of whose work on the letters appeared 30 years before Edelstein's!).

Morrow and others have defended vigorously the authenticity of the *Seventh Letter*; my own view, in fact, is that it should be regarded as genuine. I am convinced that a document of such length and containing such a detailed account of

Plato's thoughts and actions could not have been produced, as were so many other letters in the ancient world (including, no doubt, others in the collection attributed to Plato), by a Hellenistic forger. I am persuaded by the remark of Solmsen that, 'if the Letter was not written by Plato, what a remarkable individual its author must have been! In a history of Greek Literature his unique achievement would certainly qualify him for a special chapter' (p. 33). Von Fritz, in the same vein, continues:

> the author . . . is not only an outstanding Platonist, but an extremely good philosopher, a philosopher, I am inclined to say, as distinguished as Plato himself. Since this, after all, is something very rare and since nothing remarkable is otherwise known about the author of the *Seventh Letter*, if he is not Plato, this seems to me to argue very strongly in favor of identifying the author with Plato. (p. 425)

Solmsen and von Fritz argue from the literary and philosophical excellence of the letter to its Platonic authorship. I would add to their contentions that the work is also an outstanding example of biographical (or, as I think, autobiographical) writing, and on this score as well is worthy of someone of Plato's gifts. Scholars are probably fated to disagree forever on the merits of the letter, however, and therefore also on its authorship. I have therefore classified it as external evidence, not because I believe it is inauthentic but because I believe its authenticity cannot be established beyond a shadow of a doubt. I would reiterate, however, that rejection of the authenticity of the letter does not entail Edelstein's extreme views of the value of the letter as a source of information about Plato and his philosophy; these views ought to be rejected, whether or not we take the letter to be authentic.

3. His most powerful critic, of course, being Cherniss (1944). Sayre has argued at length and to my mind very effectively for a much more positive estimate of the value of Aristotle's testimony than that given by Cherniss.

4. Sayre thinks that the *Philebus* contains this later version of the Theory of Forms. I would agree that it provides evidence for the view that Plato came in his later works to think of the Forms in mathematical terms; unlike Sayre, however (who unfairly dismisses the *Timaeus* as a statement of Plato's late ontology: cf. Ch. 3, n. 4), I do not think that it is more valuable in this respect than the *Timaeus*.

5. I disagree with Aristotle on one point. As I argued in Chs. 3 and 4, I think that the Theory of Forms as Plato states it contains resources for an adequate response to the Third Man Argument. I concede, however, that Aristotle may well be correct in implying that Plato never marshalled these resources into an explicit reply to the Third Man. In that sense, though not in the former, he may have had no answer to the argument.

6. The sketch which follows is derived from Armstrong and Wallis. Detailed references to individuals and works mentioned may be found in their indices.

7. Wallis, p. 19.

8. Ibid.; cf, McKenna, p. xxxix, n. 2, and Brehier, pp. 192–4.

9. Wallis has confirmed this judgement in personal conversation.

10. Lutoslawski, pp. 36–7; Brandwood (1958), p. 4.

11. Lutoslawski, p. 52; Brandwood (1958), pp. 4–5.

12. Lutoslawski, p. 52.

13. Campbell (1867), pp. xliv–xlv.

14. Brandwood (1958) states his approval of Campbell's method in these words:

> Campbell's demonstration and the way in which he used it are beyond reproach. Certainly it can hardly be said that he overstepped the bounds of moderation in concluding that the *Soph., Pol., Phil., Tim., Crit.,* and *Laws* form the last group of Plato's works . . . (p. 16)

15. Brandwood (1958), pp. 18–19; cf. Friedländer, p. 447.

16. Brandwood (1958), pp. 118–24. Brandwood finds Ritter's work methodologically sound and his conclusion justified, including his reaffirmation of the existence of a late group consisting of six dialogues, among them the *Timaeus* (cf. Brandwood (1958), pp. 117, 124–6).

17. Guthrie (1975), p. 49. Brandwood (1958), pp. 223–46, is much harder on Lutoslawski than Guthrie; he concludes (p. 398, n. 1) that Lutoslawski's study is of 'no value'. Brandwood succeeds in showing that many of the 500 criteria Lutoslawski assembled for the evaluation of the style of the dialogues are faulty and must be rejected, but in one respect he seems to me to be an unfair critic. He claims that Lutoslawski based his comparisons on a list of 'late' characteristics drawn from all the dialogues in the late group, and not just the *Laws*. If this were so, it would give artificially high scores to the dialogues in that group and invalidate any conclusion based on such a comparison that concerned the membership of that group. Brandwood does not note, however, that, while Lutoslawski uses this set of criteria in comparing earlier dialogues to the late group, he also compares the other members of the late group to the *Laws*, using just those features of Plato's later style which occur in the *Laws* (cf. Lutoslawski, pp. 178–82). This does not vindicate Lutoslawski's method, but it does show him to have been somewhat more thorough than Brandwood's account would suggest.

18. Friedländer, p. 447.

19. Field, p. 68.

20. Ross, pp. 2–3.

21. Guthrie (1975), p. 51.

22. Ibid., p. 50.

23. Brandwood (1958), p. 400.

24. Ibid., p. 399.

25. This places Owen, I believe, in an awkward position. He wants to maintain that the *Sophist*, *Statesman* and *Philebus* are late dialogues and that the *Timaeus* and *Critias* are not. Yet even if the evidence of stylometry were totally rejected, there would remain the evidence of the historical tradition on behalf of a late (or at least mature) *Timaeus*. In the case of the *Sophist*, *Statesman* and *Philebus*, however, the *only* support for their late placement comes from those very stylometric studies which either support or presuppose a late *Timaeus*, and which Owen wishes to discredit.

26. Owen (1953), pp. 314–18.

27. Words occurring only in the *Sophist*, only in the *Statesman*, in both and in other late dialogues; Campbell (1867), pp. xxv–xxvi.

28. Ibid., p. xxxi.

29. The fact that Campbell lists words unique to the *Sophist* and *Statesman* but only those from the *Timaeus* which occur also in these two dialogues actually shifts the weight of the evidence unfairly against the *Timaeus*, a fact Lutoslawski noted (pp. 186–7). Lutoslawski dealt with this problem by recalculating the 'relative affinity' of these dialogues to the *Laws* after subtracting Campbell's data; the results were about the same as with them included.

30. Brandwood (1958), pp. 1–2.

31. Brandwood (1958), p. 340; cf. Cox and Brandwood, p. 199: on proserhythms. Brandwood (1958a), p. 133: on hiatus.

32. As I noted in Prior (1975), pp. 46–50, Lutoslawski calculated the 'relative affinity' not just of complete works, but also of various portions of the *Republic*, these portions varying in length from 7.5–60.4 pages. If we divide the dialogues into groups of equal length and compare them to these fragments of the *Republic*, the results confirm the fact that the *Timaeus* and the other dialogues of Campbell's late group were written after the *Republic*, the *Theaetetus*, *Parmenides* and *Phaedrus*

around the same time, and the other dialogues earlier. In view of the flaws in Lutoslawski's method, it would doubtless be unwise to insist on the accuracy of these results; I do think it worth noting, however, that his results can be made to conform to his stricture about only comparing dialogues of equal length.

33. Cherniss (1957), pp. 344–6. Cherniss's answer to Owen is on this point quite conclusive, I think.

34. Owen (1953), pp. 315–16.

35. Ritter's criterion of reply formulas cannot be used to date the *Timaeus* because most of the dialogue, as Owen has noted, is an essay and contains no reply formulas of any sort. Ritter did, however, note 19 other stylistic features characteristic of the *Laws*, of which 18 recur in the *Timaeus* (Brandwood, 1958, pp. 125–6).

36. Brandwood (1958), p. 280.

37. Owen (1953), p. 318.

38. Jowett and Campbell, pp. 49–50.

39. According to Brandwood (1958, p. 275), Janell suggested that the sections of the *Phaedrus* with low incidence of hiatus were those sections Plato later revised. Brandwood, perhaps wisely, offers no explanation of the *Phaedrus*'s anomalies.

40. Owen (1953), p. 315.

41. Brandwood (1958), pp. 294–343. Cf. Cox and Brandwood.

42. Skemp (1967), p. 125.

43. Billig, p. 250.

44. Brandwood (1958), pp. 398–402. Skemp, an examiner on Brandwood's dissertation committee, summarises Brandwood's position accurately:

Taking the various criteria of 'stylometry' proposed to date, and using other vocabulary tests also, Brandwood concluded that the *Timaeus*, on other criteria than hiatus-avoidance and *clausulae* as well as on these, appears to belong to the late group but may be the first of that group — i.e., that it is definitely later than the *Parmenides* and *Theaetetus*. (1967, pp. 124–5).

# BIBLIOGRAPHY

Only those works cited in the text or in the notes appear in this bibliography.

Ackrill, J. L. 'Plato and the Copula: *Sophist* 251–259' in Vlastos (1971), pp. 210–22. Originally in *Journal of Hellenic Studies* 77 (1957), pp. 1–6

Allen, R. E. (1960) 'Participation and Predication in Plato's Middle dialogues' in Allen (1965), pp. 43–60. Originally in *Philosophical Review* 69 (1960), pp. 147–64

———— (1965) (ed.) *Studies in Plato's Metaphysics* (London: Routledge & Kegan Paul)

———— (1970) *Plato's 'Euthyphro' and the Earlier Theory of Forms* (London: Routledge & Kegan Paul)

———— (1971) 'Plato's Earlier Theory of Forms' in Vlastos (1971a), pp. 319–34

———— (1983) *Plato's Parmenides: Translation and Analysis* (Minneapolis: University of Minnesota Press)

Anton, John P. and Kustas, George L. *Essays in Ancient Greek Philosophy* Albany: State University of New York Press, 1971)

Armstrong, A. H. (ed.) *The Cambridge History of Later Greek and Early Medieval Philosophy* (Cambridge: Cambridge University Press, 1967)

Ast, Friedrich. *Lexicon Platonicum* (Leipzig, 1835)

Bambrough, R. (ed.) *New Essays on Plato and Aristotle* (London: Routledge & Kegan Paul, 1965)

Bestor, T. W. 'Plato's Semantics and Plato's "Parmenides"' in *Phronesis* 25 (1980), pp. 38–75

Billig, L. 'Clausulae and Platonic Chronology', *Journal of Philosophy* 35 (1920), pp. 225–56

Bluck, R. S. 'Forms as Standards', *Phronesis* 2 (1957), pp. 115–27

Brandwood, L. (1958) *Tne Dating of Plato's Works by the Stylistic Method: A Historical and Critical Survey*, vol. I (unpublished dissertation, University College, London)

———— (1958a) Ibid., vol. II

———— (1959) See Cox, D. R., and Brandwood, L.

———— (1976) *A Word Index to Plato* (Leeds: W. S. Maney & Son)

Brehier, E. (ed. and trans.) *Plotin: Ennéades*, vol. 6, part 2, 3d ed. (Paris: Société d'Edition 'Les Belles Lettres', 1963 — Budé edition)

Brownstein, D. *Aspects of the Problem of Universals* (Lawrence: University of Kansas Press, 1973)

Campbell, L. (1867) (ed.) *The Sophistes and Politicus of Plato* (Oxford: Clarendon Press)

———— (1894) See Jowett, B., And Campbell, L.

Cherniss, H. F. (1944) *Aristotle's Criticism of Plato and the Academy* (Baltimore: Johns Hopkins Press, 1944). Reprint ed., New York: Russell & Russell, 1962

———— (1954) 'A Much Misread Passage of the *Timaeus* (*Timaeus* 49 C 7–50 B 5)', *American Journal of Philology* 75 (1954), pp. 113–30

———— 'The Relation of the *Timaeus* to Plato's Later Dialogues' in Allen (1965), pp. 339–78. Originally in *American Journal of Philology* 78 (1957), pp. 225–66

———— (1976) (ed. and trans.) *Plutarch's Moralia*, vol. 13, part 1 (Cambridge,

Mass: Harvard University Press — Loeb edition)

Cornford, F. M. (1935) *Plato's Theory of Knowledge* (London: Routledge & Kegan Paul). Reprint ed., Indianopolis: Bobbs-Merrill (Liberal Arts Press), 1957

───── *Plato's Cosmology* (London: Routledge & Kegan Paul). Reprint ed., New York: Liberal Arts Press, 1957

───── (1939) *Plato and Parmenides* (London: Routledge & Kegan Paul). Reprint ed., Indianapolis: Bobbs-Merrill, n.d.

Cox, D. R., and Brandwood, L. 'On a Discriminatory Problem Connected with the Works of Plato', *Journal of the Royal Statistical Society*, Ser. B, 21 (1959), pp. 195–200

Crombie, I. M. *An Examination of Plato's Doctrines: II. Plato on Knowledge and Reality* (London: Routledge & Kegan Paul, 1963)

Cross, R. C., and Woozley, A. D. *Plato's Republic: A Philosophical Commentary* (New York: St Martin's Press, 1966)

Edelstein, Ludwig. *Plato's Seventh Letter* (Leiden: E. J. Brill, 1966)

Else, G. F. *The Structure and Date of Book 10 of Plato's Republic* (Heidelberg: Abhandlungen der Heidelburg Akademie der Wissenschaften. Philosophisch-Historische Klasse, 1972)

Field, G. C. *Plato and His Contemporaries* (New York: E. P. Dutton and Co., 1930)

Forrester, J. W. 'Arguments an Able Man Could Refute: Parmenides 133b–134e', *Phronesis* 19 (1974), pp. 233–7

Frede, M. *Prädikation und Existenzaussage* (Göttingen: Vandenhoeck und Ruprecht, 1967)

Friedländer, P. *Plato: The Dialogues, Second and Third Periods* (Princeton: Princeton University Press, 1969)

Fujisawa, N. '*Echein, Metechein*, and Idioms of "Paradeigmatism" in Plato's Theory of Forms', *Phronesis* 19 (1974), pp. 30–58

Gallop, D. *Plato Phaedo* (Oxford: Clarendon Press, 1975)

Geach, P. T. 'The Third Man Again' in Allen (1965), pp. 265–77. Originally in *Philosophical Review* 65 (1956), pp. 72–82

Gosling, J. 'Similarity in Phaedo 73b seq', *Pronesis* 10 (1965), pp. 151–61.

Gulley, N. 'The Interpretation of Plato, *Timaeus* 49 D–E', *American Journal of Philology* 81 (1960), pp. 53–64

Guthrie, W. K. C. (1975) *A History of Greek Philosophy*, vol. 4 (Cambridge: Cambridge University Press)

───── (1978) *A History of Greek Philosophy*, vol. 5 (Cambridge: Cambridge University Press)

Hackforth, R. (1955) *Plato's Phaedo* (Cambridge: Cambridge University Press). Reprint ed., Indianapolis: Bobbs-Merrill, n.d.

───── (1959) 'Plato's Cosmogony (Timaeus 27 D ff.)', *Classical Quarterly*, N. S. 9 (1959), pp. 17–22

Hintikka, K. J. J. 'Time, Truth, and Knowledge in Ancient Greek Philosophy', *American Philosophical Quarterly* 4 (1967), pp. 1–14

Jowett, B., and Campbell, L. *Plato's Republic*, vol. 2: Essays: (Oxford: Clarendon Press, 1894)

Kahn, C. 'The Greek Verb "to Be" and the Concept of Being', *Foundations of Language* 2 (1966), pp. 245–65

Ketchum, R. J. 'Participation and Predication in Sophist 251–260', *Phronesis* 23 (1978), pp. 42–63

Keyt, D. 'The Mad Craftsman of the *Timaeus*', *Philosophical Review* 80 (1971), pp. 230–5

Lee, E. N. (1967) 'On Plato's *Timaeus*, 49D4–E7', *American Journal of Philology* 88 (1967), pp. 1–28

───── (1973) 'The Second "Third Man": An Interpretation' in Moravcsik, pp. 101–22

Lee, E. N., Mourelatos, A. P. D., and Rorty, R. (eds.) *Exegesis and Argument; Phronesis*, Supplemental vol. 1 (Assen: Van Gorcum & Comp., 1973)

Lewis, F. A. 'Parmenides on Separation and the Knowability of the Forms: Plato *Parmenides* 133a ff', *Philosophical Studies* 35 (1979), pp. 105–27

Lutoslawski, W. *The Origin and Growth of Plato's Logic* (London: Longmans, Green and Co., 1897)

McKenna, S. (trans.) *Plotinus: The Enneads* (London: Faber & Faber Ltd; 4th ed, 1969); introduction by Paul Henry

Mills, K. W. (1957–1958) 'Plato's Phaedo, 74b7–c6', *Phronesis* 2 (1959), 128–47, and 3 (1958), pp. 40–58

———— (1968) 'Some Aspects of Plato's Theory of Forms: Timaeus 49c ff.', *Phronesis* 13 (1968), pp. 145–170

Moline, Jon. *Plato's Theory of Understanding* (Madison: University of Wisconsin Press, 1981)

Moravcsik, J. M. E. (ed.) *Patterns in Plato's Thought* (Dortrecht: D. Reidel Publishing Company, 1973)

Morrow, Glenn R. *Plato's Epistles*, revised ed. (Indianapolis: Bobbs-Merrill, 1962; first edition, 1935)

Nehamas, A. 'Self-Predication and Plato's Theory of Forms', *American Philosophical Quarterly* 16 (1979), pp. 93–103

O'Brien, D. 'The Last Argument of Plato's *Phaedo*', *Classical Quarterly*, N. S. 17 (1967), pp. 198–231, and 18 (1968), pp. 95–106

Owen, G. E. L. (1953) 'The Place of the *Timaeus* in Plato's Dialogues' in Allen (1965), pp. 313–38. Originally in *Classical Quarterly*, N. S. 3 (1953), pp. 79–95

———— (1957) 'A Proof in the *Peri Ideon*' in Allen (1965), pp. 293–312. Originally in *Journal of Hellenic Studies* 77 (1957), pp. 103–11

———— (1968) (ed), *Aristotle on Dialectic: The Topics* (3d Symposium Aristotelicum Proceedings; Oxford: Clarendon Press, 1968)

———— (1968a) 'Dialectic and Eristic in the Treatment of the Forms' in Owen (1968), pp. 103–25

———— (1971) 'Plato on Not-Being' in Vlastos (1971), pp. 223–67

———— (1973) 'Plato on the Undepictable' in Lee, Mourelatos and Rorty, pp. 349–61

Parry, R. D. 'The Unique World of the *Timaeus*', *Journal of the History of Philosophy* 17 (1979), pp. 1–10

Passmore, J. *Philosophical Reasoning* (New York: Basic Books, 1969)

Plutarch. 'On the Generation of the Soul in the *Timaeus*' in Cherniss (1976), pp. 131–345

Prior, W. J. (1975) *Plato's Intellectual Development: A Critique of the Owen Thesis* (unpublished dissertation; University of Texas)

———— 'Parmenides 132c–133a and the Development of Plato's Thought', *Phronesis* 24 (1979), pp. 230–40

———— (1980) 'Relations Between Forms and "Pauline Predication" in *Euthyphro* 11e4–12d4', *Ancient Philosophy* 1 (1980), pp. 61–8

———— (1983) 'The Concept of *Paradeigma* in Plato's Theory of Forms', *Apeiron* 17, no. 1 (1983), pp. 33–42

Quine, W. V. O. *Word and Object* (Cambridge, Mass: MIT Press, 1960)

Robinson, T. M. *Plato's Psychology* (Toronto: University of Toronto Press, 1970)

Ross, W. D. *Plato's Theory of Ideas* (Oxford: Clarendon Press, 1951)

Runciman, W. G. 'Plato's *Parmenides*' in Allen (1965), pp. 149–84. Originally in *Harvard Studies in Classical Philology* 64 (1959), pp. 89–120.

Ryle, G. 'Plato's *Parmenides*' in Allen (1965), pp. 97–147. Originally in *Mind* 48 (1939), pp. 129–51, 302–25

Sayre, Kenneth M. *Plato's Late Ontology: A Riddle Resolved* (Princeton: Princeton University Press, 1983)

Seligman, P. *Being and Not-Being: An Introduction to Plato's Sophist* (The Hague: Martinus Nijhoff, 1974)

Sellars, W. 'Vlastos and "The Third Man"' in *Philosophical Review* 64 (1955), pp. 405–37

Shiner, R. A. *Knowledge and Reality in Plato's Philebus* (Assen: Van Gorcum & Comp., 1974)

Skemp, J. B. (1967) *The Theory of Motion in Plato's Later Dialogues*; enlarged ed. (Amsterdam: Adolf M. Hakkert, 1967)

——— (1976) *Plato. Greece and Rome:* New Surveys in the Classics, no. 10 (Oxford: Clarendon Press)

Solmsen, F. (1942) *Plato's Theology* (Ithaca: Cornell University Press)

——— Review of Edelstein, *Plato's Seventh Letter* in *Gnomon* 41 (1969), pp. 29–34

Strang, C. 'Plato and the Third Man' in Vlastos (1971), pp. 184–200. Originally in *Proceedings of the Aristotelian Society*, Supplementary vol. 37 (1963), pp. 147–64

Taylor, A. E. *A Commentary on Plato's Timaeus* (Oxford: Clarendon Press, 1928)

Teloh, Henry. *The Development of Plato's Metaphysics* (University Park: Pennsylvania State University Press, 1981)

Turnbull, R. G. 'Aristotle's Debt to the "Natural Philosophy" of the *Phaedo*', *Philosophical Quarterly* 8 (1958), pp. 131–46

Vlastos, G. (1939) 'The Disorderly Motion in the *Timaeus*' in Allen (1965), pp. 379–99. Originally in *Classical Quarterly* 33 (1939), pp. 71–83

——— (1954) 'The Third Man Argument in the *Parmenides*' in Allen (1965), pp. 231–61. Originally in *Philosophical Review* 63 (1954), pp. 319–49

——— (1963) 'Addendum' (to Vlastos, 1954) in Allen (1965), pp. 261–3. Dated '1963'

——— (1964) 'Creation in the *Timaeus*: Is It a Fiction?' in Allen (1965), pp. 401–19. Dated '1964'

——— (1965) 'Degrees of Reality in Plato' in Vlastos (1973), pp. 58–75. Originally in Bambrough (1965), pp. 1–19

——— (1965a) 'A Metaphysical Paradox' in Vlastos (1973), pp. 43–57. Originally in *Proceedings of the American Philosophical Association* 39 (1966), pp. 5–19. Dated '1965'

——— (1969) 'Self-Predication and Self-Participation in Plato's Later Period' in Vlastos (1973), pp. 335–41. Originally in *Philosophical Review* 78 (1969), pp. 74–8

——— (1969a) 'Plato's "Third Man" Argument (*Parm.* 132A1–B2): Text and Logic' in Vlastos (1973), pp. 342–65. Originally in *Philosophical Quarterly* 19 (1969), pp. 289–301

——— (1969b) 'Reasons and Causes in the *Phaedo*' in Vlastos (1971), pp. 132–66. Originally in *Philosophical Review* 78 (1969), pp. 291–325. Also in Vlastos (1973), pp. 76–110

——— (1970) 'Ambiguity in the *Sophist*' in Vlastos (1973), pp. 270–322. Dated '1970'

——— (1971) (ed.) *Plato I: Metaphysics and Epistemology* (Garden City; Doubleday and Company, Inc.)

——— (1971a) (ed.) *The Philosophy of Socrates* (Garden City: Doubleday and Company, Inc.)

——— (1971b) 'The Unity of the Virtues in the *Protagoras*' in Vlastos (1973), pp. 221–69. Originally in *Review of Metaphysics* 25 (1972), pp. 415–58. Dated

'1971'
———— (1973) *Platonic Studies* (Princeton: Princeton University Press)
von Fritz, Kurt. 'The Philosophical Passage in the Seventh Platonic Letter and the
   Problem of Plato's "Esoteric" Philosophy' in Anton and Kustas, pp. 408–47
Wallis, R. T. *Neoplatonism* (London: Duckworth, 1972)
Wedberg, A. 'The Theory of Ideas' in Vlastos (1971), pp. 28–52. Originally ch. III
   of Wedberg, *Plato's Philosophy of Mathematics* (Stockholm: Almqvist and
   Wiksell, 1955)
Weingartner, R. *The Unity of the Platonic Dialogue* (Indianapolis: Bobbs-
   Merrill, 1973)
White, N. *White on Knowledge and Reality* (Indianapolis: Hackett, 1976)

# INDEX LOCORUM

# INDEX NOMINUM